MATTERING PRESS

Mattering Press is an academic-led Open Access publisher that operates on a not-for-profit basis as a UK registered charity. It is committed to developing new publishing models that can widen the constituency of academic knowledge and provide authors with significant levels of support and feedback. All books are available to download for free or to purchase as hard copies. More at http://matteringpress.org.

The Press' work has been supported by: Centre for Invention and Social Process (Goldsmiths, University of London), European Association for the Study of Science and Technology, Hybrid Publishing Lab, infostreams, Institute for Social Futures (Lancaster University), OpenAIRE, Open Humanities Press, and Tetragon, as well as many other institutions and individuals that have supported individual book projects, both financially and in kind.

We are indebted to the ScholarLed community of Open Access, scholar-led publishers for their companionship and extend a special thanks to the Directory of Open Access Books and Project MUSE for cataloguing our titles.

MAKING THIS BOOK

Books contain multitudes. Mattering Press is keen to render more visible the unseen processes that go into the production of books. We would like to thank Endre Dányi, who acted as the Press' coordinating editor for this book, Joe Deville for his work on the book production, Julien McHardy for the cover design, the reviewers Andrew Barry, Adi Kuntsman and Helen Verran, Steven Lovatt for copy-editing, Jennifer Tomomitsu for proofreading, Alex Billington and Tetragon for typesetting, and Will Roscoe, Ed Akerboom, and infostreams for their contributions to the html versions of this book.

COVER

Cover art by Julien McHardy.

DEMOCRATIC SITUATIONS

EDITED BY

ANDREAS BIRKBAK

AND

IRINA PAPAZU

Mattering Press

First edition published by Mattering Press, Manchester.

ISBN: 9781912729302 (pbk)
ISBN: 9781912729128 (pdf)
ISBN: 9781912729135 (epub)
ISBN: 9781912729319 (html)
DOI: http://doi.org/10.28938/9781912729302

Mattering Press has made every effort to contact copyright holders and will be glad to rectify, in future editions, any errors or omissions brought to our notice.

CONTENTS

LIST OF FIGURES

CONTRIBUTORS

ANDREAS BIRKBAK is associate professor at Aalborg University in Copenhagen and a co-founding member of the Techno-Anthropology Laboratory (TANTLab). Andreas' research focuses on public participation and digital methods. His recent publications include 'Participatory Data Design' (book chapter in *Making and Doing*, MIT Press 2021, with Jensen, Madsen and Munk). Andreas has been a visiting scholar at multiple universities, including at the Centre for Interdisciplinary Methodologies (Warwick) and the Centre for the Sociology of Innovation (École des Mines de Paris).

JASON CHILVERS is Professor of Environment and Society and Chair of the Science, Society and Sustainability (3S) Research Group in the School of Environmental Sciences at the University of East Anglia. He is a science and technology studies (STS) scholar and geographer concerned with the changing relations between science, innovation and society in contemporary democracies, particularly in environment and sustainability contexts and in response to issues of energy, climate change and emerging technologies.

RACHEL DOUGLAS-JONES is Associate Professor of Anthropological Approaches to Data and Infrastructure at the IT University of Copenhagen, where she is Head of the Technologies in Practice research group and co-Director of the ETHOS Lab. Her recent publications include *Towards an Anthropology of Data* (JRAI 2021, with Antonia Walford and Nick Seaver) and *Hope and Insufficiency: Capacity Building in Ethnographic Comparison* (Berghahn 2021, with Justin Shaffner). She is currently PI of the Danish Research Council Project *Moving Data, Moving People*, which ethnographically studies experiences of the emergent social credit system for people on the move in China.

VÉRA EHRENSTEIN is a CNRS researcher at the Centre d'étude des mouvements sociaux (UMR 8044), École des hautes études en sciences sociales, Paris. Her research explores the relations between science, markets and politics, with a focus on climate change. Véra recently published with Daniel Neyland and Sveta Milyaeva the book *Can Markets Solve Problems? An Empirical Inquiry into Neoliberalism in Action* (Goldsmiths Press, 2019).

LOTTE KRABBENBORG is Associate Professor of Public Participation in Science and Technology Development at the Institute for Science in Society, Faculty of Science at Radboud University. Her research focuses on the ways in which new techno-scientific developments such as nanotechnology are adopted by society. The main aim of her research is to explore power dynamics and enhance empowerment of civil society actors, either individual citizens or non-governmental organisations, through involvement in deliberation and decision-making processes.

DAVID MOATS is assistant professor at Tema-T, Linköping University and research fellow at the Faculty of Social Sciences at the University of Helsinki. His research is mainly about digitisation and the role of machine learning and artificial intelligence in transforming various industries, including media, healthcare, politics and academia. He is also interested in the methodological implications of these new sources of digital data for interdisciplinary collaborations.

ANDRZEJ W. NOWAK, philosopher, academic teacher and researcher, works in the Philosophy Department of Adam Mickiewicz University, Poznań, Poland. His current research focuses on hegemonical dimensions of materiality and ontology, trying to merge the ontological sensitivity of post-humanism with the Promethean promise of modernity and Enlightenment. He is an active participant in Polish public life, occasional columnist, blogger and a devoted bike tourist as well as a marathon runner.

HELEN PALLETT is a lecturer in the School of Environmental Sciences at the University of East Anglia, and a member of the 3S (Science, Society &

Sustainability) Research Group. She is a science and technology studies scholar and geographer interested in the relationships between science, democracy and the environment, and particularly in diverse forms of public participation at these intersections.

IRINA PAPAZU is associate professor in the Technologies in Practice research group at the IT University of Copenhagen. She has published a book in Danish on *Actor-Network Theory in Practice* with colleague Brit Ross Winthereik. She heads the Agile State working group in the Center for Digital Welfare, and she splits her research time between public sector digitalisation and public participation in climate change and energy transitions.

LINDA SONERYD is professor of sociology at the University of Gothenburg, and Score Fellow at the Stockholm Centre for Organizational Research, Stockholm University. Her research focuses on environmental governance and participation. Her current work includes a forthcoming monograph (Bristol University Press, 2022) with Göran Sundqvist on science and democracy.

GÖRAN SUNDQVIST is professor of science and technology studies at the University of Gothenburg. His research focuses on interconnections between climate research and climate transitions. He is also working on a book together with Linda Soneryd on science and democracy (Bristol University Press, 2022)

ANNE KATHRINE VADGAARD received a PhD degree from IT-University of Copenhagen in 2016. Her research examines democratic and bureaucratic principles, material and technological practices and the inner workings of elections. Anne is currently working with public IT implementation and business transformation at the Danish IT consultancy firm Netcompany.

LAURIE WALLER is a researcher based at the Science, Society and Sustainability (3S) research group at the University of East Anglia. His research falls between science and technology studies, digital sociology and participation. He's interested in the ways technological controversies unsettle political forms and their potential for bringing democratic publics into closer relation with their environments.

ALEXEI TSINOVOI'S research examines the role of new media technologies in international politics. His work is influenced by science and technology studies (STS), the digital methods approach, political philosophy, and international relations theory. Alexei is currently researcher at the Department of Political Science at Lund University; he previously was a postdoctoral researcher at the University of Copenhagen, supported by the Carlsberg Foundation (project no. CF18-1015).

ACKNOWLEDGEMENTS

FIRST OF ALL, WE WOULD LIKE TO THANK ALL THE CHAPTER AUTHORS, including those whose work did not make it into the final book. Each of you have generously shared your ideas and stories with us, which has been truly inspiring. You also put up with a long publishing process and many revisions, including serving as dedicated commentators on each other's chapters. Thanks for that. We could literally not have done this without you, and this is obviously also your book.

Similar thanks go to all the participants at the workshop 'STS and democratic politics', which we hosted in Copenhagen in November 2017 to kickstart the project – and not least to Kristin Asdal and Andrew Barry for their captivating keynotes at the workshop. Thanks is also due to the European Association for the Study of Science and Technology (EASST), the Department of Management, Politics and Philosophy at Copenhagen Business School, and the Department of Culture and Learning at Aalborg University, all of which supported the workshop financially. Extra thanks go to the last institution, which in addition to workshop funding also supported the book project itself with a substantial contribution.

In addition to all the above, we would very much like to indicate our appreciation for Mattering Press. In the original book proposal, we argued that Mattering Press is unique in offering the combination of straightforward Open Access publishing and high-quality editorial support. This turned out to be true. It has been a real privilege to work with other STS scholars at each step in the publishing process. First and foremost a huge thanks to Endre Dányi, who was a rock of support, experience, and strong ideas throughout the journey from conceptualisation to printed book. Thanks also to Julien McHardy whose ingenuity made the wonderful cover possible. Finally, a big thank you to our extremely competent external reviewers, to whom this book owes a lot.

We would also like to acknowledge our many phenomenal mentors and colleagues in different locations. You are too many to mention, but you nevertheless provide the web that makes projects such as this one possible. To list some of the more institutionalised conversations: The Technologies in Practice group at IT University Copenhagen and the Techno-Anthropology/TANTLab group at Aalborg University both offered valuable feedback at internal seminars. Both James Maguire and Casper Bruun Jensen offered detailed written feedback at crucial points, which warrants special thanks. Thanks also to the participants at the 4S 2020 conference track 'Democracy in the Making', convened by Jason Chilvers and Jan-Peter Voß. Jan-Peter also invited us to Berlin for a 2018 workshop on 'Sciences of democracy', where he, Brice Laurent, and Mark Brown offered valuable feedback on the book project. Thank you. Thanks also to all the participants in the track on 'STS and democratic politics' at Nordic STS 2017, which we convened together with Linda Soneryd and Anne Kathrine Vadgaard, and which served as an important warm-up for the book project.

Anne Kathrine (AK) deserves very special thanks. She was the third person on the team in the early stages of this project. Her ideas and spirit have shaped the final book in irreplaceable ways.

ANDREAS AND IRINA
Copenhagen, August 2021

I

INTRODUCING DEMOCRATIC SITUATIONS

Andreas Birkbak and Irina Papazu, editors

AT THE TIME OF WRITING THIS INTRODUCTION, IN THE SUMMER OF 2020, we find ourselves working from home. Denmark, like most countries in the world, is in a state of partial lockdown due to the Covid-19 pandemic. This sudden state of emergency is proving an apt occasion to consider the blurring of lines between science and democracy. During this crisis, situations related to medicine and health are seemingly becoming entangled with some of the strongest tropes of democracy, such as the experience of voting in a democratic election. As a case in point, the Danish politician Bertel Haarder made the following observation in a Facebook post, after he was tested for coronavirus:

> It was almost like voting: first you give your social security number. You then receive a note to deliver at the testing booth. At the booth, they shove a stick down your throat, and then it's back out in the sunshine. We are encouraged to get tested […] and I have a bit of a dry cough (Haarder 2020, translated from Danish by the authors).

The Facebook post compares getting tested for coronavirus with voting in an election. In voting, as in medical testing, you enter a carefully controlled setup where, on the basis of your social security number, something is extracted from you and stored, and you can then move on with your life.

The voting booth, which the politician alludes to, might be one of the first objects that comes to mind when thinking about democracy. The most remarkable feature of the voting booth is its lack of distinguishing features. In Denmark, at least, you can expect a bland and uninspiring booth with an opaque, heavy curtain and a bare minimum of interior equipment. It is their homogeneity that makes voting booths capable of generating a specific register of democracy: they make the voting experience predictable and safe, almost clinical, devoid of irregularities, as our choice of one candidate over another should not be conditioned by any irregularities of the situation in which we find ourselves. The voting booth is intended to create a space purified of political influence, to guarantee that the voter is not influenced by anything at the moment of voting.

A key difference between the voting situation and the test situation is that for the purposes of the coronavirus test, the results concern the person who takes the test, and a link must be maintained between you and the trace you leave behind. In the case of voting, this logic is reversed: as soon as your vote is cast, it must be dissociated from you in order to ensure anonymity, confidentiality and, thus, the legality of the vote.

The juxtaposition of the two situations, the voting experience and Covid testing, can help us appreciate how they both exert an influence on the involved individual. While the voting booth aims for a clinical, neutral appearance, it can by no means be characterised by an absence of influence on the individual. On the contrary, this setting deliberately severs individuals from their relations in order for them to stand 'free' and 'secret' in the act of choosing between candidates (Cochoy and Grandclément-Chaffy 2005), just as the Covid testing setup has to isolate the patient in order to achieve an uncontaminated test result.

The 'proposition' (Latour 2000; Dányi et al. 2021) of the seasoned politician, which endows the experimental scientific setup of Covid testing with traits and sentiments mimicking the democratic practice of voting, is a timely prompt to consider democracy and science as mutually constitutive, and to take democracy as seriously as technoscience as an empirical object of study in science and technology studies (STS). If we are to fully appreciate the politician's experience, we must ask questions pertaining to democracy, such as: How does getting tested for Covid-19 enact the citizen in a democratic register ('we are encouraged to get tested')? And how does the test setup instil a democratic sentiment in the citizen? To address these questions is to explore how democracy is enacted and becomes part of social life with an experimentalist sentiment, emphasising that the role of technosciences in society is also one of instigating processes of enquiry and learning (Barry 2001, Latour 1987, Marres 2009), while at the same time complicating the study of the experimental test setup through its affiliation with democracy (Ezrahi 1990, 2012; Marres and Stark 2020). Part of this argument is well-known – fundamental, even – in STS: objects have politics (Winner 1980; Latour 1992; Marres 2005); politics is a socio-material phenomenon. But the juxtaposition of the two arrangements does not only tell us that *politics* is materially situated; it tells us that *democracy* is materially situated. The question that this book poses is: what makes materially situated politics *democratic*?

Democratic politics is a phenomenon understood and studied from many perspectives – as discursively organised conflict (e.g., Mouffe 2000), in terms of interests and power (e.g., Strøm 1990), as a matter of securing the right conditions for deliberation and free debate (e.g., Habermas 1985, Møller and Skaaning 2013), or as a complex of rules and institutions (e.g., Dahl 1989, Elklit 1999). Aside from a few notable exceptions in STS (such as Latour and Weibel 2005; Marres 2007), however, democratic politics has rarely been treated as a materially entangled phenomenon. Yet at least three developments characteris-ing the period we live in provide potent demonstrations of a rapidly changing, unpredictable and materially entangled Euro-American democracy: first, the pandemic's science-policy entanglements; second, the 'ongoing, irreversible, eco-logical mutation' (Latour 2020) of the earth's climate and its ability to bring into view the relationships of interdependence between the human and the natural world; and third, political events such as Brexit and Donald Trump's presidency, fuelled by a so-called post-truth new media environment mobilising populist sentiment. Science communication has become 'high politics' (Keohane and Nye 2001), and new digital technologies have become high-profile protagonists in election victories (Vadgaard 2016; Waller and Moats, this volume). If ever the ideal of Democracy, with a capital D, as an unchanging, anthropocentric and primarily discursively organised phenomenon was tenable, then it has been decisively disproven in the last couple of decades.

The aim of this book is to contribute to the study of democracy, with a small d, by investigating it as a rapidly shifting and techno-scientifically entangled moving target. Each chapter explores a specific situation in which democracy is at once given and emergent. Democracy is given in the sense that the situations carry a certain 'signature of democracy' (Agamben 2009): actors evoke concepts and tropes that can be considered part of a democratic repertoire, just as something in the setting qualifies the situation as relevant in relation to democracy. Democracy is at the same time emergent in the sense that the analyses show the practical limits and contestability of the democratic concepts and ideals evoked. Through empirical analysis of practical encounters, democracy emerges as something that fluctuates; something that must be practically coordinated and is often contested as well as mobilised for different purposes. Through such situated analysis, democracy as a singular model vanishes and becomes a multiple phenomenon – not in a harmonious offering of various dishes of democracy, but in a complicated way where multiple versions of democracy supplement, override or combine with each other (Mol 1999).

The democratic fluctuations explored in this book have to do with 1) the ways in which democracy becomes *technodemocracy* through ongoing processes of institutional, infrastructural, theoretical and bureaucratic reproduction, 2) the relationships between democracy and the technosciences, and 3) the influx of new nonhuman actors such as digital technologies. The prevalence of questions pertaining to science, technology and reflexivity in these themes, which also organise the book into sections, indicates why we believe this is a good time for STS scholars to contribute to the study of democratic politics. Key STS topics such as scientific facts, material politics and the performativity of theory can no longer be relegated to the fringes but go to the core of contemporary democratic politics and political thought.

The timing, we believe, is also good for STS as a research field. Democracy has long been 'an object of inquiry and imagination in STS' (Pallett and Chilvers, this volume). Not least, Latour and Weibel's exhibition and anthology *Making Things Public: Atmospheres of Democracy* (2005) marked a shift in the field, where the project of understanding and criticising the production of scientific knowledge was brought into conversation with the making of democratic politics. In making this shift, Latour and Weibel drew on Shapin and Schaffer's historical interrogation of the relations between science and the public (1985), Isabelle Stengers' (2005) studies of experimental science and John Dewey's pragmatist thinking about democratic politics (1927). The shift toward the study of democratic politics in STS is related, further, to pragmatist accounts of issue publics (Marres 2007), post-Foucauldian studies of political technologies and situations (Barry 2001), ANT-inspired examinations of 'the little tools of democracy' (Asdal 2008) and a wave of studies focusing on public participation in science and politics (Chilvers and Kearnes 2020; Kelty 2020).

True, 'efforts to democratise science' (Watson 2014: 75) have been present since the inception of the field of STS (Sismondo 2008). However, the abovementioned contributions notwithstanding, there were signs that some STS scholars, as Latour puts it, 'were so busy renewing some of the features of scientific practice' that 'we took off the shelf whatever political theory we had' (Latour 2007: 203). The political theory that was perhaps most often taken from the shelf was the 'assumption that ... more public participation in technical decision-making, or at least more than has been traditional, improves the public value and quality of science and technology' (Sismondo 2008: 19).

In this volume, we do not seek to re-theorise democracy, but we do aim to employ our empirical work to disturb tenets of political theory that may have travelled into STS underexamined. This analytical logic is sometimes referred to as empirical philosophy (Mol 2002), or as an empiricist approach which 'takes seriously the ways in which actors deal in practice with what are usually considered philosophical concerns: what is good, what is right, what is true, and so on' (Jensen and Gad 2009: 292). The chapters in this book, while borrowing from a variety of analytical traditions in and around STS, all start from empirical situations where actors are tackling questions concerning politics and democracy, and let these practices point to and complicate common understandings of democracy, rather than employ such understandings or theories to evaluate the practices studied. Instead of criticising, for instance, the low degree of public involvement in a technoscientific matter, several chapters question the nature and aims of specific public involvement initiatives (e.g., Krabbenborg, Soneryd and Sundqvist, Tsinovoi).

The chapters in this collection all engage with contemporary Euro-American participatory democracy, broadly conceived. This is visible in the relative familiarity of the situations explored in the chapters: Election planning (Vadgaard), NGO lobbyism (Ehrenstein), procedures for public participation (Krabbenborg, Soneryd and Sundqvist, Pallett and Chilvers), political campaigns (Waller and Moats, Tsinovoi, Nowak), ethical review boards (Douglas-Jones), community organising (Papazu), and public debate (Birkbak). These are the categories of democratic practices studied in this volume. While they all fit quite readily with commonplace notions of Euro-American democratic politics today, the chapters also highlight the changing nature of democracy. They welcome new actors to the scene, such as digital marketing companies (Waller and Moats), apps (Tsinovoi) and activist-technocrat hybrids in the EU (Ehrenstein). And they make visible the malleable, socio-material nature of classic democratic tropes, such as public debate (Birkbak) and the electorate (Vadgaard).

As the book's title indicates, we believe the work of studying democracy in practice can be furthered by a slight shift in emphasis from settings to situations. The point of thinking the phenomenon through the setting remains important: democracy is not fixed in advance of the specific socio-material settings that participate in enacting it (Gomart and Hajer 2003). But we find that asserting the significance of specific settings is not enough. As Gomart and Hajer note, it is in the *variability* of the settings that the changes and shifts that mark democracy can be observed and studied (2003: 38). If important things happen to democracy as its settings shift and transform, then it is a vital analytical task to study these multiple settings as underdetermined, locally specified, fragile and only temporarily fixed. These settings must be seen as situated and rubbing up against other settings and arrangements, the existence of which the researcher must also be alert to.

The notion of situation is at the same time more localising and more open-ended than the notion of setting, and, as such, focusing on 'democratic situations' foregrounds the fragile and relational nature of the categories and settings of democratic politics, including their vulnerabilities and dependencies on other phenomena unfolding elsewhere in place and time. Barry (2012) invokes the concept of the political situation to describe how any singular political event is always tied to other controversies, contexts and events, overspilling theoretical delineations and categorisations, and thus pointing to the relational and distributed characteristics of political events such as the ones studied in this book.

Barry's concept of the political situation also alerts the researcher to how different knowledge systems of the social, natural or technical sciences – including theories and concepts from other contexts, such as social science or political philosophy – can be activated as resources in the particular situation. This understanding of 'the situation' reminds us that events cannot be reduced to isolated case studies, just as they cannot be delimited to any *one* setting. By bringing the concept of the political situation to bear on democratic politics, democratic politics can be understood as grounded in, as well as produced by, the socio-material devices and actors (Marres 2012, Laurent 2011) and the social scientific theories and contexts (Asdal and Moser 2012) that inhabit and are invoked by or enacted in the situation. In this way, even though social scientific theories do not enter the analysis as judges called on to arbitrate democratic situations, their agency should be acknowledged as integral to the situations under study.

The chapters in this book pursue this research agenda by offering empirical inquiries into situations emphasising what happens in the cracks and interstices between the usual 'building blocks' of democracy – thereby adding new layers to our perception of those building blocks (see Dányi 2020). To foreshadow our more detailed discussion of the chapters below, Vadgaard, for instance, emphasises neither the election apparatus, nor bureaucracy itself, but instead the shifting interface between the two. Birkbak's chapter studies neither public debate nor the newspaper business alone but engages with their mutual inseparability. Pallett and Chilvers combine a study of public dialogue in the UK with observations about concurrent parliamentary politics and social scientific developments, attending to how they co-constitute each other and emerge together.

As these previews illustrate, we believe there is more work to be done with regards to the otherwise familiar categories of participatory Euro-American democracy. Such work will supplement existing STS arguments, which emphasise that democratic politics is not only present where mainstream narratives expect it to be. Three key lines can be distinguished. First, materialist approaches foreground how the complicated problems of technological societies require an openness and constant reinvention of the forms of democratic politics (Gomart and Hajer 2003, Latour and Weibel 2005, Marres 2007, Callon et al. 2009, Barry 2001), which may be taken to suggest that it is more important to study material and artistic practices than the commonplace settings of participatory democracy (Marres 2012). Second, postcolonial approaches emphasise that attention must be paid to indigenous and locally grounded political practices in order to avoid extending Western standards (Verran 1998, de la Cadena 2010, de Castro 2012, Brooks et al. 2020, Dányi and Spencer 2020), as has been common not least when it comes to the 'democratisation process' of spreading democracy beyond the Western Hemisphere (e.g., Elklit 1999). Third, feminist scholars have highlighted the problems of exclusion and standardisation involved in shining a light on the loci of power (Haraway 1988, Star 1991), alerting the reader instead to individuals (Callon and Rabeharisoa 2004), creatures (Haraway 1978), environmental issues (Ebron and Tsing 2017), invisible infrastructures (Star 1999) and ageing and obsolete technologies (Cohn 2016) in need of repair, visibility and care (Mol, Moser and Pols 2010; Puig de la Bellacasa 2017).

These are important research agendas that expand both our imagination and our understanding of the range of forms that democratic politics can take, as well as what can be qualified as political or democratic in the first place. However, here we want to stick with the more mundane situations of participatory democracy and try to render them more interesting through empirical work. We find that there is value in studying more obviously political or democratic situations, not least as these have been less well studied by STS researchers. Indeed, according to Barry, it may be this tendency of STS to be 'dominated by the study of "cases" […] whose significance for the study of politics is obscure', which has caused 'the connections between science, technology and politics' to be 'reproduced' rather than 'interrogated' (Barry 2001: 12).

The Covid testing setup described above was experienced by the Danish politician as transforming him, not only into a patient, but into a citizen doing his democratic duty. This is an example of how we are witnessing the emergence of new relations in contemporary Euro-American participatory democracy. Uncovering them requires an appreciation of the newness of the medical-political situation as well as of the ways in which one of the most well-known tropes of democracy, the voting experience, is drawn into the situation. In this way, the situation reaches out, overspills and is distributed across a wider landscape than is at first glance apparent. It is in this spirit that the chapters in this volume seek to render situations of participatory democracy, which some may think they know all too well, more *interesting* (Stengers 2000: 48), by rendering them more active, distributed and situated.

We believe this research agenda can draw on and develop three ways in which STS has taken up the theme of democracy in recent years, which coincide with the three abovementioned transformations democracy is currently undergoing. First, democratic politics in practice is co-shaped by its interfaces with more or less rigid institutions and bureaucracies. Second, the relationship between technoscience, democracy and public participation is as intricate and shifting as ever, and the distinction between technoscience (predominantly concerned with organisms and materials) and democracy (concerned with the relations between humans) is destabilised and problematised, not least in the face of the pandemic and the wider environmental crisis. Third, nonhumans play a growing role in democratic politics, which among other things problematises the figure of the autonomous human individual in the voting booth.

To a large extent, the chapters in this collection combine all these three approaches. For example, Tsinovoi asks how the particular nonhuman *device* (#3) of a smartphone app formats the *participation* (#2) of lay citizens in the state-driven institution of digital *diplomacy* (#1) by enacting a hybrid, bot-like digital-human political actor. Still, the emphasis in the chapters differs, which allows us to structure the book and our discussion of the individual chapters along these three themes.

PART I: THE INTERFACES OF TECHNODEMOCRACY

Inspired by social studies of economic markets, STS scholars have explored how social scientific techniques enact publics in 'historical, contingent and disputable' ways (Muniesa et al. 2007: 3) including how settings such as focus groups, citizen assemblies and surveys have performative effects, constructing both participants and democratic ideals in the process (Hajer 2005; Lezaun and Soneryd 2007; Law 2009; Jensen 2005; Blok 2007; Laurent 2011, Osborne and Rose 1999). A recent wave of studies focuses not on social science techniques but on the institutions and procedures belonging to the conventional domain of Politics with a capital P. Parliaments, for instance, have started to provoke substantial interest among STS scholars as sites for the empirical study of how democratic politics are assembled in practice (Dányi 2018, Asdal and Hobæk 2016, Brichzin 2020).

Extending such moves, the three chapters in this first section all take a well-defined socio-material setting – the election office (Vadgaard), the 'eco-system' of activist-lobbyists in Brussels (Ehrenstein), a national newspaper's 'debate school' (Birkbak) – as the starting point for asking how contemporary democracy is produced through political-administrative decision-making, EU lobbyism and newspaper debate. In the process, the chapters denaturalise ideals and assumptions underpinning democracy-as-democratic-theory, specifically the Weberian ideal of bureaucratic neutrality (Vadgaard), the Marxist ideal of radical resistance to capitalist arrangements (Ehrenstein), and the Habermasian ideal of the public sphere (Birkbak).

While all the chapters in this volume foreground and investigate the role of the setting in the situation under study, the three chapters in this section demonstrate this sentiment most explicitly by exploring organisational and institutional settings of democratic politics ethnographically, and by paying attention to how these both bring into play certain tropes of democracy and contribute to enacting specific versions of technodemocracy in practice. In short, they consider the diverse problems or 'facts' of democratic political practice an effect of the settings that enable their production and stabilisation and study these settings and their performative capacities in practical, socio-material detail.

A central argument from laboratory studies is that distinctions between the social and the natural world are the outcome, rather than the starting point, of scientific knowledge production (Latour and Woolgar 1979; Latour 1983; Latour 1987; Watson 2014). Bringing this logic to bear on the realm of local politics in Copenhagen Municipality, Vadgaard, in her chapter, argues that if, due to its world-making qualities, 'science is politics by other means' (Latour 1988), then 'so is bureaucracy'. Vadgaard observes how public administrators in an election office in Copenhagen Municipality work to construct a political proposition to remove and consolidate a number of polling stations with consequences for 'voter accessibility'. By following the proposition's circulation through the bureaucratic maze of political decision-making in the City of Copenhagen, Vadgaard describes how the boundary between political decisions and bureaucratic casework is performed and simultaneously constantly challenged. She points out that what counts as 'political' versus what can pass as disengaged, 'bureaucratic' work is a distinction that emerges as part of the practices of municipal procedure. This distinction, however, does not only emerge through practice: it also exists as a theoretical conception in the minds of the municipal employees who work hard to keep administration and politics apart. Vadgaard's analysis problematises the democratic ideal of bureaucratic neutrality (for a classic analysis, see March and Olsen 1989), while at the same time showing how this ideal is at play in the practices of the civil service. Vadgaard proposes the term 'technodemocracy', playing on Latour's concept of technoscience (Latour 1987), to capture how the democracy we think we know is spun into and produced through a web of socio-material practices.

With Ehrenstein's chapter, we dive further into the complicated politics of 'technodemocracy', as she investigates the 'technocratic activism' of NGO-based policy officers and analysts lobbying the EU system to modify the European Union Emissions Trading System. Ehrenstein argues that the NGO professionals she studies are neither just climate activists nor just experts in the neoliberal economics of emissions trading. The focus of these 'technocratic activists' is the political-bureaucratic procedures and practical workings and particularities of the EU system, which they navigate proficiently. With her study of EU activist-lobbyists, Ehrenstein reveals a middle ground between the classic civil society politics of participation (e.g., climate marches) and the institutionalised, techno-bureaucratic politics of the EU. In her chapter, we witness a disturbance of the dichotomy between an inside and an outside of institutionalised EU politics, with the activist-lobbyists situating their efforts somewhere in the middle. Here, in the 'zero point between dichotomies' (Star 1991: 47), the urgency of climate change activism rubs against the slow-paced temporality of the EU system, as the technocratic activists find themselves in the roles of professionals working within the framework of the EU emissions trading scheme, trying to 'make it work', rather than attacking the system and proposing 'radical' alternatives.

While the chapters in this section take well-known settings of participatory democracy as their vantage points, the accounts point to democratic politics as something that also takes place in the 'high-tension zones' (Star 1991) between the institutional settings of participatory democracy. Democratic politics may be understood as staged in various settings, but when studied as specific political situations, we encounter a 'technodemocracy' where political values and technical procedures are intertwined. Here, each situation may inhabit and affect multiple settings which, in turn, also affect the actors working within and across them, installing expectations, procedures and regulations, and conditions of possibility and impossibility.

In his chapter, Birkbak locates the phenomenon of 'public debate' in the large Danish newspaper *Politiken*'s initiative to create a 'School of Debate and Critique'. Birkbak enrols in the school, and through his engagement with this format investigates how the school stages public debate through various technologies and arrangements (Latour and Weibel 2005; Barnett 2008), such as writing assignments, feedback and presentations by public speakers. Birkbak observes how *Politiken's* staff invokes the democratic ideal of equal representation: the students must mirror the demography of the Danish population, because public debate must mirror the concerns of the population. *Politiken*, he argues, aims for the students to represent 'their generation' – a generalised and abstract concept that turns out to create problems for the newspaper: it does not generate good texts. *Politiken* then asks for texts grounded in 'personal experiences' but continues to draw on 'generalising and trite categories', such as 'the Muslim minority' or 'young people' or 'females/males'. With inspiration from Stengers, Birkbak points out the missed opportunities for slowing down 'public language and majority reasoning' (Stengers 2010: 20). Instead of revitalising 'public debate', the newspaper ends up trying to reinforce and reproduce the existing order, missing out on the generative potential of the school event. Nevertheless, the event offers a glimpse of the challenges and opportunities for a legacy newspaper in the twenty-first century, which helps situate the abstract notion of public debate in an ongoing effort to maintain and renew specific infrastructures and discourses.

A common thread running through these first three chapters by Birkbak, Ehrenstein and Vadgaard is the technical and managed form of democratic politics, which exists *between* rule-governed bureaucratic procedure and the open space of democratic freedom. In this middle-ground of technodemocracy, the chapters demonstrate how participatory democracy is simultaneously given and emergent in practice. As mentioned above, this also applies to the rest of the chapters in this volume, and this is an important consequence, we find, of thinking about democracy through situated encounters. The situations explored contain strong ideas about what democracy and related concepts consist of, and these ideas have some agency in practice. But we also see the practical limitations of these idea(l)s, and how the sheer challenge of coordinating a situation that can come close to living up to concepts about democracy endows the situations with something extra – something emergent that must be studied empirically to be detected. This is where Democracy with a capital D starts to become multiple democracies; where we notice that in each democratic situation, something distinct and different is at play that breaks with commonplace dichotomies, and which may be explored as resources for rethinking democracy through how it is done in practice.

PART II: TECHNOSCIENCES, DEMOCRACY AND SITUATED ENACTMENTS OF PARTICIPATION

STS has a longstanding interest in studying and problematising the relations between science and democracy, and the democratisation of science and technology has been a central political project since the inception of the field (Levidow 2018). This research can be seen as falling into, roughly, two parts: fora of public participation – that is, artificially constructed settings of engagement with specific topics, such as the consensus conference (Jensen 2005, Blok 2007) or the roundtable (Felt and Fochler 2010) – on the one side, and knowledge controversies on the other (Pinch 1981, Epstein 1995, Venturini 2010, Whatmore and Landström 2011).

The first group of studies investigates how citizens, scientists and policy-makers meet to discuss complex themes typically relating to the governance of science and technology in society (Cammaerts and Carpentier 2005). The purpose of these studies is often to 'criticise particular engagement activities while […] expressing a commitment to a wider principle of "democratisation"' (Irwin et al. 2013: 119). This notion that other types of knowledge and expertise besides those of established science deserve a voice is central to the branch of STS often referred to as Public Engagement with Science (PES).

The second group of studies investigates how knowledge controversies overflow their framings and sets out to map the seemingly incommensurable positions and alliances of different actors and issues involved in controversies. The intention here is to contribute to democratic politics by mapping, rearranging or staging new meetings between implicated actors and their knowledge practices. The knowledge controversy as an object of interest within STS is considered a particularly fruitful instance of politics as turning around issues, 'instead of having the issues enter into a ready-made political sphere to be dealt with' (Latour 2007: 815). Following Latour (ibid.), during the controversy 'the political' assumes different forms and is altered through interaction with changing issues and settings (Whatmore and Landström 2011; Papazu 2017); there is a moment of societal transformation, where the social is in a 'magmatic state' (Venturini 2010).

The public engagement with science literature comes face to face with controversy studies in Soneryd and Sundqvist's chapter, which juxtaposes two controversial issues: nuclear waste management and water management in Sweden. Soneryd and Sundqvist set out to investigate the limits of participation, as they find 'the usual' call for including ever-more voices in the governance of science and technology naïve, since 'participatory procedures can uphold and even strengthen already established power relations and knowledge authorities'. In this, Soneryd and Sundqvist go against the classic assumption in STS that more participation will necessarily improve the public value and quality of science and technology. Instead, they argue, in practice, efforts to organise public participation in science and technology must necessarily mix technocratic and participatory elements. By juxtaposing two profoundly different cases, with nuclear waste a 'technocratically framed process' and water management situated in 'a long tradition of local engagement', Soneryd and Sundqvist show how both areas, despite Swedish attempts to create participatory arrangements around them, are characterised by the problem that the participants perceive their participation as practically meaningless. As such, calls for 'more participation' or warnings against technocracy are insufficient. Rather than abstract ideals, what is needed are investigations of how, for whom and under what conditions participation becomes meaningful, including scrutiny of the infrastructures for linking up with other democratic situations elsewhere – such as local or governmental decision-making procedures.

In their UK-based study of the participation format Public Dialogue, Pallett and Chilvers contribute to the task of exploring links between multiple democratic situations by situating the knowledge practices of STS as *part of* the phenomenon under study; this is an approach that resonates with Barry's (2012) insistence on understanding social scientific knowledge-making as a crucial ingredient in political situations. Pallett and Chilvers argue that STS researchers may not have the privilege of coming 'before or after' democracy, as innovators, interpreters or critical observers. Instead, they argue, as a scientific field with its own agency, STS must be understood as appearing *with* democracy. Specifically, they describe how STS researchers such as Brian Wynne (1992) have taken part in the setup and execution of deliberative Public Dialogues in relation to scientific developments in the UK, and how the format of Public Dialogue has changed over time, not least through engagements with the 'participatory democratic imagination' of STS scholars.

In the following chapter, Krabbenborg describes another highly artificial setup: the Dutch Societal Dialogue on Nanotechnology. Describing societal dialogues as 'ambitious attempts, initiated by government agencies, to create large scale, in-depth, and often longer term interactions among citizens, science and technology developers and other stakeholders to inform policy makers', she argues that while this participation format may be framed as a 'democratic situation' in the theoretical sense that citizens 'are stimulated to actively participate in policy-making processes regarding new science and technology developments', the important question is '*how* a societal dialogue is actually designed and orchestrated', as this design enacts participation in a particular register and may or may not lead to involvement in the matters discussed. Krabbenborg here echoes the general commitment of the PES field to 'a wider principle of democratisation'. The setup of the Dutch societal dialogue can be understood as particularly artificial, because the participants are invited on the basis of their *lack* of prior relation to the topic of nanotechnology, invoking an ideal of unbiased participation. This ideal proves impractical in so far as Krabbenborg shows how the design of the dialogue never allows the topic of nanotechnology to become an *issue* (Marres 2005; Birkbak 2017) with relevance for participants' lives. Instead, 'awareness raising' and 'reaching as many people as possible' become the criteria of success for the organisers, leaving the participants untransformed by the experience (Stengers 2000; Gomart and Hajer 2003).

Douglas-Jones' chapter also engages in a discussion of the participatory turn in the democratic governance of science. Quoting Chilvers, she points out how STS scholars currently find themselves 'in the "tricky position" of shifting from a role of *promoting* the "democratisation of science" to critically and reflexively analyz[ing] these very same practices' (Chilvers 2017: 117). She adds that the 'move away from implicit theories of democracy towards an approach that considers the democratic as an emergent set of logics and practices aligns STS more closely with anthropologists who refuse the preconceived'. Based on her ethnography of stem cell research ethics committees (ESCROs) in the US, Douglas-Jones' chapter focuses on the largely tacit role which democratic ideals have within such spaces of research governance. Like Krabbenborg's Societal Dialogue on Nanotechnology, ESCROs are put in place to mediate questions of public concern about new scientific fields, and they 'claim to be reasoning in the public interest' (Jasanoff 2012: 5). However, the committees are not particularly participatory. They have almost no online existence, and the interviewed members admit to operating far from the public eye: 'we *say* they're open to the public, we say they're accessible, but try finding it', as a member notes. Democratic ideals of openness, transparency and accountability are constantly present in the ways committee members conceptualise their roles and responsibilities, but 'the ideals largely remain ideals'. In practice, concerns for expertise, authority and secrecy keep the public at a distance, leaving democratic and participatory ideals as mere abstractions.

Continuing Soneryd and Sundqvist's interest in what counts as meaningful participation, when and for whom, in the last chapter within this theme, Papazu investigates the story of a community-driven renewable energy transition on the Danish island of Samsø. Samsø's energy transition has become a globally renowned model for 'energy democracy': a 'recipe' for how to manage the transition from fossil fuels to locally based renewable energy technologies without sparking public resistance and making the project democratically untenable (Papazu 2017). In her chapter, Papazu argues, however, that the storytelling surrounding 'the Samsø model' focuses on communication and participation while ignoring the techno-material, financial and legal challenges of energy transitions. Papazu employs Puig de la Bellacasa's (2011) concept 'matters of care' to disturb the distinction encountered on Samsø between community-oriented action ('good') and self-interested, materially oriented action ('bad'). Turning her ethnographic gaze to a large-scale farmer who played a significant role in the island's energy transition yet remains largely unacknowledged in the popularised narrative about Samsø, Papazu argues that although the farmer seems to personify the opposite of community, democracy and communication due to his stubborn attitude and his position of 'money and power' on the island, he is deeply invested in Samsø's transition. In Papazu's alternative narration of the story, the material-affective practices of the farmer-investor are foregrounded to appreciate how 'energy democracy' is about more than communicative action and community-building. This entails recognising how virtuous stories about citizen participation can be surprisingly exclusive and insensitive to actors that do not 'fit in'.

Participation in practice is not necessarily pretty, and even when successful in reaching its goals, it may fall short of the theoretical ideals it is constantly measured against. As the chapters in this section indicate, some of these ideals may be fruitfully redefined and renegotiated through co-constitutive encounters between practical democratic situations and the theoretical tropes that inhabit them.

PART III: RECONFIGURING DEMOCRATIC POLITICS WITH NEW NONHUMAN ACTORS

The third and final section of the book consists of three chapters that explore the arrival of new, mainly digital, technologies to existing settings of democratic politics: election campaigns, public diplomacy and social movement politics. The situations are distinct from those described in Part II in that they are not set within a public participation format, such as public or societal dialogue or committee or council work. Instead, the three chapters describe how a heterogeneous set of 'movements' – an electorate (Waller and Moats), citizen-diplomats (Tsinovoi), and abortion opponents (Nowak) – are created with the use of different 'tools of democracy' (Asdal 2008).

By investigating 'more-than-social' practices of participation (Papadopoulos 2018, Nowak, this volume), the chapters in this section contribute to the central interest of STS in how political agency is delegated to objects and technologies. There are many ways to pursue this, as indicated by Marres' demonstration of 'the powers of engagement' of mundane objects like environmental teapots and eco-show homes (Marres 2012) over classic examples, like the silent but powerful politics of Winner's (1980) Long Island bridges that constrain the mobility of certain societal groups, to Latour's (1992) early reflections on car safety belts and 'sleeping policemen' capable of installing a specific state-sanctioned morality in the driver.

The chapters in this section are mostly in conversation with recent scholarship on (digital) material participation (e.g., Marres 2012). However, the situations explored do not concern spontaneous publics 'sparked into being' by specific issues (Marres 2005). Rather, the chapters show how digital material politics can be orchestrated and steered from above. Nevertheless, Waller and Moats' approach remains inspired by Marres, as they examine empirically how objects and technologies – in their case campaign software – are assigned certain democratic qualities by specific actors. The strength and difficulty of this approach, which is a difficulty relevant to this book as a whole, is that democracy is no longer available in any simple way as an external ideal that can arbitrate between 'good' and 'bad' technological practices. Instead, it is an effect of these practices, whether good or bad.

This is particularly noteworthy in relation to the three final chapters, which all describe technological developments that invite concern and critique. We depart from the liberal figure of the choice-making independent citizen and learn about how attitudes, beliefs and actions are distributed across material objects and digital technologies, which at the same time become the grounds for political struggle. The chapters all point to ways in which the democratic actor can be re-conceptualised along more relational, affective and materialist lines, as they study situations where political agencies are installed, problematised and redistributed by political and state actors, with the help of mainly digital technologies.

In the first chapter, describing how the state of Israel uses social media campaigns to improve its reputation abroad, Tsinovoi examines how new digital technologies are associated with reconfiguring the autonomy of individual citizens, as 'the communication potential of the citizens is harnessed to conduct effective public diplomacy offensives', to paraphrase one of Tsinovoi's sources. Part of this diplomatic effort involves recruiting citizens to spread positive messages about Israel using different digital devices. In one of these reputation management initiatives, Tsinovoi is approached on Twitter, as he receives an algorithmically generated message extending an invitation to join a 'digital task force' to 'help Israel fight all the Fake News about it'. This appears to be a government-affiliated initiative, which enlists citizens to help the Israeli state fight what it claims to be 'echo chambers' and 'fake news'. By joining in, he 'enables daily automatic retweets of facts about Israel' from his personal Twitter account. Tsinovoi asks what kind of participation is taking place, since, as he notes, 'unlike Marres' (2007) notion of public participation as an organic and spontaneous response to an unresolved issue, in these examples, participation is clearly the result of a strategic and calculated movement'. He suggests that we are witnessing a new mode of governmental 'action at a distance' (Latour 1987), whereby states render their publics active and governable in new ways.

Much in line with Tsinovoi's considerations of how new digital tools can be used to steer citizens from afar, Waller and Moats' contribution studies the contentious case of Brexit and the Vote Leave campaign. They examine how campaign software employing big data techniques to micro-target political messages is constructed as a 'democratising' influence on election campaigns, as it is said to enable the mobilisation of 'people who usually ignore politics' and 'level the playing field' by employing open-source software. Waller and Moats show how the alleged democratic potential of such software is articulated as part of the marketing material of software companies, revealing a version of democratisation that cannot be disentangled from the hype around big data. The chapter highlights how democratic ideals, such as equal access, bottom-up participation and transparency can be appropriated by marketing companies and campaigning politicians. At the same time, while it might be tempting to write off such uses of democratic ideals as inauthentic, the point is that to attend to the roles that technology plays in contemporary politics we need to look at how technological change plays out in practice. This becomes more evident in situations in which what counts as democracy is up for grabs.

Lastly, in Nowak's chapter, it is not notions and ideals of democracy themselves that are contested, but something more directly entangled with the body: namely, gender equality and abortion rights in Poland. Focusing on the so-called 'war on gender', Nowak traces how Catholic-conservative forces employ digital devices and material objects in an ongoing political campaign to mobilise the public against gender equality and abortion rights. He finds that this battle must be understood as a case of ontological politics (Mol 1999) employed as a performative force 'able to influence future states of the world by means of crafted objects and practices'. The 'war' is fought with material weapons and strategically brings into play gory details such as blood and foetuses: The anti-abortionists' narrative of the early foetus as a 'conceived child' is buttressed by 3D-printed tiny plastic figurines depicting the foetus, an accompanying card game, and even a tamagochi-like app that allows users to 'adopt' a foetus and nurse it through pregnancy. The pro-abortion movement, for its part, also employs material means, as the black umbrella becomes a symbol of the demonstrations against anti-abortion regulations. Nowak concludes, however, that the material means of the pro-abortion movement 'continue to work more on the conventional symbolic level of social movement politics [...] allowing the catholic-conservative forces a somewhat surprising role as the more "techno-logically enhanced" actor'.

A tension runs through these three chapters, between well-known categories of democratic politics, such as referenda and social movement struggles, and the influx of new digital technologies. The latter turn out to be more mundane in practice than allowed by digital hype cycles, while the former turn out to be more unstable and shifting than expected by democratic theory. Studying such tensions as they unfold in democratic situations allows us to reconsider distinctions or boundaries between 'old' (ideals) and 'new' (technologies) by tracing what we described above as the simultaneously given and emergent qualities of democratic politics in situated encounters.

CONCLUSIONS

It is our hope that this book will contribute to a beginning rather than a conclusion of STS engagements with democratic politics as an object of study in its own right. In this introductory chapter, we have sought to indicate our preferred direction for such a research agenda, emphasising the situated, relational and distributed qualities of democratic politics. As the book's three themes suggest, we find that STS has a lot to offer, given the field's existing engagements with 1) institutions, bureaucracies and theoretical ideals, 2) participation in the technosciences, and 3) new technological translation processes, all three of which are key components in how democratic politics unfold in practice in contemporary Euro-American societies.

To push the point a bit further, we think relational accounts of democratic situations are valuable because of their potential to render the motley settings of participatory democracy more 'interesting' in the Stengersian sense of their capacity for creating new connections (Stengers 2000). As Gomart and Hajer put it, 'the interesting setting is one where the person or creature or thing is not left alone, authentic, but transformed by what occurs, and transformed in ways which induce its interference with the project' (Gomart and Hajer 2003: 39–40). The notion of interest is thus transformed from something determining (e.g., determined by economic and political interests) to something that is opening.

In practice, there is always a tension here. Indeed, this volume seeks to show that democratic politics is both governed by interests and is also (sometimes) interesting.

Coming back to the opening example of the coronavirus test setup in Denmark and the comparison with the act of casting a vote in a Danish election, the testing booth and the voting booth are instances of settings that seemingly leave individuals 'alone and authentic', but in practice very much rely on transforming individuals from their everyday, materially implicated, distributed selves into a spit sample or a cross on a ballot (and back to normal again). Such transformations do not leave the person unaffected, and empirical and analytical work needs to be done in order to unpack the specific interferences that happen in such situations, which may again render them more interesting.

The voting booth situation is arguably a particularly hard case to redescribe since it epitomises the modern-liberal narrative of an independent mind in an individual human citizen. Many other situations of Euro-American participatory democracy are more obviously distributed and in interference with other projects, as shown for instance in the chapters concerning science and democracy and all the configurations of 'participation' that connect them. Nevertheless, even the hard case of the voting experience has been somewhat transformed by the work presented here, with Vadgaard's chapter describing the politics of the election office and Waller and Moats' contribution adding the varying democratic capacities of campaign software to the equation. This is indicative of what we mean by offering more relational, situated and distributed accounts of democratic politics.

It also points to the value of reading the collection as a whole. As editors we have deliberately aimed for a wide-ranging collection of democratic situations, because we find that our argument about the relational and distributed quality of contemporary democratic politics is furthered by the juxtaposition of heterogeneous situations, which all contain claims about democracy in one way or another. Together, the chapters attest to democracy as something that is invoked in many different places by various actors in multiple ways. And this is only a beginning, since the list of potential democratic situations is open-ended and of course neither limited to parliamentary politics, nor to the predominantly Euro-American practices studied in this book.

The fact that Euro-American participatory democracy is often upheld as an ideal for the rest of the world to follow makes it more, not less, important to study how it is itself a situated, distributed, material, emergent, heterogenous, fragile and at times faltering figure and project. Indeed, most of the chapters describe situations where democracy is not an uncomplicated, virtuous thing; and even if the chapter authors seek to render the settings more interesting by describing their situated variability, the Stengersian transformative potential of the situations is rarely actualised. So, the work is only starting, but we hope that these stories will nevertheless 'enlarge the scope of […] what interests us' (Stengers 2000: 51), and by doing so make room for surprising and inventive situations within the ordinary settings of contemporary democratic politics.

REFERENCES

Agamben, G., *The Signature of All Things: On Method* (New York: Zone Books, 2009).

Asdal, K., and B. Hobæk, 'Assembling the Whale: Parliaments in the Politics of Nature', *Science as Culture*, 25 (2016), 96–116.

Asdal, K., and I. Moser, 'Experiments in Context and Contexting', *Science, Technology, & Human Values*, 37 (2012), 291–306.

Asdal, K., 'On Politics and the Little Tools of Democracy: A Down-to-Earth Approach', *Distinktion: Scandinavian Journal of Social Theory*, 9 (2008), 11–26.

Barnett, C., 'Convening Publics: The Parasitical Spaces of Public Action', in K. Cox, M. Low and J. Robinson, eds, *The SAGE Handbook of Political Geography* (London: Sage, 2008), pp. 403–417.

Barry, A., *Political Machines: Governing a Technological Society* (London: The Athlone Press, 2001).

——, 'Political Situations: Knowledge Controversies in Transnational Governance', *Critical Policy Studies*, 6 (2012), 324–336.

Birkbak, A., 'When Financial Concerns Shape Traffic Policy: How Economic Assumptions Muted the Copenhagen Payment Zone Issue', *Science as Culture*, 26 (2017), 491–504.

Blok, A., 'Experts on Public Trial: On Democratizing Expertise through a Danish Consensus Conference', *Public Understanding of Science*, 16 (2007), 163–182.

Brichzin, J., 'Materializations through Political Work', *Social Studies of Science*, 50 (2020), 271–291.

Brooks, H., T. Ngwane, and C. Runciman, 'Decolonising and Re-theorising the Meaning of Democracy: A South African Perspective' *The Sociological Review*, 68 (2020), 17–32.

Callon, M., P. Lascoumes, and Y. Barthe, *Acting in an Uncertain World: An Essay on Technical Democracy*, (Cambridge, MA: The MIT Press, 2009).

Callon, M., and V. Rabeharisoa, 'Gino's Lesson on Humanity: Genetics, Mutual Entanglements and the Sociologist's Role', Economy and Society, 33 (2004), 1–27.

Cammaerts, B., and N. Carpentier, 'The Unbearable Lightness of Full Participation in a Global Context: WSIS and Civil Society Participation', in J. Servaes and N. Carpentier, eds, *Towards a Sustainable Information Society: Beyond WSIS* (Bristol: Intellect, 2005), pp. 17–49.

Chilvers, J., 'Expertise, Professionalization, and Reflexivity in Mediating Public Participation: Perspectives from STS and British Science and Democracy' in L. Bherer, M. Gauthier and L. Simard, eds, *The Professionalization of Public Participation* (London: Routledge, 2017), pp. 125–148.

Chilvers, J., and M. Kearnes, 'Remaking Participation in Science and Democracy', *Science, Technology, & Human Values*, 45 (2020), 347–380.

Cochoy, F., and C. Grandclément-Chaffy, (2005). 'Publicizing Goldilocks' Choice at the Supermarket: The Political Work of Shopping Packs, Carts and Talk', in B. Latour, and P. Weibel, eds, *Making Things Public* (Cambridge MA: The MIT Press, 2005), pp. 646–657.

Cohn, M. L., 'Convivial Decay: Entangled Lifetimes in a Geriatric Infrastructure', Proceedings of the 19th ACM Conference on *Computer-Supported Cooperative Work & Social Computing*, 2016, pp. 1511–1523.

Dahl, R. A., *Democracy and its Critics* (New Haven, CT: Yale University Press, 1989).

Dányi E., 'The Things of the Parliament', in J. Brichzin, D. Krichewsky, L. Ringel, and J. Schank, eds, *Soziologie der Parlamente. Politische Soziologie* (Wiesbaden: Springer VS, 2018), pp. 267–285.

——, 'Búskomor politics: Practising critique in the ruins of liberal democracy', *The Sociological Review*, 68 (2020), 356–368.

Dányi, E., and M. Spencer, 'Un/common Grounds: Tracing Politics across Worlds', *Social Studies of Science*, 50 (2020), 317–334.

Dányi, E., M. Spencer, J. Maguire, H. Knox, and A. Ballestero, 'Propositional Politics', in J. Maguire, L. Watts, and B. R. Winthereik, eds, *Energy Worlds in Experiment* (Manchester: Mattering Press, 2021), pp. 66–94.

de la Cadena, M., 'Indigenous Cosmopolitics in the Andes: Conceptual Reflections beyond "Politics"', *Cultural anthropology*, 25 (2010), 334–370.

Dewey, J., *The Public and its Problems*, (New York: Henry Holt and Company, 1927).

Ebron, P., and A. Tsing, 'Feminism and the Anthropocene: Assessing the Field through Recent Books', *Feminist Studies*, 43 (2017), 658–683.

Elklit, J., 'Electoral Institutional Change and Democratization: You Can Lead a Horse to Water, but You Can't Make It Drink', *Democratization*, 6 (1999), 28–51.

Epstein, S., 'The Construction of Lay Expertise: AIDS Activism and the Forging of Credibility in the Reform of Clinical Trials', *Science, Technology, & Human Values*, 20 (1995), 408–437.

Ezrahi, Y., *The Descent of Icarus: Science and the Transformation of Contemporary Democracy* (Cambridge, MA: Harvard University Press, 1990).

——, *Imagined Democracies: Necessary Political Fictions* (Cambridge: Cambridge University Press, 2012).

Haarder, B., Facebook post 21 April 2020, https://x.facebook.com/story.php?story_fb id=3525203384175776&id=404683979561081 [accessed 18 August 2021].

Felt, U., and M. Fochler, 'Machineries for Making Publics: Inscribing and De-scribing Publics in Public Engagement', *Minerva*, 48 (2010), 219–238.

Gad, C., and C. B. Jensen, 'On the Consequences of Post-ANT', *Science, Technology & Human Values*, 35 (2010), 55–80.

Gomart, E., and M. Hajer, 'Is That Politics?', in B. Joerges, and H. Nowotny, eds, *Social Studies of Science and Technology: Looking Back, Ahead* (Netherlands: Springer, 2003), pp. 33–61.

Habermas, J., *The Theory of Communicative Action, Volume 1: Reason and the Rationalization of Society* (Boston: Beacon Press, 1985).

Hajer, M. A., 'Setting the Stage: A Dramaturgy of Policy Deliberation', *Administration & Society*, 36 (2005), 624–647.

Haraway, D., 'Animal Sociology and a Natural Economy of the Body Politic, Part I: A Political Physiology of Dominance', *Signs: Journal of Women in Culture and Society*, 4 (1978), 21–36.

——, 'Situated Knowledges: The Science Question in Feminism and the Privilege of Partial Perspective', *Feminist Studies*, 14 (1988), 575–599.

Irwin, A., T. E. Jensen, and K. E. Jones, 'The Good, the Bad and the Perfect: Criticizing Engagement Practice', *Social Studies of Science*, 43 (2013), 118-135.

Jasanoff, S., *Science and Public Reason* (London: Routledge, 2012).

Jensen, C. B., 'Citizen Projects and Consensus-Building at the Danish Board of Technology On Experiments in Democracy', *Acta Sociologica*, 48 (2005), 221–235.

Jensen, C. B., and C. Gad, (2009). 'Philosophy of Technology as Empirical Philosophy: Comparing Technological Scales in Practice', in E. Selinger and S. Riis, eds, *New Waves in Philosophy of Technology* (London: Palgrave Macmillan, 2009), pp. 292–314.

Kelty, C. M., *The Participant: A Century of Participation in Four Stories* (Chicago, Il: University of Chicago Press, 2020).

Keohane, R. O., and J. S. Nye, *Power and Interdependence* (New York: Longman, 2001).

Latour, B., 'Give Me a Laboratory and I will Raise the World', in K. Knorr-Cetina and M. Mulkay, eds, *Science Observed: Perspectives on the Social Study of Science* (Beverly Hills: Sage Publications, 1983), pp. 141–170.

——, *Science in Action: How to Follow Scientists and Engineers Through Society* (Cambridge, MA: Harvard University Press, 1987).

——, *The Pasteurization of France.* (Cambridge, MA: Harvard University Press, 1988).

——, 'Where are the Missing Masses? The Sociology of a Few Mundane Artefacts', in W. E. Bijker, and J. Law, eds, *Shaping Technology/Building Society: Studies in Socio-Technical Change* (Cambridge, MA: The MIT Press, 1992), pp. 225–259.

—— 'A Well-Articulated Primatology. Reflexions of a Fellow-Traveller', in S. C. Strum and L. M. Fedigan, eds, *Primate Encounters: Models of Science, Gender, and Society* (Chicago, Il: University of Chicago Press, 2000), pp. 358–381.

——, 'Turning around Politics: A note on Gerard de Vries' paper', *Social Studies of Science*, 37 (2007), 811–820.

——, 'What Protective Measures Can You Think of so We Don't Go Back to the Pre-Crisis Production Model?' http://www.bruno-latour.fr/sites/default/files/downloads/P-202-AOC-ENGLISH_1.pdf [accessed 7 June 2021].

Latour, B., and S. Woolgar, *Laboratory Life: The Social Construction of Scientific Facts* (Sage Publications, 1979).

Latour, B., and P. Weibel, eds, *Making Things Public: Atmospheres of Democracy.* Cambridge, MA: The MIT Press, 2005).

Laurent, B., 'Technologies of Democracy: Experiments and Demonstrations', *Science and Engineering Ethics*, 17 (2011), 649–666.

Law, J., 'Seeing Like a Survey', *Cultural Sociology*, 3 (2009), 239–256.

——, 'The Greer-Bush Test: On Politics in STS', in M. Akrich, Y. Barthe, and F. Muniesa et al., eds, *Débordements*, (Paris: Presses des Mines, 2010).

Levidow, L., 'Science as Culture', *EASST Review Volume* 37 (2018).

Lezaun, J., and L. Soneryd, 'Consulting Citizens: Technologies of Elicitation and the Mobility of Publics', *Public Understanding of Science*, 16 (2007), 279–297.

March, J. G., and J. P. Olsen, *Rediscovering Institutions: The Organizational Basis of Politics* (New York: Free Press, 1989).

Marres, N., 'Issues Spark a Public into Being: A Key But Often Forgotten Point of the Lippmann-Dewey Debate', in B. Latour and P. Weibel, eds, *Making Things Public: Atmospheres of Democracy*, (Cambridge MA: The MIT Press, 2005), pp. 208–217.

——, 'The Issues Deserve More Credit: Pragmatist Contributions to the Study of Public Involvement in Controversy', *Social Studies of Science*, 37 (2007), 759–780.

——, 'Testing Powers of Engagement: Green Living Experiments, the Ontological Turn and the Undoability of Involvement', *European Journal of Social Theory*, 12 (2009), 117–133.

——, *Material Participation: Technology, the Environment and Everyday Publics* (Basingstoke: Palgrave, 2012).

Marres, N., and D. Stark, 'Put to the Test: For a New Sociology of Testing', *The British Journal of Sociology*, 71 (2020), 423–443.

Mol, A., 'Ontological Politics. A Word and Some Questions', *The Sociological Review*, 47 (1999): 74–89.

——, *The Body Multiple: Ontology in Medical Practice* (Durham, NC: Duke University Press, 2002).

Mol, A., I. Moser, and J. Pols, *Care in Practice: On Tinkering in Clinics, Homes and Farms* (Bielefeld: Transcript Verlag, 2010).

Muniesa, F., Y. Millo, and M. Callon, 'An Introduction to Market Devices', *The Sociological Review*, 55 (2007), 1–12.

Møller, J., and S. E. Skaaning, *Democracy and Democratization in Comparative Perspective* (New York: Routledge, 2013).

Osborne, T., and N. Rose, 'Do the Social Sciences Create Phenomena? The Example of Public Opinion Research', *The British Journal of Sociology*, 50 (1999), 367–396.

Papadopoulos, D., *Experimental practice: Technoscience, Alterontologies, and More-Than-Social Movements. Experimental Futures, Technological Lives, Scientific Arts, Anthropological Voices* (Durham, NC: Duke University Press, 2018).

Papazu, I., 'Nearshore Wind Resistance on Denmark's Renewable Energy Island', *Science & Technology Studies*, 30, (2017), 4–24.

Pinch, T. J., 'The Sun-Set: The Presentation of Certainty in Scientific Life', *Social Studies of Science*, 11 (1981), 131–158.

Puig de la Bellacasa, M., *Matters of Care: Speculative Ethics in More Than Human Worlds*, Vol. 41 (University of Minnesota Press, 2017).

——, 'Matters of Care in Technoscience: Assembling Neglected Things', *Social Studies of Science*, 41 (2011), 85–106.

Shapin, S., and S. Schaffer, *Leviathan and the Air Pump: Hobbes, Boyle, and the Experimental Life* (Princeton, NJ: Princeton University Press, 1985).

Sismondo, S., 'Science and Technology Studies and an Engaged Program', in E. J. Hackett, et al, eds, *The Handbook of Science and Technology Studies*, 3rd ed., (Cambridge, MA: The MIT Press, 2008).

Star, S. L., 'Power, Technologies, and the Phenomenology of Conventions: On Being Allergic to Onions', in J. Law, ed., *A Sociology of Monsters? Power, Technology and the Modern World* (London and New York: Routledge, 1991), pp: 26–56.

——, 'The Ethnography of Infrastructure', *American Behavioral Scientist*, 43 (1999), 377–391.

Stengers, I., 'Another Look: Relearning to Laugh', *Hypatia*, 15 (2000), 41–54.

——, 'The Cosmopolitical Proposal', in B. Latour and P. Weibel, eds, *Making Things Public: Atmospheres of Democracy*, (Cambridge MA: The MIT Press, 2005), pp. 994–1003.

——, 'Including Nonhumans in Political Theory', in B. Braun, and S. J. Whatmore, eds, *Political Matter: Technoscience, Democracy, and Public Life* (Minneapolis: MN: University of Minnesota Press, 2010).

Strøm, K., 'A Behavioral Theory of Competitive Political Parties', *American Journal of Political Science*, 1990), 565–598.

Vadgaard, A. K. N., 'The Election Machine – Generating Danish Democracy' (PhD Dissertation, IT University of Copenhagen, 2016).

Venturini, T., 'Diving in Magma: How to Explore Controversies with Actor-Network Theory', *Public Understanding of Science*, 19 (2010), 258–273.

Verran, H., 'Re-Imagining Land Ownership in Australia', *Postcolonial Studies: Culture, Politics, Economy*, 1 (1998), 237–254.

Viveiros de Castro, E., *Cosmological Perspectivism in Amazonia and Elsewhere* (Manchester: HAU, 2012).

Watson, M. C., 'Derrida, Stengers, Latour, and Subalternist Cosmopolitics', *Theory, Culture & Society*, 31 (2014), 75–98.

Whatmore, S. J., and C. Landström, 'Flood Apprentices: An Exercise in Making Things Public', *Economy and Society*, 40 (2011), 582–610.

Winner, L., 'Do Artifacts Have Politics?', *Daedalus*, 109 (1980), 121–136.

Wynne, B., 'Misunderstood Misunderstanding: Social Identities and Public Uptake of Science', *Public Understanding of Science*, 1 (1992), 281–304.

PART I

THE INTERFACES OF TECHNODEMOCRACY

2

THE PROPOSITION: COMPILING AND NEGOTIATING DEMOCRACY IN A DANISH MUNICIPALITY

Anne Kathrine Vadgaard

DEMOCRATIC POLITICS TYPICALLY RELIES ON ELECTIONS FOR THE APPOINT-ment of political representatives, which involves the highly visible work of political campaigning and mobilisation of voters. But elections are also dependent on the largely invisible work of bureaucrats and temporary staff, who organise the electoral process and record and count the votes. On election day, citizens are transformed into voters, and ballots into political authority. This is only possible when polling stations are accessible, political candidates are registered and ballots are counted. All these nitty-gritty bureaucratic practices make democratic elections possible. At the same time, a particular kind of democracy appears from this invisible, taken-for-granted 'electoral infrastructure', which needs to be assembled and maintained in practice (Bowker and Star 2000).

The purpose of this chapter is to explore the kind of democracy that is situated in the electoral infrastructure of municipal elections. While the work of electoral bureaucrats can seem mundane and reproductive, it can also be responsible for re-assembling or transforming this infrastructure. Following such work with ethnographic methods allows for a productive unsettling of the distinction between bureaucracy and politics, as it becomes apparent that the dividing line between the bureaucratic and the political is both a political and a technical question.

Helen, a Danish bureaucrat, and my main informant during my 2013 field-work at a Copenhagen municipal election office, made this reflection on her work with organising polling stations:

> We could decide not to send the proposition to reduce the number of polling stations to the local City Council for further investigation. This would make it an administrative decision. But we chose to pursue a political assessment. After all, it is the politicians who govern.

Here, Helen offers a glimpse into a performance of democracy where the divide between political and administrative responsibilities is perceived as given, but where the status of a problem as political or administrative is at the same time left to the discretion of the bureaucrats. In what follows, I explore the work surrounding a written proposition to reduce the number of polling stations in Copenhagen Municipality. I dwell on the socio-material practices through which municipal democracy appears, is negotiated, and becomes entangled with idea(l)s about bureaucratic work. In doing so, I approach representative democracy as a practical achievement by the public administration. More specifically, my focus is on the bureaucrats' attempts to produce a proposition that is politically viable. This emphasis on the mixing of bureaucracy and politics is a way of recognising and appreciating democracy as 'technodemocracy' – with inspiration from Latour's foregrounding of the social and material realities of science in action that led him to approach science as 'technoscience' (Latour 1987).

My approach builds on two claims about democracy. The first is that there is no decontextualised or pure form of democracy. This is not to say that there are no situated democratic ideals. In the case of Denmark, the ideal of a deliberative and representative democracy can be traced back to debates between theologian Hal Koch and solicitor Alf Ross in the years following the Second World War (Ross 1946; Koch 1991[1945]; Togeby et al. 2003). However, this chapter focuses on how democratic ideals and principles are intertwined with practices, concepts and procedures in public administration. The focus on electoral practices allows me to avoid treating democracy as a set of ideals separate from lived reality. According to this approach, ideals are not pure democratic principles that 'get dirtied in the harsh and messy social world when they are "applied" in practice' (Mol and Berg 1994: 248). Rather, ideals emerge entangled with local practices. In my case, they appear as the work on the proposition progresses. Throughout this chapter, I follow how the issue of the accessibility and cost of polling stations is negotiated and rearranged as part of the work on the proposition. In the words of Asdal and Hobæk (2020: 255), I seek to highlight how election office work includes 'not only knowing the issue but also the ability to work on and *modify* issues'. Democratic politics happens partly through bureaucracy, and democratic ideals are situated in these practices.

My second claim about democracy is that constructions of democracy are 'as social – and material – as anything else' (Mol and Berg 1994: 248). Following a long tradition of ethnographies of bureaucracies and documents (see Hull 2012; Frohmann 2008; Harper 1998; Riles 2006; Strathern 2006), I explore the rearrangement of political, organisational and legal concerns through the writings of the proposition. Through techniques and technologies, document-ing practices and archival work, a democratic order emerges which is detached from the political document that is produced. Although the work of the politi-cal administration tends to be hidden and is usually considered apolitical and mundane, these technologies and practices are by no means neutral (Barry 2001). On the contrary, they are generative of modern forms of knowledge, expertise and governance (Riles 2006).

In what follows, I will first briefly explain the background of the proposi-tion up until the point when I started my fieldwork. I will then tell the story of the election office bureaucrats Ida and Helen, with an emphasis on how their efforts to ensure the political viability of the proposition also complicated it.

COMPILING AND COMPLICATING

The proposition is a three-page document. The document lists six arguments for reducing the number of polling stations in the municipality. This is the result of a long process. Since early 2012, drafts of the proposition have been circulating between meeting rooms and offices, employees and committees in the munici-pality. It all started when the politicians in the Election Committee asked the election office to investigate the possibility of reducing the number of polling stations in order to cut down on the costs of the election. Two months later, at the next meeting of the Election Committee, the election office presented a proposition to reduce the number of polling stations from 54 to 38. The elec-tion team presented a rough draft as they wanted to know whether to continue in this direction before they put more effort into it. While the politicians were happy with the work, several members emphasised that it was important not to remove polling stations from districts with low voter turnout. The election team was requested to revise the proposition with this in mind. The Election Committee also emphasised the importance of broad political agreement on this matter. So, in November 2012, the local group leaders of the political parties represented in the City Council were involved in the process. At this point, the reduction of polling places in the proposition had been revised to 40 follow-ing the suggestions made at the initial meeting with the Election Committee. The majority of party leaders, however, did not support a reduction of polling stations based on the prospect of financial savings. The politicians argued that democracy is expensive by nature and that it would be important that any reduction in polling stations would not affect voter participation. It was decided only to look into mergers of polling stations that would improve accessibility.

The work on the third version of the proposition started at the time I began my fieldwork in the election office. For six months, I followed the 'immense labor and negotiating skill that lies behind the formulation of every sentence' (Strathern 2006: 196) of the final proposition.

Learning bureaucratic argumentation

How do you write a municipal proposition? This was the question Ida, a recently hired municipal employee, faced one cold January morning in the election office. As a recent university graduate, she had little experience of municipal bureaucratic work, and she had never written a proposition before. She turned to Helen, sitting next to her, for help. Helen had worked in the municipality for many years and had also written the previous two versions of the proposition. First, Ida found the latest version of the proposition in the municipal case and document management system, along with the document template. With these key elements in view on the screen, Helen taught her some basic formats for a proposition. Ideally, a proposition should be no longer than three pages and contain only four to five arguments. This concise format was a result of the politicians' tight calendars, Helen explained, which only left them an hour for committee meetings and even less time to prepare. If documents were imprecise or too lengthy, the politicians would be unable to make informed decisions. Helen used the term 'strategic argument' to explain what should make up a significant part of a proposition. A strategic argument would align with the objections made earlier by the Election Committee and the City Council. Yet Helen also expressed an aversion against being too 'strategic', as she did not like the connotation of technocratic coercion. The goal of the proposition is not to coerce the politicians, she argued, but to provide the foundation for them to make an informed decision.

The previous version of the proposition, which Ida now opened, proposed splitting one polling station into two in an area with a growing population and new housing projects. This version pointed out that despite the growth of the area, the polling station was still located in the same old building, and the polling station had problems with long queues on election day. it was therefore proposed to add a second polling station. For strategic reasons, Ida underlined that setting up a polling station in a centrally located and entirely new public building would future-proof the polling station with regards to location and increased capacity, as well as offer easier access for voters. Furthermore, it would 'contribute to solidarity and local identity in the new neighbourhood', Ida wrote. Strategically reframing the argument of the proposition to meet concerns about accessibility and long queues was an important way in which the election office sought to make the proposition politically viable and thus reorganise the electoral reality.

Working with these arguments, Ida learnt to navigate between administrative reasons for fewer polling stations and political objections to these plans. She learned to use politically 'safe' expressions such as accessibility, instead of problematic notions such as financial cost. In doing so, she aligned with the Election Committee's concern with the democratic ideal of accessibility.

Complicating the proposition

One afternoon, about one week into the revision process, I found Ida glancing at a large map of Copenhagen that hung in the middle of the office. The floor-to-ceiling map showed nine different voting districts and 54 different polling station areas in the municipality, each outlined with coloured lines. Small dots showed the 54 current polling stations, and small arrow stickers highlighted the polling stations under consideration for change. Ida needed an overview, as she was in the process of adjusting the arguments so the reduction would only be from 54 to 50 stations instead of the 38 or 40 stations that the first two versions of the proposition had suggested.

As it turned out, cost and accessibility were no longer the only concerns in play. The election team had discovered several irregularities in the current setup. The election law states that each of the 54 areas must be associated with a polling station. Although it is not specified, Ida and Helen took it that polling stations must be located within the area they are associated with. This did not apply to three stations, so these irregularities had to be dealt with first. Ida therefore visited potential sites for new polling stations around the city to get a sense of their accessibility, and she discussed the matter with employees in the department that governs the portfolio of municipal buildings. Back in the office, she stared at the map to try to unite all the different requirements and mumbled: 'By now, the arguments have almost got me blocked. They have been in the making for so long'.

She put her finger on the polling station in district 1, and I asked her about the arguments for removing it. First, Ida stated, the polling station is not even located in district 1, but in district 3. Secondly, the school that hosts the current polling station is not particularly accessible. It is undergoing reconstruction, and as a result the entrance is not at the level of the surroundings, making it difficult to access for the walking impaired. She had not been able to find any alternative locations in the area. Instead, she explained, the polling place should be merged with another that was both accessible and more centrally located. This is what Ida eventually suggested in the proposition, along with the removal of four other polling stations by merging them with already existing polling stations: two of them due to similar district irregularities and one because it was located at a school that was closing and thus unavailable for the next election. The last polling station was deemed to have very low accessibility, and as it was situated very close to two other polling stations, the election team proposed to merge all three. In the end, despite the fact that legal concerns were clearly the main reason for taking a closer look at these polling stations, the proposition highlighted the accessibility of the merged polling stations rather than issues of legality.

In short, while strategic arguments about accessibility were important, the writing of the proposition was not simply a matter of aligning with the interests of the political committee. The election team followed up on a multitude of concerns, discovered new site-specific problems and opportunities, and discussed many different scenarios. In the process of working on the proposition what was initially raised as a financial question was complicated to include concerns regarding accessibility, waiting time, legal regulations and hopes for urban development.

Circulating the proposition

One afternoon in late February 2013, Ida stated, 'it doesn't get any better now' and sent the proposition to Marie, the head of the election office, for review. Ida had finished constructing her six arguments: five arguments for merging the five polling stations and one argument for setting up a polling station at a new location in a new neighbourhood. The proposition was now ready to be circulated through multiple political and bureaucratic units for approval, before getting the final verdict in the City Council. Two days later it was on the Election Committee's agenda, and during this meeting, the Lord Mayor and chairman of the committee again focused on the issue of voter accessibility. Marie and Ida from the election team, who were present at the meeting, clarified that some of the changes were due to legal regulations. The election team eventually agreed to go over the suggested changes to clarify how they affected accessibility. With that settled, the Election Committee unanimously approved the proposition.

The next stop after the Election Committee's approval would be another municipal committee, the Finance Committee. The road to the Finance Committee, however, was bumpy. High-ranking employees in the Finance Administration now needed to look at the document. For each step up the political ladder that the proposition travelled, a parallel step was needed in the administration. This approval process was slow, and the proposition got stuck on the Financial Director's table.

While awaiting his approval, the previously discarded concern about costs re-emerged. Part of the reason was that the Department of Citizen Services, including the election team, had recently been moved to the Finance Administration. This move effected an increased focus on finances and costs, which in turn affected the approval process for the proposition. So, while the proposition remained stuck on the Financial Director's table, several employees closer to the director in the organisational hierarchy emphasised a concern with costs, which had been the original driver behind the proposition to reduce the number of polling stations. To accommodate this concern, Ida added a rough estimate of potential savings to the proposition. In 2013, the savings were projected to balance out with the added cost of an information campaign. Potential savings for 2014 were more difficult to estimate. The overall budget for the elections to come in 2014 was not available this early, and Ida struggled to calculate the numbers. At this moment, the election team was trying to figure out how to rein-corporate the previously discarded concern with costs without compromising the Election Committee's dismissal of financial arguments. The uncertainties of the election budget came to the foreground when the Finance Administration questioned the election team's method of calculation. Ida had calculated the costs based on the expenses of establishing a polling station, whereas the Finance Administration suggested that the calculations should be based on the yearly costs of running a polling station. Ida revised the proposition accordingly and added a new section named 'Economy'.

This new version of the proposition with the section about costs won approval from the Finance Administration. The proposition was, however, still not ready for the Finance Committee's agenda. After reviewing the document, the secretary had requested that the proposition be sent to the political group leaders of each party in the City Council for further discussion. The opening quote of this chapter relates directly to this suggestion. Helen and Marie discussed who should handle this request: 'We could decide not to send the proposition to reduce the number of polling stations to the local City Council for further investigation. This would make it an administrative decision', Helen said. In her opinion, sending the proposition to the political group leaders was yet another time-consuming detour. But instead of going with an 'administrative decision', they decided to go for a 'political assessment', which implied asking the politicians in the Election Committee. 'After all, it is the politicians, who govern', as Helen had explained.

Fortunately for the election team, the Election Committee decided not to redirect the proposition to the political group leaders. After three months of circulating between different political and bureaucratic units in the municipality, the three-page proposition was finally ready to be discussed at the meeting of the Finance Committee in May 2013. Here, it was recommended by 11 out of 12 members of the committee and on 4 June the proposition was on the agenda at the City Council meeting, awaiting final approval.

Disengaged responsibility

When the proposition finally reached the City Council, all the revision work and the time-consuming circulation up and down the organisational hierarchy was erased. Only the final document made it to the politicians. In contrast to the election team, which had been reconfiguring polling stations for more than twelve months, these politicians had never seen the proposition before. They encountered the polling stations through the short and highly selective way in which the administration had chosen to present the new electoral infrastructure on three pages of paper.

In scientific practices of fact-production, the world is also packed into words, but in ways that differ from the political decision-making procedures described here. Latour's (1999) work on 'circulating reference' shows the processes through which information from the Brazilian Amazonas is translated into a scientific paper. Following his presentation of botanists' and soil scientists' investigations into whether the savanna is encroaching upon the forest or vice versa, he explores how scientists collect samples and transport and transform these from objects into words. For instance, small samples of branches brought back from the forest, neatly stored and rearranged in a cabinet in Manaus, are slowly transformed into notes and botanic categories in the hands of the botanist, as she looks for emerging patterns in the leaves. But even within this botanist's collection, where the forest is reduced to its simplest expression, the reverse process is never far away; the simple expressions can 'quickly become as thick as the tangle of branches from which we started' (Latour 1999: 39). Thus, while some original context may be lost in the transformation and simplification, the reference back to the forest remains intact, and the chain of reference between the forest and the scientific paper is always reversible (Latour 1999).

References do not circulate with the same kind of reversibility in the municipal decision-making process. While the politicians are provided with an appendix of maps of the polling stations, which allows them to track some of the arguments in the proposition back to specific areas in Copenhagen, these short referential chains are rarely explored further, nor are they supposed to be. The politicians keep themselves within what is narrowly defined as 'the issues in the file'. The task of the municipal employee collecting the file is therefore not to create the kind of two-way path seen in scientific research practices. Rather, the task at hand is to provide the politicians with a number of unquestionable and thoroughly investigated arguments. Ida's assignment in the election office was to create 'strategic' arguments from which a decision could easily be reached. This was not done by accumulating more and more data, as would be the approach of the scientific researchers Latour describes. Instead, Ida produced a narrow, coherent document by linking and unlinking the issues of cost and accessibility in different ways (Latour 2010).

An instrumental part of this mode of referring to the electoral reality is the election team's ability to rearrange arguments in the face of conflicting and changing concerns. When performing this task of (un)linking and rearranging the issue, Ida could not afford to be married to any of the arguments. She needed to move into a disengaged position from which she could recognise a plurality of concerns, complicate matters if necessary, and rearrange the issue according to new and shifting conditions. While Ida was passionate about her work, her focus was on the bureaucratic craftsmanship of constructing arguments that would make the proposition 'go all the way', rather than on any particular aspect of the proposition.

The bureaucratic detachment from the political decision-making process was intact when the proposition was approved on 4 June 2013. The election team had been working on the proposition since May 2012, so when Ida told me about the final approval, I thought about congratulating her on the success. But with my observation of detachment in mind, I just replied: 'That's good'? Ida must have been able to read the implicit question mark after my hesitant remark as she merely responded, 'it is certainly new'.

Later, however, when I talked to Ida about the entire process, she did mention that by the time the Election Committee requested and decided to move on with the proposition to reduce the number of polling places, it had become a criterion of success for the election office that the proposition would be approved. But a successful outcome would require, Ida stressed, that everybody involved in the process be heard. Long and time-consuming procedures were not a sign of failure, she pointed out, but a prerequisite of approval. It follows that the indifference I noted towards the outcome does not reveal a lack of care for the document. It is about not being attached to any particular arguments so that their smooth unlinking, rearranging and reformulation is possible. The disinterest can thus be seen as a necessary lack of concern with political arguments, decisions, ideals, political schemes or hopes for the city and its citizens. These are rather the concern of politicians, whereas the bureaucrats simply carry out the tasks imposed on them, whether relating to accessibility or reducing costs. By continuously performing the relationship between the election team as responsible for the *basis* of the decision, and the politicians as responsible for the *decision itself*, the election team creates a small, disengaged space for manoeuvre in which multiple, diverse and shifting political concerns can be taken into account.

THE POLITICS OF THE PROPOSITION

As should be clear by now, the process of compiling, negotiating and making the proposition 'go all the way' involved time-consuming work. At the same time, in the circulation of the document, a boundary was drawn between political decision-making and bureaucratic casework. This was explicated several times during my conversations with the election team, as exemplified by the opening quote. Here, Helen emphasises that it is the politicians who govern and make assessments, in contrast to the work of the bureaucracy.

Following Matei Candea's analysis of the non-politics of language activists in Corsica, the election team can be perceived as creating a non-political space through which they can attend to the proposition in a disengaged manner (Candea 2011). They collect and test arguments that form the basis on which the politicians make decisions. Through this work, Ida and the team enact the administrative and the political worlds as distinct from one another. In other situations, however, such as the discussion over who should decide on the circulation of the proposition to the group leaders, the borders between the political and the non-political are less clear-cut and are, indeed, frequently renegotiated. The political and the non-political emerge as opposed performative projects, rather than figure and ground (Candea 2011: 321).

I would suggest, however, that accepting a fluctuating yet rather straight-forward opposition between the political and the non-political risks missing some of the complexity of the situation. When the election team makes sense of its work as non-political and as opposed to the politics of the City Council, this is done in terms that resembles a fixed idea of political power based on a four-year policy cycle, where citizens, by means of elections, delegate authority to politicians who then govern and make decisions. This understanding of politics follows democratic principles of representative democracy and is in its ideal form independent of (administrative) practices.

In other instances, however, the dichotomy between the political work of the City Council and the non-political work of the bureaucratic offices appears ambiguous. Ida had to weigh and balance conflicting bureaucratic and political concerns. The financial administration emphasised costs, but the politicians were more concerned with accessibility. According to the politicians, costs were to be explicitly disregarded as an argument for changing the structure of the polling stations. The first version of the proposition was rejected by the City Council because it argued for reducing the number of polling stations based on the prospect of financial savings. In my reading of the situation, the administrative crafting of the proposition does not precede political concerns or decision-making in a linear fashion. Throughout the process of revising the proposition, Ida paid attention to the political concern with maintaining voter participation regardless of costs. Yet she eventually included a small paragraph on the expected savings of reducing the number of polling stations. A political move, one might say, to appease the finance administration and get the proposition accepted. Through the process of building the proposition, administrative and political concerns were mutually brought into being and adjusted. They sometimes collided when arguments regarding costs encountered arguments of accessibility, with accessibility trumping costs as a political concern. At other times, and in the final version of the proposition, they were combined (Law 2004). In this situation, the domain of politics was both emergent and given, site-specific and not-yet-located, both worked on and perceived as something independent of the administration, but still dictating and framing the work performed there.

COMPILING AND NEGOTIATING DEMOCRATIC 'GOODS'

Instead of settling on one definition of the political, which may or may not include an idea of the non-political, I suggest we keep all the different meanings and notions of 'the political' alive as markers of democracy in situated practice. The continuous negotiations and circulations of the proposition presented in this chapter suggest that ontologically different political and non-political realities and 'goods' may co-exist (Law and Mol 2002; Mol 1999). The proposition's concerns with accessibility and costs could be seen as universal democratic goods. But this would miss how several goods were at stake in the situation. The compilation of the proposition illustrates how different political and bureaucratic concerns were constantly brought into play in unforeseen ways. They clashed and competed when the proposition was sent from the Election Committee to the Finance Administration and back. They overlapped when closing old polling stations would reduce costs *and* improve accessibility. They were both disrupted by legal concerns about polling station regulations.

As the proposition twisted and turned its way through the political and bureaucratic hierarchy in the municipality, it was impossible to single out a universal and explicitly 'good' democratic polling station solution. Instead, the election team's work on the proposition can be viewed as an emergent heterogeneous practice that shapes democratic 'goods' and political decisions on polling stations in relation to concerns over accessibility and costs. Thus, as the proposition slowly emerged in the election office, a situated approach to democracy emerged with it and eventually appeared in the final three-page-long proposition. Here, accessibility and voter mobilisation weighed heavily, but were inseparable from legal and financial concerns. Democratic decision-making was performed as something different from bureaucratic casework, as the election team made sense of its work with reference to itself as a pre-existing, non-political, disengaged administrative entity. And as a result, in the neatly ordered proposition, the laborious socio-material practices of rearranging concerns, the ambivalent moments characterised by shifting tensions, the colliding democratic and bureaucratic ideals, and the inevitable twists and turns of the proposition, were erased. As Kimberly Coles (2007) remarks in her study of elections in Bosnia-Herzegovina, the myth of democracy hides the reality of democracy-making.

REFERENCES

Asdal, K., and B. Hobæk, 'The Modified Issue: Turning around Parliaments, Politics as Usual and How to Extend Issue-Politics with a Little Help from Max Weber' *Social Studies of Science*, 50 (2020), 252–270.

Barry, A., *Political Machines: Governing a Technological Society* (London: The Athlone Press, 2001).

Bowker, G. C., and S. L. Star, *Sorting Things Out. Classification and Its Consequences* (Cambridge, MA: The MIT Press, 2000).

Candea, M., 'Our Division of the Universe: Making a Space for the Non-Political in the Anthropology of Politics' *Current Anthropology*, 52 (2011), 309–334.

Coles, K., *Democratic Designs: International Intervention and Electoral Practices in Postwar Bosnia-Herzegovina* (Ann Arbor, MI: The University of Michigan Press, 2007).

Frohmann, B., 'Documentary Ethics, Ontology, and Politics' *Archival Science*, 8 (2008), 291–303.

Harper, R., *Inside the IMF: An Ethnography of Documents, Technology and Organisational Action* (New York: Academy, 1998).

Hull, M. S., *Government of Paper. The Materiality of Bureaucracy in Urban Pakistan.* (Berkeley, CA: University of California Press, 2012).

Koch, H., *Hvad Er Demokrati* (Copenhagen, DK: Gyldendal, 1991).

Latour, B., *Science in Action* (Cambridge, MA: Harvard University Press, 1987).

——, *Pandora's Hope. Essays on the Reality of Science Studies* (Cambridge, MA: Harvard University Press, 1999).

——, *The Making of Law: An Ethnography of the Conseil D'État* (Cambridge: Polity Press, 2010).

Latour, B., and S. Woolgar, *Laboratory Life. The Construction of Scientific Facts* (Beverly Hills: Sage Publications, 1979).

Law, J., *After Method: Mess in Social Science Research* (London, UK: Routledge, 2004).

Law, J., and A. Mol, 'Local Entanglements or Utopian Moves: An Inquiry into Train Accidents', *The Sociological Review* 50 (2002), 82–105.

Mol, A. 'Ontological Politics. A Word and Some Questions', in J. Law and J. Hassard, eds, *Actor Network Theory and After* (Oxford, UK: Blackwell Publishing, 1999).

Mol, A., and M. Berg, 'Principles and Practices of Medicine' *Culture, Medicine and Psychiatry* 18 (1994), 247–265.

Riles, A. 'Introduction: In Response', in A. Riles, ed., *Documents: Artifacts of Modern Knowledge* (Ann Arbor, MI: The University of Michigan Press, 2006), pp. 1–41.

Ross, A. *Why Democracy* (Cambridge, MA: Harvard University Press, 1946).

Strathern, M., 'Bullet-Proofing: A Tale from the United Kingdom', in A. Riles, ed., *Documents: Artifacts of Modern Knowledge.* (Ann Arbor, MI: The University of Michigan Press, 2006).

Togeby, L. et al., *Power and Democracy in Denmark. Conclusions.* (Aarhus: Magtudredningen, Aarhus University, 2003).

3

TECHNOCRATIC ACTIVISM: ENVIRONMENTAL ORGANISATIONS, CARBON MARKETS AND EUROPEAN BUREAUCRACY

Véra Ehrenstein

WHEN READING THE NEWS IN THE AUTUMN OF 2019, ONE COULD NOT ignore how politicised the issue of climate change has become. Throughout the year, pupils and students organised school strikes for the climate in a movement called Fridays for Future, flight shame spread among an ever-larger number of people and civil disobedience took hold in several big cities. At the United Nations climate summit in New York in September 2019, the Swedish activist Greta Thunberg reminded the world's heads of state and government of their political responsibilities vis-à-vis younger generations. A month later, 150 French citizens started auditioning experts to formulate policy propositions on how to reduce the nation's greenhouse gas emissions without jeopardising social justice. Around the same time, on the other side of the Channel, Extinction Rebellion activists were multiplying disruptions, blocking London City Airport and spraying fake blood on the Treasury's building in order to push the British government to declare a climate and ecological emergency.

Whether it is through performances convening a broader public via the media (Barry 1999) or elected governments resorting to *ad hoc* technologies of participation (Laurent 2016), the issue of climate change is, it seems, in need of more democracy. This therefore raises the question of already existing forms of democratisation. To start exploring this question, I propose to look at the making of climate policy in the European Union and foreground the work of environmental non-governmental organisations. I will refer to their lobbying of European institutions, including the democratically elected Parliament, as *technocratic activism*. This is a discreet mode of political action that stands in sharp contrast to the highly visible mobilisations witnessed recently (e.g., Extinction Rebellion and Fridays for Future, see de Moor et al. 2020). In fusing civil society advocacy, technical expertise and a knowledge of bureaucracy, environmental lobbying in Brussels offers, I suggest, a striking example of what the editors of this volume refer to as 'technodemocracy'.

The cornerstone of European climate policy is a market mechanism called the European Union Emissions Trading System (EUETS). Operational since 2005, the EUETS is an evolving piece of legislation. The research on which this chapter is based was carried out in 2016–2017, when the revision of the EUETS for post-2020 was under discussion. As I was doing fieldwork in Brussels, I was expecting to see industrial lobbyists participating in the legislative process. The European Commission is known for having always encouraged the involvement of business associations in policy-making (Laurens 2018). Lacking the legitimacy of elections and dealing with economic questions related to the single market project, the new bureaucracy has made stakeholder participation a key aspect of EU politics. While I did meet business lobbyists, though, my attention was drawn to the environmental non-governmental organisations that had also been actively involved in the revision of the climate policy. I then decided to conduct a series of interviews with these activists.[1] Our conversations revolved around their experience of lobbying the EUETS and the legislative matters that, at the time, they were most concerned about (the future value of the emissions cap and the problem of the surplus of allowances). But before turning to these technical questions, I will first situate this piece within the STS literature on publics and further introduce the EUETS.

FROM EMERGENT PUBLICS TO TECHNOCRATIC ACTIVISTS

In STS, there is now a substantial literature on emergent publics. Scholars in the field have been particularly keen to explore processes whereby citizens and consumers become politically active, from the formation of concerned groups triggered by technoscientific issues and their overflows (Callon et al. 2009), through the enrolment of laypeople in participatory initiatives aimed at eliciting collective concerns (Voß and Amelung 2016) to everyday 'material participation' in domestic settings (Marres 2012). This interest in emergent publics has been extended to climate change through the study of personal carbon accounting devices (Marres 2012) and deliberative panels on geoengineering (Bellamy and Lezaun 2015), to cite only two examples. Looking for new politics, STS scholars have tended to pay less attention to more conventional forms of political engagement.[2] Like other contributions in this volume, my chapter shifts this focus: the main protagonists of the story are environmentally minded professionals bearing job titles such as 'policy officer' and 'analyst'. We will see them navigating a set of policy-making institutions, which one of them termed the 'Brussels ecosystem', and witness their concern about the capacity of the EUETS to be effective as a climate policy. While their advocacy can also be traced online (e.g., Blok 2011), I attend to their work *in situ*.

In order for us to understand what matters to these environmental advocates, we need to know a little more about the technicalities and the short history of the policy under scrutiny. MacKenzie's piece (2009a) on the EUETS is a good place to start. It shows that EU policy-makers adopted a somewhat experimental approach when they decided to implement the market mechanism through a phased structure (on carbon markets as sites of experimentation, see Callon, 2009). The policy was launched in 2005 for a pilot phase, followed by a second phase from 2008 to 2012. Phase 3 started in 2013 and ended in 2020, while in December 2017 the rules for a fourth phase (2021–2030) were agreed on. This sequential dynamic has led to quite a few changes in the policy. Mackenzie wrote his account of the EUETS at the beginning of phase 2, when key aspects were still decided nationally. His analysis unpacks disputes about the stringency of the policy in which national governments were opposing the European

Commission. As the EUETS entered its third phase, it was further harmonised. Brussels became the main locus of policy-making and lobbying by business associations and environmental organisations. Discussions were particularly intense in the periods when the legislation, or some aspects of it, were being renegotiated, as was the case in 2016 and 2017 when I carried out this research.

Since 2013 (the start of phase 3), the EUETS has regulated the emissions of more than 11,000 industrial sites in 31 countries,[3] from oil refineries and coal-fired power generators, to cement plants and blast furnaces. The total quantity of CO_2 that these sites are allowed to emit in a year is capped, and for the current phase (2013–2020) the value of this EU-wide emissions cap has been fixed in advance. Each year, an amount of emissions allowances equivalent to the cap (one allowance represents one tonne of CO_2) is created in an electronic registry. Some allowances – about 40% of the cap – are transferred for free to regulated facilities according to common allocation rules established, again in advance, for the whole phase. The rest is sold in auctions by member states. Companies are responsible for monitoring how much CO_2 is emitted across their sites, and subject themselves to audit. Emissions reports must be submitted annually to national authorities, and allowances must be surrendered electronically, to assess whether they match the reported emissions levels. As the EUETS is a market, companies short of allowances can buy some from those having excess allowances. Overall, allowances are expected to be scarce, creating incentives to invest in cleaner technologies. Given that they can be traded, emissions abatement is expected to take place where it costs the least, and so the cap would be met at the lowest possible aggregated cost. Hence the cost-effectiveness of emissions trading praised by economists and EU policy-makers.

It is commonplace to talk about the European Union as a technocracy, and the EUETS does not deviate from the highly technicised regulatory style that has come to characterise European action (Barry 2001; Laurent 2019). Lobbying the EUETS, therefore, is a matter of technicality. As one interviewee put it, 'there is no scenery, no visual that captures the very dry, technical policy and data-driven ETS. It's not something that fires people's imagination'. The policy appears unsuitable for the visual approach of environmental campaigning (think of images of orangutans displaced by palm oil plantations) and disruptive performances. Instead, the 'policy officers' and 'analysts' I spoke to were engaged in what I call *technocratic activism*. With this term, I insist both on the arcane procedures of European bureaucracy they need to master and the technicalities of the climate policy, which they also have to come to grips with. The EUETS is a highly technical piece of legislation. Models and statistics are used to inform key decisions (on the value of the cap and the allocation of allowances) and various indicators and thresholds are developed, and revised, to implement those decisions. Any attempt to change policies must engage with the numerical artefacts through which the EUETS is given effect. The absence of a 'European public' these activists might appeal to provides further reason for adopting a 'gentler approach' that embraces technicality but at the cost of 'downscaling' radicality (Bomberg 2012: 414). As this chapter suggests, technocratic activists are experts less in the rallying of crowds or the economics of emissions trading – the practices, respectively, of grassroot environmentalists and economists – than in the practical workings of a market-based policy customised to the particularities of EU politics.

CRITICAL SCRUTINY RATHER THAN IN-PRINCIPLE REJECTION

When I conducted this research, three organisations appeared to be most active with regard to the EUETS.[4] The first organisation is a well-established non-governmental network operating as a coordination platform for climate advocacy. Its Brussels-based secretariat is composed of about twenty people closely following EU policy discussions. It is then able to inform constituent organisations of the issues at stake and help build common positions. This network also has the capacity to mobilise its membership to get an idea of how the EUETS is experienced locally, and pressure national politicians. Created a decade ago, the second organisation active on the EUETS has, from the start, scrutinised the use of carbon markets as climate policy. The EUETS being the largest emissions trading system to date, it is a major focus for the advocacy work of the ten people or so in the core team in Brussels. A eurocrat I interviewed at the Directorate General for Climate Action considered it to be the reference environmental organisation. The third organisation involved in lobbying the EUETS when I conducted this research was based in London. Also set up a decade ago, it started as an online platform providing information about the market mechanism and allowing anybody to buy and cancel allowances. Drawing on a high level of technical skills, this organisation distinguished itself as the 'number cruncher', to quote one of its 'analysts'. At the end of 2019, it shifted its focus from 'working to reform and improve the EU carbon market' to accelerate 'coal phase-out'. While I was not able to inquire into what motivated such a shift, it seems reasonable to posit that the UK leaving the EU could be one of the reasons.[5]

My interlocutors within these organisations were European citizens – German, Dutch, British, Lithuanian – with varying experience in environmental advocacy, from enthusiastic university graduates in their mid-twenties to knowledgeable longstanding climate activists. Some had previously worked for Members of the European Parliament (MEPs) and consultancy firms, while others were initiating a reverse move, leaving the world of non-governmental activism to become parliamentary assistants and consultants. The youngest ones were educated in anthropology, physical geography and economics, with one having a PhD and another willing to finish the doctoral research they started in parallel to their environmental lobbying. Positioned at the interface between politics and expertise, my interviewees insisted on qualifying their advocacy as 'evidence-based'.

For these technocratic activists, the everyday was that of a lobbyist: following the EU agenda, conducting online research, writing reports, releasing statements, tweeting, organising and participating in policy events in Brussels. Most importantly, their efforts were attuned to the legislative process, trying to 'influence' the European Commission when it produces its proposals, before turning to MEPs and their assistants once the legislation is in their hands. Obtaining face to face meetings was said to be essential. As one interviewee put it, 'if somebody agreed to commit 15 minutes of their Brussels schedule to listen to what you have to say, they are unlikely to ignore what you are saying'. Although all three organisations were also active online, physical co-presence is essential to the practice of technocractic activism.

If some differences could be identified in the content of their advocacy – for example, whether carbon capture and storage should be supported by EU climate policy – the activists I met nevertheless agreed on what was wrong with the EUETS. The bottom line was that the policy is not stringent enough to bring down CO_2 emissions. Without being market enthusiasts, my interlocutors advocated a system 'that does what it says it should' and considered that 'carbon markets in theory can work, if there is a political will'. To support this claim, references were made to academic research in economics showing 'how [emissions trading] could be made to work'. There was a general understanding that the EUETS could be designed in a way that ensures that its economic logic delivers the promised transformative changes.

The activists I interviewed aimed to exert what they call a form of 'democratic control', which they equated to bringing in 'a different perspective [to that of] industrial lobbyists'. Indeed, the EUETS is a piece of legislation to which business associations devote plenty of time and money, often to limit its stringency. But my interlocutors also felt that their own difficulties in creating interest 'from the civil society side', as 'other NGOs doubt that their engagement can make a difference', meant that their voice might be lacking sufficient legitimacy. A few years ago, I was told, there was more activism. Large environmental organisations, such as Greenpeace's and WWF's European offices, used to be involved 'in trying to improve the ETS'. Out of disappointment with its lack of ambition, they gradually diverted their attention away from climate policy. The three organisations mentioned above were left alone in their efforts to stimulate the political will they thought was missing to make carbon markets work.

One should not rush to conclude that this reformist attitude is naïvely optimistic. The challenges facing technocratic activists in their dealings with EU climate policy are similar to those faced by transnational climate activists vis-à-vis the United Nations' climate talks: an 'efficacy dilemma' (de Moor 2018) seems to come with the territory. 'Should I stay or should I go' provides a good summary. A long-time activist explained:

> We always have this discussion: at what point does it make more sense to spend your effort elsewhere? At what point do you lose your credibility if

you support a tool that, basically, you already know, with the revisions [the rules for phase 4 and other regulatory adjustments that will be discussed below] that are proposed, it's not going to work until at least 2030? [...] On the other hand, if you say, 'scrap it', you don't influence anything. So I have been saying 'this is a policy that is not going away, if you like it or not, so we better engage with it to some extent'.

The 'scrap it' refers to the slogan 'scrap the ETS' of a campaign led in 2013 by a coalition of environmental organisations. The campaign was launched as the European Commission was preparing a reform to address a major problem in the EUETS, namely the accumulation of a surplus of allowances (more on this in the next section). The advocacy message was simple: the market mechanism cannot be 'fixed' and should just 'be abolished no later than 2020 to make room for climate measures that work' (letter, no date). While the 'scrap the ETS' campaign mobilised a coalition of organisations known to be against the principle of market-based policy, it created controversy among less radical activists about the meaning and usefulness of their own engagement with the policy.

One advocacy success, however, was mentioned to me several times: the ban in phase 3 (from 2013 onwards) of CO_2 offsets from projects destroying industrial gases. When the EUETS was established, it was linked to another carbon market, the Clean Development Mechanism (CDM), set up by the United Nations' climate talks (MacKenzie 2009b). The CDM was an international project-based offsetting system, through which emissions reduction activities implemented in so-called developing countries could yield offsets that EU policy-makers decided to render fungible with allowances. Companies were thus authorised to import these reductions into the EUETS and use them to cover a limited share of their emissions. The linkage was justified as further decreasing the cost of compliance. A few projects hosted by chemical plants in China and India turned out to provide the majority of offsets bought in Europe, attracting the scrutiny of environmental activists. Online research, data gathering and calculations revealed that the plant owners seemed to be increasing their production solely for the purpose of reducing the pollutants and selling offsets.[6] Reports and press releases were published in what became a victorious campaign that succeeded in outlawing the controversial offsets. As an interviewee summarised:

> I think there was just too much publicity around it and it was so, I mean it was so extreme! They really manipulated these projects, manipulated their emissions to maximise credit generation. That was something that could be sold to the press very easily. So there was an outcry about this, that's why it was then changed, because there was enough pressure.

Yet despite the pressure and the publicity, 'some made sure that those changes didn't come too fast'. Large companies, in particular the French and Italian electricity producers EDF and Enel, actively resisted the move as their trading desks had large financial stakes in the sale of the now infamous offsets (Bryant 2016). Their lobbying might have delayed the ban. A massive influx of cheap reductions was brought in the EUETS and used for compliance before the decision entered into force. For the activists I talked to, though the ban was a victory, it left a bad taste.

The three main environmental organisations active on the EUETS that I introduced earlier in this section were all committed to critical scrutiny. Unlike more radical anti-market activists, they rejected in-principle rejection of the EUETS, because the policy was considered to be 'here to stay'. The efficacy of their lobbying was, nevertheless, a source of debate. Campaigning against the problematic offsets had been successful but the circumstances were particular: 'it was so extreme' that it almost amounted to fraud. Among my interlocutors, at least when we spoke in 2016 and 2017, the general feeling was weariness more than irritation, as the latest revisions of the EUETS, which I will turn to now, had not produced the hoped-for changes.

TIMING AND POLITICAL SCENES

A major concern for the activists I spoke to was how many allowances were in circulation in the market and how many more would be added in the coming years. This decision would directly affect the environmental impact of the EUETS given that, in such a system, emissions levels ought to be constrained by the total quantity of allowances made available. All my interviewees argued that the policy had not been ambitious enough for quite some time. Two issues needed to be better addressed: the surplus and the value of the emissions cap.

The surplus refers to unused allowances that have accumulated in the accounts of regulated industrial sites and companies in the last decade. In 2013, its value exceeded two billion tons of CO_2, the equivalent to two years of emissions of all the facilities covered by the policy. The problem was that from 2008 onwards the quantity of allowances created each year has exceeded by far what was being released into the atmosphere. The substantial size of the surplus, and the very low price at which allowances were traded in the early and mid-2010s, resulted from generous national allocation during the second phase of the policy, a decline in industrial activities and in demand for energy due to the economic recession, and a move towards cleaner energy sources encouraged through policy incentives. Environmental activists explained to me that the difficulties in dealing with this issue are a matter of temporal rigidity. This rigidity was created by the phased structure of the EUETS and the pace of decision-making in the EU. When the recession happened, the EUETS just entered its second phase (2008–2012). By then member states had established their own caps, based on growth projections made at a time of high levels of industrial activity in Europe. This temporal mismatch between expected and actual emissions was reinforced when the cap for phase 3 was agreed on. Its linearly declining value from 2013 to 2020 was derived from a policy target set by the European Council in 2007, just before the crisis (a 20% cut in CO_2 emissions in 2020 compared to 1990, as part of a broader climate and energy policy package). I was told that changing what has been endorsed by all heads of state and government is hard. The European Commission tends to *de facto* endorse the European Council's policy directions when it develops its policy proposals. To launch the revision of the EUETS for phase 3, the Commission took the 20% emissions cut target for granted. The legislative process ended in 2009 with a directive whereby the amount of allowances to be distributed more than ten years into the future was fixed in place, based on a policy objective that might have appeared ambitious in 2007 but was clearly not constraining enough a couple of years later. Thus, even as the recession continued to bite, a growing surplus had been committed to.

As the imbalance between supply (issue allowances) and demand (reported emissions) became obvious, around 2010, environmental organisations started being vocal. They argued for the cancellation of excess allowances to be distributed in the future, as anticipated by the already known value of the cap. The measures eventually introduced were less radical. A first emergency measure, called backloading, was passed that consisted in delaying the issuance of allowances meant to be auctioned between 2014 and 2016 to later in phase 3. After lengthy negotiations, a more structural adjustment, the Market Stability Reserve, was adopted. The Reserve would keep a percentage of allowances out of the market every year so that companies looking for allowances could buy them from companies owning the surplus. Once the value of the surplus would be reduced to a reasonable amount, set in advance, allowances kept in the Reserve could be made available again. When it was first envisioned, the idea of a Reserve had found some support among environmental activists. But the actual measure proved disappointing. In 2016, as the rules of the Reserve were finalised, my interlocutors still attempted, with moderate optimism, to influence the outcome. As explained below, their position was consistent with their initial advocacy message in favour of cancellation:

> Now, one of our proposals around that was to say, either limit the size of the MSR [Market Stability Reserve] and cancel anything that enters it that's over, we suggested a limit of 1 billion, because that would give you 10 years of return back to the market at 100 million a year. Another way of limiting the size of the MSR would be to say that allowances expire after they've been in there for 10 years.

In order to be heard in Brussels, arguments for a more constraining climate policy must be articulated in numbers and thresholds. This is technocratic activism. The regulatory measures eventually adopted did include the possibility of cancellation, but according to conditions that environmental organisations considered too limiting. The fight about the surplus was not over, however, as the functioning of the Reserve was expected to be renegotiated in 2021.

When I was conducting this research, advocacy for a tougher EUETS also focused on the value of the cap in phase 4. The revision of the policy for the 2021–2030 period relied on policy targets decided, once again, by the European Council far in advance (in 2014). The Commission used this target in its Impact Assessment to calculate potential values for the future cap. What could not have been foreseen was the global momentum taking over the United Nations' climate talks in December 2015. The Paris Agreement endorsed by almost all the countries of the world, including European member states, provided techno-cratic activists with a new argument: according to climate models and emissions scenarios, to meet the ambition announced in the treaty, the European Union would need stronger commitments, including a lower 2030 cap for the EUETS. This was not just an environmentalists' crusade: the European power associa-tion articulated the same message. While their motivations no doubt differed, environmental organisations and business lobbyists were momentarily speaking in unison to support a tougher climate policy. The Commission's proposal for phase 4 was finalised in the summer 2015 when it was handed to a small group of parliamentarians, the European Parliament's Committee on Environment, Public Health and Food Safety. A tighter cap for 2030 gained traction within this committee of 50 or so MEPs. It was included in its report to the parliament. But at the plenary, amendments were introduced, and, in February 2017, a majority voted to come back to the initial value of the cap, in accordance with the target set in 2014.[7] An activist made sense of the U-turn as follows:

> Just before the vote we heard that the conservatives wanted to move away from the compromise. We tried to persuade the socialists to stick to their commitment, but the socialist group split, and 20% voted against the most ambitious elements. […] We heard from a German NGO that a very influ-ential MEP from Saarland had a lot of pressure from the steel lobby that sent out a letter five days before the vote. We tried to write a response and meet with the MEP and their assistants; we were also in touch with the socialist

shadow rapporteur, but the pressure from the steel industry spread out, and it created an alliance with trade unions in Saarland.

For technocratic activists, closely monitoring MEPs' twists and turns in order to tune their advocacy in real time is essential, although in this case it did not work. The vote in Strasbourg was shaped by what was going on in Saarland, Germany, where public demonstrations against a too stringent EUETS took place. Environmental technocratic activism was overtaken by old school representative democracy and trade union politics.

A local workers' movement, national electoral reasons and coalition dynamics in the Parliament led to a vote against what my interviewees described as the 'most ambitious elements' of the legislation, namely a lower emissions cap and revised rules for the allocation of allowances to industrial sectors, such as steel plants. In phase 3, the latter were receiving large supplies of (surplus) allowances for free.[8] The Commission had suggested restricting access to free allowances after 2021, but the Parliament amended the proposition. Voicing their disappointment with the revised Directive, environmental organisations found only limited interest in the media (on the lack of EU-wide media coverage of the EUETS, see Bomberg 2012).[9]

The three organisations active on the EU ETS did not, however, abandon further intervention. Whereas they considered they had so far mostly 'tried to act through technical details' (e.g., the value of the cap and the rules of the Market Stability Reserve), their pressure could also target international politics in order to 'make sure there is a discussion about the adequacy of the ETS for the Paris objectives'. My interlocutors saw a 'policy window' to strengthen the market mechanism in a series of forthcoming events. The first was the release in 2018 of an IPCC report about what should be done to ensure that the average temperature at the Earth's surface stays below a 1.5-degree increase compared to pre-industrial times, a target mentioned in the Paris Agreement. United Nations' meetings, during which national commitments taken as part of the new global agreement would be assessed, were another potential arena for triggering changes in EU climate policy. These meetings tend to attract media attention and are also places where diplomatic reputations are at stake, which is why climate activists keep attending them (de Moor 2018). Under international pressure, European heads of state and governments might modify what, as the European Council, they or their predecessors had decided back in 2014. Bringing the EUETS in line with the Paris Agreement was a simple message that technocratic activists hoped would be effective, even though some had already been told by MEPs that 'the ambition' they called for was 'unrealistic'.

To practice technocratic activism, one needs to understand the technicality of an increasingly complicated mechanism and navigate the temporal rigidity of EU policy-making. 'Things are updated infrequently', complained an activist as we were talking about how long it took for the problem of the surplus to be addressed through a technical fix, the Market Stability Reserve, they found unsatisfactory. And yet, this procedural slowness is what allows EU policy to be negotiated among a wide range of parties, members states, hundreds of elected politicians and a bureaucracy committed to the participation of stakeholders, including environmental organisations. Given the disappointing results of their lobbying on the fourth phase of the EUETS, some were planning to shift focus from EU technocracy to climate diplomacy. Advocacy requires a certain art of timing, and here this meant knowing when to switch to another political scene.

STIRRING PUBLIC OUTRAGE?

In addition to intervening in the slow-paced policy-making process on the EUETS to strengthen the cap and reduce the surplus, some activists also concerned themselves with the fate of these excess allowances. As we shall now see, asking 'who owns the surplus?' leads to more confrontational advocacy, the purpose of which appears to be stirring public outrage.

As early as 2010, an environmental organisation decided to make public the large quantities of unused allowances owned by a handful of 'carbon fat cats'. It singled out two industries, steel and cement, where companies had received large quantities of allowances in excess of their needs. This was a consequence of the recession having a lasting negative impact on the construction sector in the second phase of the EUETS, while free allowances kept been distributed to cement and steel plants based on their emissions levels measured in

2005–2007 – that is, before the crisis. When I say the issue was made public, I do not mean that confidential information was revealed. Calculating a company's surplus allowances can be done using two datasets: the annual emissions levels reported for all the industrial sites owned by a company and the quantity of allowances these sites received for free. Both datasets are available online, but in a format that does not make easily visible who owns how much. Technocratic activism here took the form of collating the data to present them in a readable manner with a catchy narrative that was picked up in the British media: 'fat cats' are making 'windfall profits' from an unequal distribution of unneeded allowances.[10]

When I was doing fieldwork, the same organisation went on to investigate the cement industry in more depth. Its analysts were taking inspiration from papers published by academic economists to conduct more elaborate calculations using trade statistics. The aim was 'to emphasise how the ETS was creating the wrong kind of incentives'. A 2016 report showed that cement plants were exploiting a regulatory loophole to maximise the amount of free allowances they were entitled to, keeping production artificially high in countries with low demand and exporting excess products within the European Union and beyond. The purpose of the report was not just to shame the industry. It discussed the technical difficulties of trying to reduce the CO_2 emissions released by the manufacturing of a material essential to infrastructures and urbanisation. While environmental activists had wanted to initiate a dialogue with the industry, the European cement association did not appreciate the gesture. It circulated a press release 'trying to trash the report' and phoned the organisation to tell them they were 'being juvenile'. Such a 'high level of mistrust' came as a surprise for one of my interviewees.

> Let's imagine I had written that the cement sector is able to reduce its emissions by 90% easily, that would have been a nightmare for them, and for us! Because they would have spent months to go and tell MEPs that what [the organisation] has written is rubbish, and that would have been bad for [our] reputation.

Even if their capacity to shape the EUETS had been limited, activists rightly believed that their word could durably damage reputations. They had therefore expected a more cooperative attitude from the cement industry and its business association, which they thought had 'missed an opportunity to educate [them]'.

Several of my interlocutors agreed that asking who unashamedly benefits from the surplus is a topic that 'could be sold to the press'. One can see why: it is a story of a public good (allowances that, if auctioned, would provide revenues to governments) being appropriated by private interests (industries lobbying to get them for free). The issue featured, for example, in a French TV programme about 'multinationals' climate bluff' broadcasted in May 2016.[11] One of the investigated multinationals was the cement producer Lafarge. Lafarge appeared on the 'carbon fat cats' list and its surplus of allowances was the topic the journalists decided to inquire into. The programme was clearly sympathetic to environmental organisations, who blamed the multinationals. The programme featured an interview with an activist taking apart the rhetoric of a leaflet of the cement association, involving printed spreadsheets full of numbers and the views of Brussels' European quarter: these were the visuals of technocratic activism. It may all have been slightly underwhelming if not for the outraged tone of the commentator arguing that the EUETS had shifted from the 'polluter pays' principle to a 'polluters are paid' policy.

We see here that environmental organisations have been looking to exert pressure beyond the EU bureaucracy and MEPs, and to take aim directly at regulated industries. While attempts to initiate a dialogue with the cement association failed, the classic strategy of shaming well-known companies for owning surplus allowances found some echo in the media. Windfall profits derived from the EUETS are more prone to stir popular outrage than the rules of the Market Stability Reserve or the mismatch between the cap in phase 4 and the Paris Agreement. But one can doubt whether headline grabbing advocacy has a lasting, productive effect and should supersede technocratic activism. For technocratic activists, the aim ultimately remains to shape the dry and technical policy that is the EUETS.

.   .   .

After reading these pages, one might ask why environmental organisations should continue to lobby the European Union Emissions Trading System. Certainly, this chapter has shown that these organisations often do question the efficacy of the effort invested, sometimes wasted, in technocratic activism. And yet, these activists simultaneously defended the need for a reformist attitude, especially in contrast to the more radical position of organisations in favour of rejecting market-based policy and scrapping the EUETS altogether. Engaging with the technicalities of emissions trading produces a more nuanced critique: it reveals how hard it is to make such a market mechanism deliver on its promises.[12] The environmental activists featured in the chapter considered that emissions trading was 'here to stay', in the European Union, and in other jurisdictions where similar policies are being implemented. By providing evidence of the failed promises of the EUETS, the activists hoped to prevent emissions trading from being seen as a simple, unproblematic policy model, which is how economists have tended to advertise it. It seems that, so far, environmental organisations have had limited success in countering industrial lobbying and electoral manoeuvres. Taking to the streets to march for the climate, and boycotting polluting companies might give more political leverage. It would be interesting to further tease out the characteristics of technocratic activism in the EUETS and contrast it with environmental justice movements in California, for example, where activists lobby the state's cap and trade policy, linking climate change to more tangible problems, such as air pollution, that affect poorer social groups (Mendez 2020). Yet, in both cases, it is hard to see how policy-making can be completely bypassed. Demands on policy-makers must be made in a specific manner, fit into a potentially complex regulatory architecture and be adjusted to the pace of bureaucracy. In Europe, a middle ground seems needed between popular movements and the EU's technocratic machinery, and this is how we can conceive of what the techno-democratic practice of technocratic activism, as sketched out in this chapter, is trying to achieve.

ENDNOTES

1 I met with two members of each of the three environmental organisations most active on the EUETS in 2016 and 2017. Fieldwork also included extensive documentary research, interviews with staff members of the European Commission, parliamentary assistants, national civil servants, academic economists and industrial representatives, and participation at policy events in Brussels. This research was supported by the European Research Council (grant no: 313173) and I would like to thank Daniel Neyland.

2 This is not entirely correct (cf. Barry 2001); see also the recent special section on parliaments in *Social Studies of Science* (Dányi 2020). On the EU turning to non-governmental organisations to stimulate forms of European citizenship in domains such as the environment and consumer rights, see Warleigh (2000). On the involvement of environmental activists in the United Nations' negotiations on climate change, see Betsill and Corell (2001) and de Moor (2018). On environmental justice movements and the Californian cap and trade policy, see Mendez (2020) and for a comparison between climate activism in the United States and the European Union, see Bomberg (2012).

3 The 31 participants are the 28 member states of the EU (before Brexit) plus Iceland, Lichtenstein and Norway.

4 In order to guarantee the anonymity of my interlocutors I decided not to give the names of these organisations.

5 Both the second and third organisations belong to the European non-governmental network. Although their structure and political capacities differ from one another, all three organisations rely on donations.

6 These projects aimed to reduce hydrofluorocarbon-23 emissions released by the production of refrigerant gases and nitrous oxide emissions released by the production of adipic acid (for nylon manufacturing). The two gases were associated with (very) high Global Warming Potential. Reducing one tonne of hydrofluorocarbon-23 could yield more than 11000 tonnes of offsets (MacKenzie 2009b).

7 In parallel to being amended by parliamentarians, the legislative draft was discussed by ministers, who also approved the cap initially proposed.

8 In phase 2, most allowances were handed out for free. This changed in phase 3, as electricity producers were required to buy their allowances in auctions. Free allocation was maintained for 'industrial' sites. The justification was that these produced goods traded internationally and might be exposed to 'carbon leakage due to loss of competitiveness' as foreign competitors would gain a higher market share through cheaper imports (Ehrenstein and Neyland 2021).

9 One of the most environmentally minded newspapers in the UK just mentioned in passing that 'environmental campaigners claim that the reformed ETS does still

not do enough. https://www.theguardian.com/environment/2017/feb/28/reform-of-eu-carbon-trading-scheme-agreed (accessed 10 April 2020).
10 https://www.theguardian.com/environment/2011/jun/19/emissions-trading-manufacturing-industry; https://www.theguardian.com/environment/damian-carrington-blog/2013/feb/14/carbon-emissions-carbon-tax (accessed 10 April 2020).
11 The TV programme is available at: https://www.youtube.com/watch?v=N_DUArvLO-U (accessed 10 April 2020).
12 As mentioned by a reviewer, this approach resonates with the work of STS scholars committed to unpacking the nitty-gritty aspects of markets and public policy, which requires, to some extent, suspending the urge to criticise. But while the latter pause and step back, trying to re-problematise what it is all about, technocratic activists follow a different tempo (that of the EUETS), gathering only actionable knowledge that quickly becomes out-of-date.

REFERENCES

Barry, A., 'Demonstrations: Sites and Sights of Direct Action', *Economy and Society*, 28 (1999), 75–94.
——, *Political Machines: Governing a Technological Society* (London: The Athlone Press, 2001).
Bellamy, R., and J. Lezaun, 'Crafting a Public for Geoengineering', *Public Understanding of Science*, 26 (2017), 402–417.
Betsill, M. M., and E. Corell, 'NGO Influence in International Environmental Negotiations: A Framework for Analysis', *Global Environmental Politics*, 1 (2001), 65–85.
Blok, A., 'Clash of the Eco-Sciences: Carbon Marketization, Environmental NGOs and Performativity as Politics', *Economy and Society*, 40 (2011), 451-476.
Bomberg, E., 'Mind the (Mobilization) Gap: Comparing Climate Activism in the United States and European Union', *Review of Policy Research*, 29 (2012), 408–430.
Bryant, G., 'The Politics of Carbon Market Design: Rethinking the Techno-politics and Post-politics of Climate Change', *Antipode*, 48 (2016), 877–898.
Callon, M., 'Civilizing Markets: Carbon Trading between In Vitro and In Vivo Experiments', *Accounting, Organizations and Society*, 34 (2009), 535–548.
Dányi, E., 'The Insides and Outsides of Parliamentary Politics', *Social Studies of Science*, 50 (2020), 245–251.

de Moor, J., 'The "Efficacy Dilemma" of Transnational Climate Activism: The Case of COP21', *Environmental Politics*, 27 (2018), 1079–1100.

de Moor, J., M. De Vydt, K. Uba, and M. Wahlström, 'New Kids on the Block: Taking Stock of the Recent Cycle of Climate Activism', *Social Movement Studies*, 5 (2020), 619–625.

Ehrenstein, V., and D. Neyland, 'Economic Under-Determination: Industrial Competitiveness and Free Allowances in the European Carbon Market', *Journal of Cultural Economy*, 14 (2021), 596–611.

Laurens, S., *Lobbyists and Bureaucrats in Brussels: Capitalism's Brokers* (London: Routledge, 2018).

Laurent, B., 'Political Experiments That Matter: Ordering Democracy from Experimental Sites', *Social Studies of Science*, 46 (2016), 773–794.

——, *European Objects. The Troubled Dreams of Harmonization* (Habilitation à diriger des recherches, Institut d'Etudes Politiques de Paris, 2019).

MacKenzie, D., *Material Markets: How Economic Agents are Constructed* (Oxford: Oxford University Press, 2009a).

——, 'Making Things the Same: Gases, Emission Rights and the Politics of Carbon Markets', *Accounting, Organizations and Society*, 34 (2009b), 440–455.

Marres, N., *Material Participation: Technology, the Environment and Everyday Publics* (Basingstoke: Palgrave MacMillan, 2012).

Mendez, M. A., *Climate Change from the Streets: How Conflict and Collaboration Strengthen the Environmental Justice Movement* (New Haven, CT: Yale University Press, 2020)

Voß, J. P., and N. Amelung, 'Innovating Public Participation Methods: Technoscientization and Reflexive Engagement', *Social Studies of Science*, 46 (2016), 749–772.

Warleigh, A., 'The Hustle: Citizenship Practice, NGOs and "Policy Coalitions" in the European Union - the Cases of Auto Oil, Drinking Water and Unit Pricing', *Journal of European Public Policy*, 7 (2000), 229–243.

4

USE YOURSELF, KICK YOURSELF! LEARNING FROM A NEWSPAPER HOW (NOT) TO DO GOOD PUBLIC DEBATE

Andreas Birkbak

INTRODUCTION

ACCORDING TO THEORIES OF DELIBERATIVE DEMOCRACY, PUBLIC DEBATE IS a cornerstone of democratic politics. It is in public debate that individuals are thought to emerge as citizens and contribute to the formation of public interests (Habermas 1989). How can this idealised notion of public debate be grounded and specified in concrete democratic situations? In the autumn of 2013, I enrolled in something called the 'School of Debate and Critique', initiated by the Danish newspaper *Politiken*. According to the organisers, the purpose of the school was to educate a 'new generation' of participants in 'public debate' in Denmark. I joined 149 other students below 30 years of age, selected based on written applications. Once accepted, we could participate in half a year of fortnightly evening talks given by the newspaper staff and various high-profile guest speakers. In addition to attending these 'inspirational evenings', as the organisers called them, the school involved a series of written assignments, a couple of full-day workshops, a diploma upon completion and the prospect of writing a letter to the editor that was 'sharp enough' to be printed in the paper.

On my first evening at the school, I found myself sitting on a black folding chair in *Politiken*'s building across from the City Hall in the centre of Copenhagen. The large, square room could barely hold 150 people. Moments before, I had been part of a long and crowded line on the pavement outside, where we waited to be individually admitted by two security guards. Their presence reminded me that security at *Politiken* had been dramatically increased after the Muhammed cartoon crisis in 2005. Once inside, I had a sensation of being one of the chosen few – despite the fact that the room was crammed. I had been admitted into the halls of one of the oldest and largest newspapers in Denmark, which cultivates an image of being a pillar of Danish democracy. I also sensed hesitation and scepticism in my own chest, and among my co-participants: Would this 'school' be worth our time, or was it simply a marketing stunt? Soon, the editor-in-chief entered the stage, and the room settled down. From the podium, he explained that the school was a project designed to 'improve the quality' of 'the debate out there in our democracy'.

I find this short statement to be indicative of a certain way of thinking about public debate, where it is assumed to always already exist in an abstract and idealised way. Modern liberal democracy in its mainstream version seems to depend on this narrative of a civic sphere with its own existence, independent of the state and the market (Somers 1995a, 1995b). In this chapter I am interested in a different way of thinking about public debate, which considers it to be not primordial, but completely artificial in the constructivist sense that public debate is staged with the help of specific technologies and arrangements (Latour and Weibel 2005, Barnett 2008). Such a perspective can draw on work in STS on public participation, which has studied the enactment of publics with techniques such as focus groups (Lezaun and Soneryd 2007), surveys (Law 2009), and citizen hearings (Jensen 2005, see also Krabbenborg 2020, Pallet and Chilvers 2020, in this volume). However, my case also differs from these, since it is about how media dynamics rather than social science techniques establish a reference to 'the public'. Media actors such as *Politiken* explicitly seek to not just represent the public or public debate, but also intervene in how public debate is organised, as the school initiative illustrates.

Specifically, *Politiken* expressed a wish to intervene by including more young people in newspaper debate, because they perceived young people to be under-represented (as well as interesting as potential future customers). At the same time, *Politiken* wanted to qualify newspaper debate and make sure it lived up to certain editorial standards long cultivated by *Politiken*, such as being well-written, eye-catching and able to spark further debate. In the following, I will explore *Politiken*'s dual ambition of including a 'new generation' in public debate and improving a public debate that is thought to already exist 'out there'. I will argue that there is a tension in this agenda between trying to come to terms with a new and, for *Politiken*, apparently rather exotic phenomenon ('young people today') and already knowing what the proper technique and arena will be ('sharp' and 'improved' newspaper debate). To what extent is *Politiken* willing to adjust itself in order to connect with these youngsters who have caught its attention, and to what extent will it remain in a business-as-usual mode of doing newspaper debate in the way it already believes is right?

What is at stake here may be explored with Isabelle Stengers' distinction between governance and politics (Stengers 2010). For Stengers, governance is the continuation of the existing 'majority repertoire' (ibid.: 23) or, differently put, conformity with the existing public order (ibid.: 16). Politics, on the other hand, involves a *hesitation* with respect to what is of importance. As indicated, *Politiken*'s aims were twofold: to include new actors in public debate and to ensure a proper public debate. As such, there is no reason to believe that *Politiken* was prepared to restrain itself to only practise hesitance. To the contrary, *Politiken* was seeking to define and demonstrate its version of good public debate against the backdrop of less well-informed and well-written contributions on social media, for example (see Birkbak 2018 for a comparison of debate on Facebook and debate in *Politiken*). From the onset, then, it seemed that *Politiken* veered toward 'governance' rather than 'politics', in Stengers' terms.

Yet the question of Stengersian politics and hesitation is crucial, because this is arguably where democracy is at stake in the sense of expanding political agency through moments where hitherto muted actors are taken into account on their own terms (Stengers 2005). In addition to describing the democratic situation of *Politiken*'s school, I wish to raise the question of to what extent *Politiken* in the process stumbled upon opportunities for hesitation that might have allowed it to learn something about young people on their own terms. To the extent that moments of hesitation took place, *Politiken's* school may be said to have contributed to democratic politics in a Stengersian sense, whereas if hesitation and learning did not happen, *Politiken* remained in a mode of governing the status quo of newspaper debate. The purpose of raising this question with Stengers is to avoid the assumption that 'high quality' newspaper debate is automatically a contribution to democratic politics. Instead, I wish to use the specific democratic situation of *Politiken's* school to open up scrutiny into how exactly newspaper debate can be said to contribute to democratic politics – or not.

In the following, I will first describe and discuss the recruitment of participants, then move on to the ideas taught at the school, and finally turn to a few aspects of how the school was organised in daily practice. I base the analysis on my field notes from the autumn semester of 2013, interviews with participants and organisers at the school, and newspaper content (see Birkbak 2016 for an overview of the material).

RECRUITING A DIVERSE ELITE

From the beginning, *Politiken's* staff emphasised that they wanted the process of securing a spot among the 150 participants at the School of Debate and Critique to be highly selective. As a result, the organisers were anxious to receive enough applications. In order to attract participants, *Politiken* issued an open call for written applications through its printed paper, various social media channels, and through a network of 20–30 young people who it already knew and understood to be well-connected. The organisers ended up receiving around 300 applications, which they saw as an acceptable number. Here is what the assistant hired by *Politiken* to help run the school told me about the selection process:

> Those who have shown an amount of creativity or an exceptional language ability [in their applications], they have landed a spot, so that has actually been the first round of selection. That is not very many. Then there is a lot in the middle, where we have tried … in part, there is a gender-related balance,

where we preferred fifty-fifty. Luckily that turned out to not be so difficult, because the applications have been almost fifty-fifty. Then there is age. We filtered out many of the younger people who applied [...] Apart from the age factor, there was a geographic factor and a demographic factor. If there is anyone who have applied from Aarhus or Aalborg [other major cities in Denmark], then let them get in [...] If there were anyone who were not university students, but electricians or primary school teachers, then we would probably give a little more weight to their application [...] There was also the ethnic factor, which we took into account.

This quote suggests that the organisers of the school saw the recruitment of the 150 students as a balancing act between talent and representativeness. This reflects an ambition expressed by the main organiser of the school to assemble 'the sharpest minds and the sharpest pens', while also reaching for diversity in relation to a conventional set of variables: gender, age, geographical location, education level, ethnicity. The two ambitions first seemed opposed to me. However, the organisers found the two things to be connected, since they found texts written by demographic outliers more likely to be interesting and suitable for publication due to these writers' supposedly 'unique perspective on social life'. The school assistant explained how pursuing not just a talented, but also a diverse, group of young people was connected to what *Politiken* is trying to achieve with its opinion pages more generally:

There needs to be something for every taste when you make a debate section; the editor of debate cares very much about that. There needs to be something related to one agenda and something related to another agenda. There needs to be some heavy politics, but there also needs to be something lighter. Lifeworld, trends, and so on. There should also preferably be some men and some women represented, some older and some younger. It is these kinds of balancing exercises that you try to take into account all the time in order to catch the attention of different readers, because *Politiken* has quite a lot of readers. It is the same balance we have tried to... there is a very strong connection between the debate section and the School of Debate and Critique.

In other words, the organisers saw the school as part of a more general effort to provide a varied newspaper diet and cater to different segments of *Politiken*'s readership. The school organisers were worried about recruiting a cohort of students that was too homogenous, not so much due to a social scientific concern with representativity, but because of a more practical concern that a homogeneous group would not deliver newspaper content deemed extraordinary and varied enough to be printed. In other words, while *Politiken* tried to achieve broad representation in a way that resembles how citizens are recruited for public participation events like consensus conferences (Jensen 2005), it also broke with this logic and sought to actively include demographic outliers because of their qualities as 'obviously interested parties', to quote Jensen (2005: 226). In a sense, 'bias' was a good thing at *Politiken*'s school, at least against the backdrop of a core readership and pool of participants sharing similar upper middle-class ideas and values.

As suspected, achieving the desired diversity turned out to be difficult. Many of the applications came from what the organisers saw as the same group of people: Copenhagen-based social science students at the university level, deeply interested in current affairs, but all with quite privileged backgrounds and similar ambitions. In order to compensate for this, the recruitment process prioritised students who 'stood out', as the organisers put it. As the school commenced, the organisers continued to highlight the value of the few demographic outliers among the participants, such as the one participant who attended a vocational school, and the one who flew in from Aalborg more than 300 kilometres away.

Here, it is useful to know that *Politiken* understands itself as part of a 'cultural struggle', as several of the editors put it when talking at the school sessions. The struggle refers to a liberal reform movement dating back to the 'Modern Breakthrough' in Scandinavian literature and education in the 1870–90s (Bredal 2009). The landscape of Copenhagen intellectuals at that time included two of *Politiken*'s co-founders, Viggo Hørup and Edvard Brandes. To this day, *Politiken* remains a social-liberal newspaper catering to the urban, educated upper middle-class located on the centre-left of Danish politics. The fact that the school organisers actively promoted students who were either right-wing, workers, not from Copenhagen, or belonged to ethnic minorities, indicates that they were concerned with being inclusive, yet in a specific way that continued their identity as an open-minded urban elite newspaper.

I would like to highlight the failure to recruit a more heterogenous group of participants as a first opportunity for Stengersian 'learning'. *Politiken* did 'hesitate' in the sense that it was concerned with how to recruit participants from under-represented backgrounds. However, the hesitation did not translate into action. The failure could have prompted *Politiken* to slow down and hesitate more in an attempt to consider why so few young people with unskilled, 'provincial', right-wing or other-than-Danish backgrounds applied. However, starting the recruitment process with 20–30 young people who were already 'friends of the house' comes across as the opposite of trying to reach beyond the urban elite. The open call for written applications also favoured young people who were already well connected and confident writers. As such, the recruitment process never really broke with *Politiken*'s own terms. This is, however, not the only way to go about recruiting participants for a debate school. Other organisations in Copenhagen have set up initiatives similar to *Politiken*'s, which specifically target people usually under-represented in a newspaper debate, such as those with a vocational background (CEVEA 2019). For *Politiken*, the main emphasis seems to have been on assembling an elite group capable of 'quality' writing. Indeed, one of the organisers put it this way during one of the school evenings: 'The school is elitist – and all the better for being so'. In short, some demographic outliers were included, but on the terms established by *Politiken*.

By assuming to already know what constitutes quality newspaper debate and by not trying to learn from under-represented groups how to reach out to them, it may be argued with inspiration from Stengers that *Politiken* missed an opportunity to learn something new about young people as a central target group of, and contributor to, public debate. *Politiken* wanted to reach what for it counted as 'minorities', but in practice only welcomed those that were well connected and able to take part in an elitist project. To contribute to democratic 'politics' in Stengers' sense, the school would have had to involve minorities on their own terms. It follows that when it comes to recruitment, *Politiken*'s school was more an act of governance than of politics. Moving on to the content of the school teaching will allow me to explore this further.

LEARNING TO 'KICK INWARDS'

During the first evening, we were told that there would be a series of writing exercises with different themes. The first theme was 'the underclass'. Two public figures, who had both grown up in underclass families, were invited to come and speak as a source of inspiration. We were then instructed to each write individual letters to the editor of maximum 800 words in length, on the topic of the contemporary Danish underclass. Two weeks later, when the next meeting took place, we learned that *Politiken* planned to move seven or eight of the letters forward towards potential publication, which could indicate that the writing assignment had been a success. However, the exercise also came across as incongruent with *Politiken*'s idea that school participants should speak from their personal 'perspectives on life' – the very perspectives on the basis of which they had been recruited. Instead, 150 young people, most of whom had no direct experience of the living conditions of the lower classes, were asked to write about the rather crude theme 'the underclass'. Moreover, those invited to talk on behalf of the underclass were those that had 'made it' and become public figures. So, while the choice of topic (the underclass) was somewhat aligned with the ambition found in the recruitment process of bringing under-represented voices and themes into public debate, *Politiken* continued to stay within the existing 'majority repertoire' of those already present in the media and the elite (Stengers 2010: 23).

The theme for the next writing exercise was 'the biggest problem for our generation'. This was arguably more in line with the logic of writing from personal experience, since all participants could claim some sort of direct experience with being a member of 'the younger generation'. At the same time, we were explicitly asked to generalise about *everyone* in our age cohort rather than write from our specific standpoint. In a way, we were asked by *Politiken* to perform the vague phenomenon of a 'new generation' that they sought to give a voice in public debate.

I found the first two writing assignments difficult, as did many of the other students I talked to. I dutifully invented an opinionated argument about the underclass and about my generation's biggest problem and wrote 800 words about each, but the writing processes did not connect well with any of my personal experiences or concerns. At the third evening meeting, we were told that, moving forward, the assignments would no longer have a fixed theme. The argument made by the main organiser of the school, who was also the editor of debate at *Politiken*, was that we 'should not feel tied down'. So far, many of the opinion letters submitted by the students gave a 'too strong feeling of responding to a fixed question' and of 'trying too hard to live up to the expectations of *Politiken*'. In the eyes of the organiser, this resulted in 'a lack of originality, focus, and a lack of a clear stance'.

This shift can be understood as another opportunity for 'hesitation' on the part of the organisers, in the sense that the quality of the written assignments was not as high as they had hoped, which made them reconsider their setup. But the moment of hesitation did not last long. The main organiser swiftly concluded that the problem was an overly fixed task, and decided to abandon the pre-given topics. The organisers could have slowed down more and asked themselves why exactly the two first writing assignments did not deliver enough texts that *Politiken* could recognise as being of high quality. The more specific problem may have been that we were asked to write about topics that did not affect us, and, as such, we were not able to draw on personal experience in our writing in a convincing manner.

While *Politiken* did not explain its shift in tactics in this way, it seemed aware of this line of thinking in its general writing advice to us. The instructors said they were looking for texts that were 'more personal' and 'less predictable'. A good letter to the editor, we were taught, is not only well argued and timely, but it is also written from a deeply personal vantage point. As one of the participants at the school expressed it in my interview with him:

> They ask for personal voices. Hyper-personal. Some who speak from their own standpoint. I have an impression that they say they go for sharp opinions, but they really go for the personal standpoints, a mass of [personal] experience. If [an applicant] just wrote an impersonal application... I do not at all think [they] would get through with [it].

It seems that the staff at *Politiken* understood the importance of cultivating different voices speaking from their own particular standpoints, but at the same time they insisted on defining the terms for how to make this happen, rather than slow down and try to learn from young people on their own terms. This argument can be expanded by looking more closely at the instruction we received at the school. The recommended form of an opinion letter was to start with a deeply personal experience and then broaden out towards a societal issue. To be sure, making the jump from private to public matters of concern is a stable part of the craft of opinion letter-writing (Boltanski 2012). However, a high premium was put on arguments which the instructors characterised as 'kicking inwards' in the sense of criticising or going against the grain of one's own socio-demographic group. For instance, when a participant wrote a piece on being genuinely but secretly interested in religious questions, this was held up as surprising and as an example to follow, because the organisers perceived 'the young' to be generally uninterested in religious matters. Another letter that was put forth as a good example was written by a person of Muslim heritage who wrote critically about childrearing in Muslim families. Yet another letter claimed that there were an increasing number of 'castrated males' in today's society dominated by 'feminine values'. This letter was foregrounded as 'kicking inwards' because it was written by a man who included himself in the category of (figuratively) castrated males.

These letters, held up at the school as examples to follow, indicate that *Politiken* was looking for a certain kind of argument, perceived to have the specific quality of being able to surprise the reader of the newspaper. Against predictable statements from predictable sources – such as the business leader arguing for lower taxes, or a left-wing politician arguing for reduced CO_2 emissions – the key to catching the eye of the reader was to make oneself vulnerable by drawing on personal experiences and going against the grain. During our interview, the debate editor explained that at the newspaper, they were amazed by how much traction personal stories were able to gain, especially on social media (Bennett 2012). In 2013, *Politiken* was perhaps in the process of discovering – together with many other media companies across Euro-American countries – that identity politics can be good for business in a world where getting many social media reactions means increased readership and ad revenue. This can also be seen as a defensive move, since social media jeopardise the business models of newspapers, and since the rise of identity politics in Denmark in recent decades arguably threatens the elite liberal outlook of *Politiken*.

The hyper-personal, against-the-stereotype letters that we were encouraged to write offer a quite specific vision for good public debate which differs from, for instance, the Habermasian idea that good arguments come from a disinterested perspective and concern the general public good. In *Politiken*'s vision for high-quality public debate, personal attachment did not disqualify participants as 'biased' by personal interests, but qualified their contributions in valuable ways (see also Papazu 2017). Following Stengers, *Politiken* seemed to be interested in setting up a situation where readers could learn things about young people and their attachments that they could not have predicted. At the same time, however, we were asked to embody and write from the vantage point of generalising and trite categories, such as 'the Muslim minority' or 'young people' or 'females/males' that *Politiken*'s staff and readers could quickly and effortlessly recognise. This is not just my assessment. While *Politiken*'s school was running, a professor of rhetoric went on record in another newspaper to criticise this tendency to stereotype:

> It is as if it is the media who tells you what to do to break through [in public debate]. And it is often by being extremely aggressive and typically by writing letters that are very generalising and dominated by what we call straw men. Which is to put up a caricatured and generalising image of the attitudes of a whole group (Christian Koch, quoted in Abrahamsen 2013).

In fact, the teaching at *Politiken* not only emphasised the need to write in an aggressive and generalising way – what teachers called a 'sharp' manner – we were also taught to prepare for the backlash. While speakers emphasised that if we did not have something antagonising to say, we might as well remain silent, a number of guest speakers also told us stories about how they had received hateful comments after being published in the paper. For the organisers, the point was clearly not to scare us away, but to prepare us for what it could mean to become a figure in newspaper debate. Politiken's staff repeatedly referred to public debate with mechanical metaphors such as 'the debate mill' and 'the debate train', suggesting it is hard to stop or escape once it has commenced. This was not portrayed as a bad thing *per se* – after all, the slogan on which Politiken was founded in the 1870s, and which was often reiterated at the school, holds that 'it is the *clash* of opposed opinions that makes us think'. In this light, some amount of personal sacrifice was simply considered to be 'part of the game'.

By staying with, and locking the participants to, a pre-existing repertoire of antagonising identity categories, however, *Politiken* arguably missed the chance to learn about emerging ones, and worse, missed the chance to learn about issues that did not fit the 'hyper-personal', individualised style promoted at the school. Here is another instance where Stengers' distinction between governance and politics becomes relevant. *Politiken* to a large extent stayed in a mode of governance based on the categories already perceived to be in circulation among its readership and staff, rather than enter a mode of politics by hesitating with respect to which categories and issues might be of importance. Indeed, the daily cycle of receiving a large stack of letters and having to quickly find out which ones to print does not accommodate hesitation very well (Czarniawska 2011), as some of the *Politiken* staff indicated in the way they spoke about their work. This brings me to the practical organisation of *Politiken*'s school, including some of the material constraints that were present.

ORGANISING AN EFFICIENT SCHOOL

In my interview with him, the main organiser of the school asserted that one thing that *Politiken* had achieved was to assemble a crowd of participants who could attract guest speakers from the 'highest shelf':

> What we can offer right now is that we can get somebody like Helle Thorning-Schmidt [the then prime minister] to come [to speak at the school]. That is simply because it is an interesting group. If you say that there are 150 interesting opinion formers, the voices of the future, who

sit here, the sharpest debaters of their generation, then generally speaking no one has said no.

It is noteworthy how the organiser relies both on the argument that the participants represent the absolute elite and on the magnitude of the number 150. As it turned out, the volume of 150 students may have been more important than the selective recruitment process, because while it continued to be difficult for many of these supposedly elite 'voices of the future' to actually get published in the newspaper, the number could have been a deal breaker in the eyes of the editor of debate:

> Someone has said, why can we not just be 30-40 who really get nursed? But then we would certainly not have had Helle Thorning-Schmidt here today... or the others. When they come, when it is an attractive group for them, then it is because there are 150.

Somehow the number 150 was perceived as striking the right balance between an elite-enough group and a large-enough group. However, the quote also shows an awareness that the teaching at the school came across as too hierarchical and unidirectional for some participants. As one of the participants I interviewed put it in a critique of the material arrangement and the opportunity for feedback at the school:

> [There was this] laughable concept where you must bring your letter and discuss it with the person next to you. 'You [only] have five minutes, because now [name of a famous politician] will be speaking on stage'. Sometimes I did not even finish reading the other person's letter before... also before people started chatting. It was useless. If you wanted to do it seriously, then you would need different facilities. Because there are 75 people speaking at the same time.

Here, the trade-off between a high number of participants and the work it requires to develop good writing comes to the fore. The facilities at the school were limited to 150 seats in rows, facing a stage, in a crammed room. There was no real space for group work or peer feedback sessions, not to mention interaction between the students and the speakers. To illustrate this, during the first three-hour long evening at the school, I counted only six times a student was able to say something in plenum, and all six comments were solicited by the organisers in a carefully controlled manner. In general, the feeling I had as a student was that of attending a show rather than participating actively.

When the organisers became aware of this problem half-way through the semester, they tried to compensate for the one-way communication by putting us into smaller study groups that were encouraged to self-organise and meet outside 'school hours' to work on our materials together. However, it varied a lot whether these groups actually managed to meet (my group never met), and the process was not facilitated. As students, we were in practice (though not always in discourse) treated more like another segment of readers or customers than as a group worth listening to, and even when time was set aside for students to contribute actively, there was always another important guest speaker waiting to take the stage, as the quote above also suggests. Although the main organiser of the school showed awareness of the problem of the overly hierarchical setup, the key indicator of success for him continued to be his ability to convince famous guest speakers to talk, not to cultivate participation. One might say that if famous and powerful people were convinced that *Politiken* had assembled a relevant sample of 'the new generation' and successfully made itself the gate-keeper of this entity, then it did not matter much how the students felt about it. This raises the question whether *Politiken* was out to promote itself more than to reinvigorate public debate. The narrow scope for participating shaped the kinds of contributions students were able to make, which again calls into question the kind of contribution that *Politiken*'s school as a whole was able to make to public debate and democratic politics in Denmark. *Politiken* may have supplied newspaper debate in Denmark with more letters from young people, but as long as these young people were addressed in a mode of one-way teaching, any contribution to *politics* in the Stengersian sense of challenging the existing majority repertoire is doubtful.

CONCLUSION

This chapter has introduced the Danish newspaper *Politiken*'s 'School of Debate and Critique' as a democratic situation worth paying attention to. In short, the school is *Politiken*'s attempt to demonstrate and renew 'high quality' public debate in practice. I have unpacked three aspects of these efforts: The effort to recruit a 'diverse elite', the teaching of the craft of writing opinion letters that 'kick inwards', and the pros and cons of having as many as 150 students. Overall, the analysis suggests that although public debate is often considered a democratic aim in itself (Barnett 2008), in practice public debate does not necessarily contribute to democratic politics in a Stengersian sense. It depends instead on whether well-established institutions such as *Politiken* are willing to 'hesitate' and *learn* from otherwise muted actors how to treat them.

Politiken missed its chances most of the time. The capacity for 'slowing down' and 'hesitating' with respect to important issues was very limited at the school. It is clear that *Politiken* from the outset considered itself an important actor in Danish public life and wanted to present itself as a competent institution with certain standards based on a long history of cultivating newspaper debate among the urban elite. The result was a highly controlled process of eliciting arguments from the young people it recruited, which included drawing on pre-existing majority language categories and encouraging an antagonising rather than hesitant argumentative style. To a large extent, the style of debate found at *Politiken* prevented learning anything from its young students.

It may therefore be tempting to simply dismiss *Politiken*'s school as a continuation of the existing public order – as governance rather than politics. However, it may be more valuable to practise a bit of scholarly hesitation here. My account suggests that *Politiken*'s staff were at least somewhat aware that hesitation could lead to 'high quality' newspaper content. This is visible in the wish to attract young people from under-represented backgrounds who can say surprising things due to their hitherto unaccounted-for personal experiences. It is also visible in how *Politiken* eventually wanted us participants to bring unexpected arguments to the table rather than write about pre-chosen and generic themes.

Such opportunities – even missed ones – should be foregrounded and expected to be present in events such as *Politiken*'s school, in so far as practice always overspills pre-existing ideas. To be sure, any public debate 'depend[s] upon pre-existing infrastructures of communication and circulation' (Barnett 2008: 15, paraphrasing Warner 2002: 105–6). But this also means that there are no 'pure' situations of democratic politics to resort to elsewhere. A situated understanding of democratic politics means, among other things, taking into account how practices related to the enactment of democracy are always shaped by infrastructures and socio-material dynamics located at different sites and prior in time (ibid.). At the same time, these infrastructures must also be constantly renewed, which means there is a constant potential for openings towards non-majority terms and perspectives that may be attended to and explored by STS scholarship.

As shown in this chapter, *Politiken* operates such an infrastructure, albeit subject to certain routines and constraints, such as being Copenhagen-based and coming from a social-liberal tradition of elitist public debate. *Politiken* started its school with a specific hypothesis that public debate might benefit from including young people to a greater extent. The opportunity for democratic politics that the school event represented was shaped by specific ideas, such as asking young people to write about personal experiences and identity politics, partly because this content circulates well on social media. The opportunity was also shaped by specific constraints, such as *Politiken* only reaching a somewhat homogeneous and privileged body of students and deciding to keep teaching relatively unidirectional. However, these processes also sparked moments of hesitation and opportunities for learning along the way, such as the organisers of the school pondering the aridness of generic headlines like 'the underclass' or 'my generation'. If properly attended to, such reflections may inform future experiments with public debate. As such, *Politiken*'s newspaper debate may provide one imperfect infrastructure among many for emerging democratic situations that instigate public surprise and learning.

REFERENCES

Abrahamsen, S., 'Meninger til salg', *Information*, 30 October 2013.

Barnett, C., 'Convening Publics: The Parasitical Spaces of Public Action', in K. R. Cox, M. Low, and J. Robinson, eds, *The SAGE Handbook of Political Geography* (London: Sage, 2008), pp. 403–417.

Bennett, W. L., 'The Personalization of Politics: Political Identity, Social Media, and Changing Patterns of Participation', *The ANNALS of the American Academy of Political and Social Science*, 644, (2012), 20–39.

Birkbak, A., 'Caring for Publics: How Media Contribute to Issue Politics' (PhD thesis, Aalborg University, Copenhagen, Denmark, 2016).

——, 'Shitstorms, bobler eller sags-orienterede offentligheder? Digitale metoder og kontroverser på sociale medier', *Dansk Sociologi*, 29 (2018), 37–61.

Boltanski, L., *Love and Justice as Competences* (Cambridge: Polity, 2012).

Bredal, B., *Politiken mod Politiken* (Copenhagen: Politikens Forlag, 2009).

CEVEA, 'Meningsdanneruddannelser [Opinon former courses]' https://cevea.dk/uddannelse [accessed 18 October 2019]

Czarniawska, B., *Cyberfactories: How News Agencies Produce News* (Cheltenham: Edward Elgar Publishing, 2011).

Habermas, J., *The Structural Transformation of the Public Sphere: An Inquiry into a Category of Bourgeois Society* (Cambridge: Polity Press, 1989).

Jensen, C. B., 'Citizen Projects and Consensus-Building at the Danish Board of Technology on Experiments in Democracy', *Acta Sociologica*, 48 (2005), 221–235.

Latour, B., and P. Weibel, eds, *Making Things Public: Atmospheres of Democracy*, (Cambridge, MA: The MIT Press, 2005).

Law, J., 'Seeing Like a Survey', *Cultural Sociology*, 3 (2009), 239–256.

Lezaun, J., and L. Soneryd, 'Consulting Citizens: Technologies of Elicitation and the Mobility of Publics', *Public Understanding of Science*, 16 (2007), 279–297.

Papazu, I., 'Nearshore Wind Resistance on Denmark's Renewable Energy Island', *Science & Technology Studies*, 30 (2017), 4–24.

Somers, M. R., 'Narrating and Naturalizing Civil Society and Citizenship Theory: The Place of Political Culture and the Public Sphere', *Sociological Theory*, 13 (1995a), 229–274.

——, 'What's Political or Cultural about Political Culture and the Public Sphere? Toward an Historical Sociology of Concept Formation', *Sociological Theory*, 13 (1995b), 113–144.

Stengers, I., 'The Cosmopolitical Proposal', in B. Latour, and P. Weibel, eds, *Making Things Public: Atmospheres of Democracy* (Cambridge, MA: The MIT Press, 2005), pp. 994–1003.

——, 'Including Nonhumans in Political Theory', in B. Braun, and S. J. Whatmore, eds, *Political Matter: Technoscience, Democracy, and Public Life* (Minneapolis, MN: University of Minnesota Press, 2010).
Warner, M., *Publics and Counterpublics* (New York: Zone Books, 2002).

PART II

TECHNOSCIENCES, DEMOCRACY AND SITUATED ENACTMENTS OF PARTICIPATION

5

LEAKS AND OVERFLOWS: TWO CONTRASTING CASES OF HYBRID PARTICIPATION IN ENVIRONMENTAL GOVERNANCE

Linda Soneryd and Göran Sundqvist

INTRODUCTION: WASTE AND WATER

FOR MORE THAN FOUR DECADES, FINAL DISPOSAL OF NUCLEAR WASTE HAS been a controversial issue in Sweden. In 1977 the industry presented a multi-barrier technical concept, in which the waste is encapsulated in copper canisters, surrounded by bentonite clay and stored in deep bedrock. The research, development and demonstration process, including finding a proper site, has been led by the industry, reviewed by government authorities and from the start framed in a technocratic manner strictly focusing on calculations of risks and safety. In the mid-1990s, however, this approach was substantially transformed and subjected to a participatory turn, due to strong resistance from people who lived near the proposed disposal sites, local politicians and environmental organisations. All of this led to the substantial involvement of a new actor: the municipality. This resulted in a range of new activities, meetings and arenas for public discussion. Inhabitants in municipalities which voluntarily agreed to site investigations could learn about nuclear waste and proposed disposal methods in school, at the Christmas market and at exhibitions. Environmental organisations were active in the consultation process, raising demands for more transparency, and involved municipalities asked critical questions of the nuclear waste company about safety, responsibility and municipal benefits.

Water management is a policy area very different from nuclear waste management. In Sweden there is a long tradition of involving a broad set of local actors and users in water management. Local engagement has primarily taken place in local water organisations, which were already established in the 1950s. These organisations are composed of a variety of actors such as farmers, fishers and environmental organisations, and activities are organised for the general public, such as water walks and quizzes and other outdoor activities that combine information exchange and socialising. The local water organisations have been important for water management and have functioned as a reference group for the authorities having formal responsibility for water management.

In this chapter, we explore participation in the contrasting policy areas of water management and nuclear waste management. Both examples concern participatory politics in relation to natural resource management in Sweden, but they are also fundamentally different. Nuclear waste must be managed in a way that keeps it far from people and environments, while water flows through and near people, activities and environments. What these two cases seem to have in common is a focus on stimulating and enhancing citizen participation, but this participation comes in different mixes of old and new styles of governance expressed in specific democratic situations.

Our ambition in this chapter is to explore extended participation in relation to environmental governance. Extended participation is a longstanding topic within science and technology studies (STS). It is important to note, however, that STS supporters of extended participation have been accused of being indiscriminate and naïve. Alfred Moore (2010: 793) claims that the STS argument in favour of participation can be summarised in the formula: 'the technical is political, the political should be democratic, and the democratic should be participatory'. In this allegedly naïve approach, there are no limits to the extension of participation; more voices are always better. Yet, in contrast to the approach identified by Moore, we find a more critical and almost cynical approach to extended participation among STS scholars, as participation procedures in practice often fall short of the ideal. Brian Wynne (2001), for instance, has vigorously criticised the frequently technocratic framing of participatory processes, which is a framing that is also found more generally when experts communicate with publics. This critical strand recognises the ways in which new participatory governance styles are often hijacked by old technocratic governance structures (Irwin 2006).

A productive way of going beyond the two stereotypes – the naïve, which indiscriminately embraces extended participation vs. the critical approach, which discards any effort to invite a broad set of participants – is to focus on the empirical situations in which participation processes play out. We have already mentioned that our two cases, water and nuclear waste management, differ in how they combine old and new styles of governance. Nuclear waste management started as a technocratically framed process, and then opened up to a more participatory style, whereas water management is characterised by a long tradition of local engagement. Our main argument in what follows is that an important contribution from STS is to engage with an open mind in empirical studies of how conflicts are managed through the extension of participation.

Our research into the nuclear waste case is based on many years of close ethnographic work, including participatory observation at public consultation meetings in municipalities subject to site investigations, interviews with key actors and document analysis (Sundqvist 2002; Soneryd and Lidskog 2008; Elam et al. 2010; Sundqvist 2014; Konopasec et al. 2018; Barthe et al. 2020). Our research on water management stems from a research project focusing on transboundary risk governance and participatory water governance in Sweden, in which we conducted interviews with local actors involved in water management, as well as participatory observation (Prutzer and Soneryd 2016; Soneryd 2015).

ANALYSIS: WHERE ARE THE CONFLICTS, HOW ARE THEY OPENED UP, WHY AND FOR WHOM?

The authority and legitimacy of scientific governance cannot be taken for granted. This means to acknowledge, at least in principle, the possibility that established issue framings can be challenged, changed or replaced. Michel Callon's (1998) conceptual pair of *framing* and *overflows* neatly captures this dynamic between established and challenged orders. We suggest that extended participation is needed for the management of controversial issues, assuming that conflicts imply issues characterised by overflows in relation to an established framing. This means that overflows can neither be contained nor managed by the established framework. But how do these conflicts which lead to overflows arise? How do they become problematic, and to whom? How do governing bodies respond, and how do they interpret problems as challenges to the established framework? In the following sections these questions are explored in relation to our two cases of water and nuclear waste.

Waste management: Interpreting overflows as leaks

During its more than 40 years of existence the Swedish solution to the nuclear waste problem, despite many conflicts associated with it, has achieved a position as a world-leading role model for geological disposal (Anshelm and Galis 2011). The key factor in nuclear waste management is safety, which gives experts a crucial role. Technical experts must assure that both the method and site for a repository are safe, and expert calculations of safety projecting very far into the future are needed. Swedish legislation demands that a final repository can be projected to be safe for 100,000 years. The response from the industry has been an expert-driven technical programme, which means that a technocratic framing has been dominating the issue since the 1970s.

By definition, technocracy means that issues are framed by experts and that this framing is also crucial for decision making. Framing is a way of simplifying and creating order in a complex world; some aspects of a problem are seen as relevant, while the framing excludes other aspects. If a narrow technical framing is agreed upon among experts and accepted by outsiders, no overflows arise. However, when objects that seem perfectly understood inside the laboratory and at the drawing board of a technical engineer are placed in new and perhaps more complex contexts, there is always a risk of overflows. Overflows are signs that the framing does not hold. Consequently, the original framing will be acknowledged, at least by some, as an inadequate simplification. As unintended consequences or externalities, overflows must be internalised by being explicitly recognised and taken care of if the project – for instance a nuclear waste technical programme – is to survive. In short, the frame has to be modified.

During the 1970s and 1980s the nuclear waste problem in Sweden was reduced to, or simplified as, a question of finding the best bedrock conditions for safe storage of the waste. However, the geophysical investigations, often including test drillings, encountered strong opposition in almost every location they were performed. A technocratic siting strategy – searching for the best bedrock in the nation – was not accepted by the people living at sites of potential interest, who had no influence on and almost no information about what happened in their home surroundings.

Massive local protests severely challenged the whole process, and the site investigations were stopped. The industry acknowledged that the technocratic approach did not work – something needed to be changed. As a reaction to the situation, the industry introduced local acceptability as a new guiding principle for repository siting, modifying the requirement of the geological barrier from 'best bedrock' to 'good enough bedrock' (Sundqvist 2002: 113f). Voluntariness and community ownership now became part of a new style of governance, coordinated by so-called 'feasibility studies', carried out by the industry in close cooperation with the local community to assess the suitability of potential sites – this 'suitability' including local acceptability. This has become the well-known and world-famous Swedish model for nuclear waste management (Sundqvist 2014). The reframing of the nuclear waste issue to include concerns for safety and local acceptability indicates that extending participation is an effective way of taking care of problematic issues (Callon et al. 2009: 32–33). Framing the siting of a final repository for nuclear waste as a purely technical issue is hard to maintain in the face of sustained local protests. Creating a space where a greater number of actors can express themselves becomes crucially important.

Extending participation is not a simple move. Governing bodies have an interest in maintaining the existing order and excluding actors that challenge it. Thus, we need to attend to how groups in charge draw boundaries between invited and uninvited participants, and how they attempt to avoid overflows by limiting participation. If governing bodies accept overflows, they have to reframe both the issue and who they consider relevant participants. With our nuclear waste case, we can nuance this spectrum of denial and acceptance: there is also the possibility for governing bodies to interpret overflows as leaks, which do not demand reframing but rather repair (Elam et al. 2010).

In 1992 the nuclear waste industry came up with a proposal to deal with overflows in practice. This was the so-called 'feasibility studies' – a new instrument for communicating with municipalities. All Swedish municipalities were at this time invited to take part in such studies, but take-up was low. After discussions with a few sparsely populated municipalities in the northern part of the country, which led to heated discussions between different groups and among inhabitants, the industry found it in its interest to only move forward with municipalities already hosting nuclear facilities and a few of their closest neighbours. In total, eight feasibility studies were carried out between 1993 and 2000. During these studies, the industry listened to the concerns of local people, politicians as well as lay people. As well as adopting an attentive attitude towards the municipalities subject to site investigations, local presence and communication, the industry also opened up its underground laboratory and performed full-scale public demonstrations of the technical concept. After the year 2000, the industry continued with site investigations at two sites and intensified local communication with the respective municipalities. This led to an internationally unique situation in which two municipalities, which were both already hosting nuclear facilities, were competing to host the waste (Sundqvist 2014: 2072).

Despite this radical change to both the technical concept and the siting process, which meant that the role of the geological barrier was reformulated, and the industry turned to a voluntary approach, the nuclear waste industry still did not acknowledge that the issue was as much a social problem as it was a technical one. A continued separation between technical and social issues remained: geological conditions and technical problems were left for the industry to deal with, while assessments of socio-economic consequences were considered by the industry to be 'municipal concerns' for the hosting municipality to handle (Svensk Kärnbränslehantering 1995: Ch.10).

Nevertheless, the turn towards voluntariness came to be seen as a world-renowned success story for the nuclear industry in Sweden. This opened up the siting process for the involvement of municipalities, but the multi-barrier system at the technical core of the situation never became an issue for deliberation. Municipal actors did not take part in the sensitive issue of adapting the assessment of the bedrock from 'the best bedrock' to a 'good enough bedrock' located in municipalities willing to host a waste repository. The feasibility studies became a tool for recognising the importance of the local community, a way of creating well-ordered surroundings for a technical programme that was in this way transformed from a controversial to an accepted project. The stepwise process initiated with the help of feasibility studies is firmly embedded in an old technocratic style of governance, which has even been strengthened by the new, added style of participatory governance.

What we learn from this case is that there are not just two options for how governing bodies can respond to overflows challenging a technocratic framing: denial or acceptance. The vigorous protests against test drilling at site investigations challenged the existing framing of the nuclear waste issue. But the challenge was not treated and responded to by the nuclear industry as overflows but rather as leaks that could be repaired and managed with a voluntary, participatory approach and a modified multi-barrier system, which downplayed the importance of the geological barrier. The multi-barrier concept *was* thus negotiated, but only internally by the nuclear industry itself, as the technical core remained non-negotiable to outsiders, despite public protests having been the catalysts for this change.

Nuclear waste management, in Sweden as in other countries, is historically characterised by a strong expert culture that is hard to destabilise even after overflows have occurred. The technocratic framing seems non-negotiable, even as parts of the issue are opened up to new participants. What remained non-negotiable in this case was the core of experts and a sharp boundary between invited and uninvited publics (cf. Welsh and Wynne 2013). Municipalities and local residents were invited through the new style of voluntariness and the principle of local acceptability, but nationally mobilised environmental groups drawing on alternative expertise were left outside. The industry intensified the communication with the concerned municipalities, who were invited for regular consultation meetings as well as to meetings between industry and government authorities. This made it possible for the municipalities to follow the progress of the project, and it gave them some access to the technical discussions. This was not the case for environmental organisations, who complained about this boundary-making. By attending to invited and uninvited publics, as well as to the distinctions made and upheld between technical and social elements of the process, we can study how overflows are managed. The concerns raised by external protesters were taken care of by the industry, who successfully transformed these into a question of acceptance or non-acceptance, and thereby circumvented extended participation in technical decision making (Sundqvist and Elam 2010).

In 2011, the nuclear industry handed in an application to the government to implement the suggested solution for a final repository. Responsible authorities assessed the application to have been completed by 2016. In 2018, however, the Swedish Environmental Court disapproved the project on the basis that uncertainties still prevailed (Swedish Land and Environmental Court 2018). Just as in 1979, doubts about whether the repository is safe enough still remain, even after the final decision was taken by the government in January 2022.

The nuclear waste case shows that there have been many opportunities for redrawing the boundaries of expertise, but thus far these have not been seized by the nuclear industry, as no outsiders have been invited to negotiate with the industry. However, due to the long delay in the planning and review process – a unique situation in Swedish environmental planning – this strategy of limiting participation can still be questioned. The possible corrosion of the copper canisters, the main reason for the Land and Environmental Court declining the application in 2018, is yet another example of overflows that challenge the entire framing of the issue.

We will now turn to our second example: water management. Since it is characterised by a long tradition of local participation, it can almost be seen as an opposing case in relation to the nuclear waste case.

Water management: An overflow of overflows

We have already asserted that extended participation is needed for the management of controversial issues. The reason for this is that conflicts indicate that there are issues and concerns that overflow an established framing. A narrow technical framing assumes that technical issues can be separated from social issues. When overflows are recognised, this also means that issues are recognised as hybrid – in other words, that the social and the technical are seen as inevitably intertwined. The support of a heterogeneous set of participants in the area of water management by European as well as national legislation means that issues related to water are at least to some extent recognised by regulatory institutions as hybrid issues, and thus not amenable to governance by technical experts alone. This recognition, however, does not imply that water issues are free from conflict. On the contrary, hybrid forums are usually the product of struggles and conflict. Callon et al. (2009: 154) argue that hybrid forums, even though they challenge established powers in the first place, if they are left alone risk reproducing patterns of power and leading to 'the exclusion of the weakest'. So, what do the hybrid forums in water management look like, and do they manage to give voice to those who are hard to hear?

The overall purpose of the EU Water Framework Directive (WFD), introduced in 2000, is 'to protect European waters and achieve a good ecological status of all waters […] and to get citizens and stakeholder organisations actively involved in the water management process' (Hammer et al. 2011: 211). In Sweden there is a tradition of active involvement of citizens and stakeholders in the local water organisations, gathering local people, the industry and farmers. Many of these local water organisations have existed on a voluntary basis since the 1950s. Today, there are more than 125 local water councils in Sweden that have their base in the old local water organisation. The water councils are expected to monitor and describe the water status, identify activities that affect water quality, contribute to identify goals, solve problems, support proposed actions and be a point of contact for the national Water Authority.

An important task for the water councils is to make other water users, decision makers and a wider public attentive to water issues. One small-scale farmer engaged in a water council, for instance, was particularly interested in the freshwater pearl mussel. These mussels can live to a great age. The oldest known example was found in Jokkmokk in northern Sweden and determined to be 256 years old. For the freshwater pearl mussel to reproduce it needs clear water, oxygenated, low in nutrients and with a stable pH value. Because of this, special measures are needed in order to get viable stocks of freshwater pearl mussels. In the river basins that this farmer was concerned with, there are no freshwater pearl mussels younger than 50 years old, indicating that the water is not of a standard that enables the reproduction of the mussel. Due to the farmer's special interest in the mussel, the water council organised 'water walks' – public walks in a river area with a focus on the freshwater pearl mussel. Several water councils conduct inventories of the freshwater pearl mussel. Since it is intolerant of pollutants, its presence is seen as a good indicator of water quality. The mussel can even be seen as part of the hybrid collectives that take form through the work in water councils; such collectives could start with an engaged farmer, who applies for funding to enable an inventory of the mussel. The discovery of freshwater pearl mussels in a river basin can motivate further measures such as making sure that there are fish to serve as hosts for the mussel larvae. In addition, water walks can be arranged so that the collective grows to include local citizens who then learn about the mussel and its importance for other species, as well as the fact that Sweden has the richest viable freshwater pearl mussel population in Europe.

One could say that these hybrid forums are successfully giving voice to a threatened species and that the local activities are potentially increasing its chances of survival by improving the quality of the water. However, this is a continuous struggle with uncertain outcomes. There are many uncertainties and potential threats: some threats are connected to agricultural or industrial activities that are environmental damaging – thus, activities performed by the very same actors that are represented in a water council; another threat is the frailty of the water councils themselves.

Farmers are often targeted by water quality improving measures, since their cooperation must be secured in order to minimise pollution from farming activities. Structural liming is an issue that has been organised collectively among farmers in a water council. Structural liming is a widespread agricultural method to reduce eutrophication (excessive richness of nutrients) of water sources by spreading structural lime on fields after harvesting. An engaged small-scale farmer, who was also the chair of a water council, applied for funding to organise collective structural liming among farmers. She tells us how she negotiated with a company to reduce the price of structural lime, and to speed up its delivery and spread. She advertised in the local newspaper and organised a field excursion and expert information on structural liming. Yet this points to a weakness of the water councils: almost all work in these councils is initiated by unpaid labour undertaken on a voluntary basis.

The examples above – the survival of the freshwater pearl mussel and eutrophication – illustrate water councils both attending to problems and initiating the measures to deal with them. To some extent, these practices align with the EU WFD policy that water management should be open for people to influence the outcome of plans and working processes, improve decision making, create awareness of environmental issues and increase acceptance of and commitment towards the mooted plans.

The participatory approach encouraged by the WFD is framed both through an instrumental value – namely, the aim to ensure effective implementation and achievement of the environmental objectives of water management – and a substantial value, which is that local actors should collaborate in order to improve water quality in the area. The effectiveness of the water councils is tenuous, however. They seem to be hybrid forums that to a great extent are left alone, and thus are examples of distributed responsibility without any centrally coordinated efforts to ensure or balance their powers to act. Our fieldwork indicates that there is a feeling among local water council members that the position of the councils is weak, with too few resources and engaged actors. A vision of the water councils as a collective force has been expressed by some actors, but the stories about how they actually work are far from encouraging. This suggests that in certain institutional contexts, participatory reforms such as the EU WFD may revive problems rather than solve them. The WFD set a goal for the water to be of high quality by 2021, but in many river basins in Sweden this is still not the case, and the measures undertaken are highly dependent on a few engaged individuals.

Overflows is a concept that has been used to refer to moments where the framing of an issue is challenged. It calls for reframing and reorientation but remains vague about how and in which direction. In the case of water management, we can see that there are many negotiable issues. Whether the freshwater pearl mussel is attended to or whether there are measures to reduce eutrophication depend on negotiations taking place within water councils between actors with diverging interests, varying engagements and different competences. So where are the overflows?

The challenges that participants express are related to responsibilities that are not accompanied by the power or resources needed to address them. This is especially true of the problematically loose coupling between local engagement in the water councils and decision-making. These issues are, we argue, typically non-negotiable. The unfortunate result is a mix of old and new styles of governance – the tradition of local participation and a decentralisation of water issues without adequate provision of resources. This problem – which is quite unintentional – is very difficult to remedy. As part of overarching shifts in power relations and subject formation, processes of responsibilisation are hard to grasp and turn into explicit objects of critique. At the same time, dispersed responsibility without dispersed resources creates overflows. There is thus a vulnerability built into the local participatory approach in the case of water management in Sweden. The fact that voluntary unpaid work to improve water quality is conducted by a few engaged individuals who are happy to be involved, but at the same time disappointed and worn out, will lead to continuous overflows, that is, problems that are difficult to manage without resources or political mandate.

DISCUSSION: WHAT IS NEGOTIABLE AND FOR WHOM?

As we have seen in the analysis, in our study of nuclear waste management a traditionally expert-led process has been mixed with a new element of voluntariness on behalf of the municipalities. This was a new principle introduced by the nuclear industry in order to deal with overflows in relation to strong protests against the siting process. By this principle, the nuclear industry managed to transform overflows into manageable leaks and still keep technical issues within a narrow expert frame. In the case of water management, while participatory elements had been in place for a long time, the new elements were rather connected to a new context for extended participation: from local self-governance to local responsibilisation.

We have argued that processes of extended participation need to be studied empirically in order to know what the mixes of new and old governance styles look like, which historical framings new participatory elements are embedded in, and how conflicts understood as overflows are taken care of. In our interpretation, this means that we need to attend to what is negotiable and what is not (Barthe et al. 2020). Protests and conflicts often reveal that a narrow technocratic framing does not hold. Extended participation can thus facilitate the acknowledgement of problems. This is also in line with how STS approaches to the democratisation of science and technology have often been seen as a form of oppositional activity. We have argued that a key focus for empirical studies of participation needs to be on how to discover negotiable and non-negotiable issues. A way to do this is to attend to invited and uninvited publics. It is important to see how industries and governments draw the boundary between who is a legitimate participant (invited) and who is not (uninvited) in order to analyse how they define non-negotiable issues.

This raises questions about how governing bodies respond to challenges: do they interpret the conflict as a challenge to a narrow expert framing, and do the challenges lead to changes or an entire reframing of the issue? Or do governing bodies interpret challenges as leaks which can be repaired without reframing issues or relevant participants? The distinction between leaks and overflows helps us to point to an in-between response by governing bodies, whereby overflows are neither denied nor accepted, but give rise to a reinterpretation of overflows as manageable leaks. As we discussed in relation to our cases, leaks can be clogged and repaired without changing the framing or the overall composition of the sociotechnical network, while overflows, if admitted as such, challenge the entire framing and composition.

As we show in the nuclear waste case, it is of great importance to analyse how actors understand overflows and the strategic reasons for actors to try to transform overflows into more manageable leaks. And of course, as also shown in this case, the outcomes of such processes have consequences for participation. The industry in this example negotiated the technical concept 'in-house' and thereby maintained the technical core closed for public deliberation. If the industry had admitted overflows, this could have opened up a renegotiation of legitimate participants, which could have led to changes in how the municipalities and environmental organisations participate and interact with industry and authorities about issues assessed by the industry as 'technical'.

In the water management case, local participation facilitated an awareness of water-related problems, which led to the discovery of overflows, but an overarching governing body that could direct attention to such overflows was lacking. Participation, in this case, is introduced in a context of responsibilisation without resources and power. This leads to an overflow of overflows, since the acknowledgement of problems happens at a faster pace than anyone can manage.

These two cases show the importance of distinguishing between the relationship between publics that attend to overflows and governing bodies that interpret and respond to such overflows. It is in making these connections that we can talk about democratic situations. We thus suggest that it is important to focus on how the governing bodies respond to the problems voiced by publics when we explore democratic situations. This implies a need to take conflicts seriously and understand them as part of a foundation for new social arrangements – what we have referred to as hybrid forums. In short, overflows need be taken care of within a context of public deliberation, which requires cultivating discussion as well as new actor constellations.

From this we can conclude that the feasibility studies set up by the nuclear industry to establish good contacts with municipalities have not given rise to the cultivation of a more open participatory process, since they had a clear instrumental focus on achieving the acceptance of expert work and ready-made technical solutions.

The water management case is a good illustration of an ambition to create space for hybrid communities and to expand the middle ground between expert work, the public and traditional political institutions. Such a space is lacking in our technical-democratic societies, as exemplified by the failure identified in the water case to bridge this divide. The support for this ambition, it turned out, was fragile; too many of the water councils' activities were dependent on the voluntary engagement of individuals, and too little support and resources were provided by the authorities to support these engagements.

If governing elites are only interested in stopping leaks, then increased dialogue with invited publics can be enough. However, if overflows need to be acknowledged and managed, then decision makers need to be responsive to challenges to the entire framing of an issue and be prepared to make more fundamental changes in how they approach the problems at hand. In the nuclear waste example, we can conclude that the responsible actors are unwilling to acknowledge overflows. On the other hand, if the authorities have no problem accepting overflows but push responsibilities downwards, there will be too much overflowing. This is the situation in the example of water management, in which local actors get engaged and try to do most of the work themselves in the absence of governing bodies handling the overflows.

While our study is very much in line with what other STS scholars have already shown (for example, Callon et al. 2009), we believe that our attention to old and new styles of governance, our focus on the power distribution and mechanisms of inclusion and exclusion that these new combinations imply, and not least how overflows can be interpreted and taken care of in different ways are valuable developments in order to approach hybrid participation in a critical as well as constructive way.

STS scholars can point to the need for decision makers to be attentive to the challenges involved in addressing controversial issues, either by giving voice to protests of the uninvited, or by facilitating attentive listening to the quieter dripping and rippling that could be a first sign of serious leaks and overflows. The aim of such research should be to show different understandings and conflicts in relation to overflows and leaks, based on the assumption that they need to be taken care of with the help of wide participation. Our two cases have shown that the crucial relationship is between publics that attend to overflows and the governing bodies that interpret and respond to such overflows. It is when this relation is dynamic, and when the public can actually be part of negotiations of how to change and improve the governance of issues, that participation becomes meaningful.

REFERENCES

Anshelm, J., and V. Galis, '(Re-)Constructing Nuclear Waste Management in Sweden: The Involvement of Concerned Groups 1970–2010', in S. Kumar, ed., *Integrated Waste Management, Volume II* (Rijeka: InTech, 2011), pp. 401–430.

Barthe, Y., M. Elam, and G. Sundqvist, 'Technological Fix or Divisible Object of Collective Concern? Histories of Conflict over the Geological Disposal of Nuclear Waste in Sweden and France', *Science as Culture*, 29 (2020), 196–218.

Callon, M., 'An Essay on Framing and Overflowing: Economic Externalities Revisited by Sociology', in M. Callon, ed., *The Laws of the Markets*. (Oxford: Blackwell Publishers, 1998), pp. 244–269.

Callon M., P. Lascoumes, and Y. Barthe, *Acting in an Uncertain World: An Essay on Technical Democracy* (Cambridge, MA: The MIT Press, 2009).

Elam, M., L. Soneryd, and G. Sundqvist, 'Demonstrating Safety–Validating New Build: The Enduring Template of Swedish Nuclear Waste Management', *Journal of Integrative Environmental Sciences* 7 (2010), 197–210.

Hammer, M., B. Balfors, U. Mörtberg, M. Petersson, and A. Quin, 'Governance of Water Resources in the Phase of Change: A Case Study of the Implementation of the EU Water Framework Directive in Sweden' *Ambio*, 40 (2011), 210–220.

Irwin A., 'The Politics of Talk: Coming to Terms with the 'New' Scientific Governance', *Social Studies of Science*, 36 (2006), 299–320.

Konopasek, Z., L. Soneryd, and K. Svacina, 'Lost in Translation: Czech Dialogues by Swedish Design', *Science and Technology Studies*, 31 (2018), 5–23.

Moore, A., 'Beyond Participation: Opening Up Political Theory in STS', *Social Studies of Science*, 40 (2010), 793–799.

Prutzer, M., and L. Soneryd, *Samverkan och deltagande i vattenråd och vattenförvaltning, rapport Havs och Vattenmyndigheten*, Rapport nr. 20016:35 (Göteborg: Havs- och vattenmyndigheten, 2016).

Svensk Kärnbränslehantering, *Feasibility Study for Siting of a Deep Repository within the Storuman Municipality*, TR 95-08 (Stockholm: Swedish Nuclear Fuel and Waste Management Co, 1995).

Soneryd, L., and R. Lidskog, 'Accountability, Public Involvement and (Ir)Reversibility', in M. Boström, and C. Garsten, eds, *Organizing Transnational Accountability* (Cheltenham: Edward Elgar Publishing, 2008), pp. 194–209.

Soneryd, L., 'What's at Stake? Practices of Linking Actors, Issues and Scales in Environmental Politics', *Nordic Journal of Science and Technology Studies*, 3 (2015), 18–23.

Sundqvist, G., *The Bedrock of Opinion: Science, Technology and Society in the Siting of High-Level Nuclear Waste* (Dordrecht: Kluwer Academic Publishers, 2002).

—— '"Heating Up" or "Cooling Down"? Analysing and Performing Broadened Participation in Technoscientific Conflicts', *Environment and Planning,* 46 (2014), 2065–2079.

Sundqvist, G., and M. Elam, 'Public Involvement Designed to Circumvent Public Concern? The "Participatory Turn" in European Nuclear Activities', *Risk, Hazards & Crisis in Public Policy,* 1 (2010), 203–229.

Swedish Land and Environmental Court, *Opinion of the Environmental Court. Nacka District Court, Land and Environmental Court.* Case, no. M 1333-11, Act document no. 842. Unofficial English translation of the summary of opinion at http://www.mkg.se/en/translation-into-english-of-the-swedish-environmental-court-s-opinion-on-the-finalrepository-for-sp. [2018]

Welsh, I., and B. Wynne, 'Science, Scientism and Imaginaries of Publics in the UK: Passive Objects, Incipient Threats', *Science as Culture,* 22 (2013), 540–566.

Wynne, B., 'Creating Public Alienation: Expert Cultures of Risk and Ethics on GMOs', *Science as Culture,* 10 (2001), 445–481.

6

STS AND DEMOCRACY CO-PRODUCED? THE MAKING OF PUBLIC DIALOGUE AS A TECHNOLOGY OF PARTICIPATION

Helen Pallett and Jason Chilvers

DEMOCRACY HAS LONG BEEN STUDIED AND THEORISED IN SCIENCE AND technology studies (STS) in relation to technoscience (Ezrahi 1990; Latour 1993; Jasanoff 2004). However, a growing body of work treats democracy and participation as objects of study and experimental interventions in their own right (Laurent 2017; Chilvers and Kearnes 2016; Lezaun et al. 2017; Voss and Freeman 2016). In this chapter we seek to make to two contributions to these 'co-productionist'[1] STS engagements with democracy and democratic situations.

The first is to demonstrate how STS can take democracy – specifically, approaches to public participation – as an object of study in its own right. In doing so we focus on participatory forms of democracy that have emerged in response or in relation to representative and neoliberal democratic arrangements. We do this by tracing the democratic situation in which 'public dialogue' – a model of public participation based on deliberative workshops involving citizens and experts working towards consensus – became established as a dominant mode of public engagement with science policy in Britain. For more than 15 years public dialogue has been promoted and supported by the UK government-funded body

Sciencewise as a way of democratising science policy. Through our account we trace the emergence, construction, institutionalisation and waning of British public dialogue as a 'technology of participation' (see Lezaun and Soneryd 2007; Laurent 2011; Chilvers and Kearnes 2016; Voss and Amelung 2017).

Second, we aim to situate the field of STS as part of, rather than apart from, crucial constitutional shifts in democracies (see Jasanoff 2011) and remain attentive to the role played by STS knowledges and concepts 'in the wild' (see Callon et al. 2009). In doing this we suggest that in democratic societies STS – or any other (inter)discipline, for that matter – is always co-produced *with* democracy. This necessitates humility and reflexivity on the part of STS scholars, to acknowledge both the deep influence of democratic practices and systems on our knowledge-making, but also to recognise the role played by STS theories and knowledges in the empirical sites and contexts we study. These insights force us to question the apparent uniqueness of the findings and arguments of STS, and to consider and anticipate the broader effects of our ideas and interventions.

Existing studies of technologies of participation have taken classic STS questions on the portability, circulation and mobility of the technosciences (Latour 1987) to consider how particular public participation methods and democratic innovations move from localised practices to become technologised and circulate transnationally (Voss and Amelung 2016), or how they become established in a particular democratic setting and then travel to be replicated and reperformed in another political culture (Soneryd 2016). Our analysis of UK public dialogue offers an altogether different view into the dynamics through which technologies of participation form, circulate and become established across cultures. Rather than focus on the innovation journey of a single technology of participation, our case reveals how multiple established technologies of participation and their associated expert communities (Chilvers 2008) – including STS scholars – intermingled to form a composite technology of participation at a key constitutional moment in British political culture and within the specific organisational setting of Sciencewise.

Through this case we show how particular democratic situations matter to the formation, standardisation, effects and threats to any one technology of participation – through their relations with other (often competing) democratic innovations, institutional settings and longer-standing constitutional relations between citizens, science and the state. We narrate the story of the development and effects of public dialogue as a technology of participation through two key moments: the first being the construction and formalisation of public dialogue as a standardised approach to public engagement in science policy-making in the mid to late 2000s, linked to the formation and institutionalisation of Sciencewise (Chilvers 2013) and the broader political dynamics of the moment; and the second being the challenging of this deliberative model in the 2010s with the emergence of alternative democratic innovations and imaginaries, and the subsequent broadening of approaches to public dialogue in UK science policy (Pallett 2018). For each of these moments we describe the status of public dialogue, the broader constitutional shifts related to it and the dominant participatory democratic imaginary within relevant STS work at the time, in order to illustrate our argument about the co-production of STS and democracy.[2]

Our argument about co-production is not only that the study of democratic politics has been at the heart of crucial developments in STS, but that developments in parts of the STS field and the 'real world' practices and structures of democracy can be considered to be co-produced or co-constitutive of one another. In our analysis we show how the two aforementioned key moments in the development of British public dialogue coincide with and are closely intertwined with both broader constitutional developments in British democracy and also democracy as an object of enquiry and imagination in STS itself. In other words, we are calling out – in a partial and situated way – the democratic situations with/in STS.

Throughout this story of the making and unmaking of public dialogue, STS scholars take up diverse positions and roles as analysts, ethnographers, theorists, methodologists, facilitators, consultants, advisors, distant critics and so on (see Chilvers 2013). However, it is not as simple as saying STS is present and thus implicated and entangled in the co-production of British science and democracy. Clearly there are important instances where STS scholars acted as forerunners, making instrumental and normative interventions that offered new models of two-way dialogue and upstream engagement (e.g., Rowe and Frewer 2000; Wilsdon and Willis 2004). We also see STS scholars and others engaging with the democratic situation of public dialogue 'after the event' in more critical or interpretive modes of intervention (see Irwin et al. 2013). Our main point, though, is that STS does not come before or after – but is always *with* – democracy, even though STS scholars sometimes present themselves as being distant and removed from the democratic situations they study. This alerts us to how STS is shaped by and responds to much larger shifts and constitutional developments in science and democracy, while also forcing reflexive consideration of the democratic constitutions of STS itself, in terms of imagined forms of democracy which become prevalent (but often tacit) assumptions at different times and places in the field's development.

Both of the present chapter authors have through various projects conducted extensive semi-structured interviews with most of the main actors involved in the setting up and running of the Sciencewise programme, and analysed relevant documents (Chilvers 2010, 2017; Chilvers and Macnaghten 2011; Pallett and Chilvers 2013; Pallett 2018). We draw on some of this data in the following account.

THE FORMATION OF PUBLIC DIALOGUE

Public dialogue was formally adopted as a practice of UK science policy and proceduralised from 2004 onwards, with the creation of the Sciencewise-ERC (Expert Resource Centre) as an arm's length government body to promote and support greater public involvement in science policy- making. The House of Lords Select Committee on Science and Technology's *Science and Society* report (2000) was the first to make explicit use of the term 'public dialogue' with reference to approaches of deliberative public engagement and consultation (including the techniques of consensus conferences, citizens' juries and stakeholder dialogues), stating that 'direct dialogue with the public should move from being an optional add-on to science-based policy making [...] and should become a normal and integral part of the process'. The British STS scholar Brian Wynne, who had been a prominent critic of the Public Understanding of Science programme pursued by the Government in the 1980s and 1990s, was involved as a key expert witness in the creation of this report. Gary Kass, a civil servant at the time, was a key interlocutor behind the scenes of the creation of this report and acted as an ally of Wynne. During a subsequent secondment at the Parliamentary Office of Science and Technology (POST) Kass reiterated this message and promoted deliberative public dialogue through further reports (POST 2001; 2002). At the same time, both James Wilsdon and Jack Stilgoe, former PhD students in the STS department at University College London, were working at the left-wing think tank Demos, and authored a series of pamphlets advocating deliberative public dialogue at the heart of science policy. A number of these pamphlets were co-authored with STS scholars (e.g., Kearnes et al. 2006).

In 2004 Kass helped to draft the 2004–2014 Science and Innovation Investment Framework, which resulted in the creation of Sciencewise. The contract to run the new body was awarded to AEA technology, the former atomic energy authority (now a private body and a commonly used government contractor). To make up for AEA's lack of specific expertise in deliberative public engagement, a number of freelance engagement practitioners were brought in to help manage public dialogue projects. Many of these expert practitioners had previously worked on supporting a stakeholder dialogue model of engagement at the Environment Council, which had a strong reputation for resolving high-profile environmental controversies (see Grolin 1999). Thus, they had expertise in running deliberative processes, but little direct experience with public engagement. Some of the early practitioners involved in Sciencewise also had connections to the academic field of STS through graduate study or working as researchers. This new concept of 'public dialogue' represented a hybridisation of the two previously distinct models of public *deliberation* – namely, the consensus conferences being developed and used by the Danish Board of Technology at the time – and stakeholder *dialogue* – as developed by conflict resolution organisations like the Environment Council (Chilvers 2017).

Initially the Sciencewise programme funded and supported some very experimental practices of public engagement covering a wide range of formats. These included a card-based discussion game which could be used to facilitate conversations about climate change in diverse contexts, to feed into a 2003 White Paper on energy policy (Pallett and Chilvers 2013). However, in the period from 2006 onwards, after Sciencewise was formally relaunched as an

'Expert Resource Centre', 'public dialogue' was more clearly formatted as a more prescriptive technology of participation as the organisation of Sciencewise and actor roles within it also became increasingly formalised. Reflecting on how UK public dialogue developed after this initial period, interview participants described the stabilisation of a clear model of public dialogue after 2005. This took the form of an invited 'mini-public' deliberation model where small groups of publics reflecting key demographic characteristics are enrolled as 'innocent citizens' with little prior interest in or knowledge of the issues under discussion (see Irwin 2006; Lezaun and Soneryd 2007).

A particular definition of public dialogue was agreed on and formalised by the Sciencewise steering group – comprising representatives from government, industry, participatory practice and academia (including STS scholars) – and was stated in published guidance as:

> a two-way conversation with members of the public, to inform [...] decision-making on science and technology issues [...] [It] is a process during which members of the public interact with scientists, stakeholders and policy makers to deliberate on issues likely to be important in future policies (Sciencewise-ERC 2009).

THE INSTITUTIONALISATION OF PUBLIC DIALOGUE

A series of devices and procedures became established within the organisation – including best practice guidelines and principles, evaluation frameworks and methodological toolkits – which served to inscribe and codify this particular definition of public dialogue and the formats, configurations and skills necessary to realise public dialogue as a technology of participation (Chilvers 2017). In the words of a participatory practitioner in a social research company, Sciencewise began to 'mainstream all this a bit more effectively' and sought to grow and promote 'best practice' in public dialogue. The Sciencewise model was further inscribed through training courses, mentoring schemes and knowledge exchange mechanisms, including a web-based knowledge hub (Chilvers 2013). Sciencewise's Dialogue and Engagement Specialists – the programme's expert practitioners – worked to ensure that the organisations commissioning and undertaking public dialogue projects followed the 'script' (Warburton 2010).

Another element of this formatting and proceduralisation of public dialogue was its increasing professionalisation (see Chilvers 2008). Where initially independent facilitators and smaller groups, including charities and academic social scientists, had taken on mediator roles in the development of UK public dialogue, many interview participants noted that the field had latterly become increasingly 'captured' by larger consultancy and market research companies, such as the British Market Research Bureau (BMRB), Ipsos-MORI and Opinion Leader Research (OLR). Such companies were able to take advantage of the introduction of framework contracts by UK government departments and agencies – recognised lists of organisations deemed qualified to bid for contracts to undertake Sciencewise dialogues – and build on their already close ties to government and long track records in providing evidence of public opinion. There was a sense that such mechanisms served to privilege the so-called 'big players', which 'obliterated all the rest of the range of different approaches' (Participatory practitioner, independent consultant), further stabilising networks around a specific version of Sciencewise public dialogue (Chilvers 2017).

Since its inception in 2004 Sciencewise has supported the orchestration of more than 30 public dialogue processes around pressing issues in British science policy, including climate change, flood risk, gene science and biodiversity. The efficacy of these attempts to codify and institutionalise a specific Sciencewise technology of public dialogue was reflected across most dialogue projects co-sponsored by the organisation between 2005 and 2010. Ten of the 13 public dialogues active in this period closely replicated this model by enrolling lay public participants who interacted with expert witnesses in small-group deliberative events, each held in different regions across the UK, which were subsequently all brought together in a final workshop at a central UK location (see Chilvers 2010, 2017; Macnaghten and Chilvers 2014; Warburton 2010). Many of these processes have had concrete and traceable impacts on policy decisions – in apparent contrast to the otherwise similar case discussed in Krabbenborg (this volume) – such as the change to the regulation of research involving animals in 2014, the decision in 2010 to fund more than 50 'low carbon communities' in support of the community energy movement, and the decision to allow the creation of so-called 'three-parent' children using mitochondrial DNA in a limited number of circumstances. Public dialogue has also in a more general sense been an important front in advancing the formal means through which citizens can engage with government processes and decisions, and has become a model which has been used by research councils and other government agencies such as local authorities, the devolved parliaments and bodies including the National Health Service.

Sheila Jasanoff has pioneered the study of the relationship between science and democracy at a constitutional level and has made the UK one of her primary study sites. Through this work she has identified nationally specific institutional structures, styles of reasoning and modes of public knowledge-making which are associated with very different configurations of the relationship between science, citizens and the state. She has characterised the UK's civic epistemology as 'communitarian', with embodied service-based styles of public knowledge-making and a relational understanding of public accountability (Jasanoff 2005). This is particularly characterised by a respect for long-serving expert voices, and a preference for empirical demonstrations of a fact in order for it to be believed (ibid).

However, the 1990s saw a number of important ruptures in this configuration, opening up the possibility of what Jasanoff refers to as a 'constitutional moment' (Jasanoff 2011) where the relationship between science, citizens and the state may change. One significant factor in this moment was the coincidence of a number of major and high-profile failures of public science advice, such as the government response to the BSE ('Mad Cow Disease') crisis. Increasing public protest around the government's policies towards nuclear power and specific siting decisions also increasingly challenged the default 'Decide-Announce-Defend' approach of much infrastructure and technology policy. These crises were judged to have damaged public trust in key policy-makers and formerly respected government experts, and were perceived as a threat to the science and technology-led progress successive governments bombastically pursued. The shift from the established model of Public Understanding of Science (PUS) which had been pursued from the mid- 1980s (Miller 2001) towards a more dialogic model of public engagement can be read as a response to these ruptures and the constitutional moment which emerged.

In parallel with public dialogue's standardisation as a technology of participation, there were broader constitutional shifts in the UK which help to explain its broad take-up and popularity. In 1997 the UK voted in a 'New Labour' government which was in power for 13 years, heralding the start of a more conciliatory and dialogue-based approach, which has been labelled 'third way' politics. Some of the key actors behind this political approach, such as Charlie Leadbetter and Geoff Mulgan (who founded Demos), as well as the sociologist Anthony Giddens, had long been calling for forms of deliberative democracy to be part of government, and they subsequently became important figures in this new government (Thorpe 2010). They had reportedly used focus group methodologies widely during the 1997 election campaign. In this context the STS scholars who advocated and developed deliberative technologies of participation can be seen as responding to and forming part of a movement which saw expanded participation as a necessary response to greater social and economic prosperity and freedom and wanted to foster a more active and engaged citizenry (Thorpe 2010). This meant that by the early 2000s there were many actors in government who were sympathetic to arguments for the greater dialogic involvement of citizens in policy-making (ibid).

Another aspect of this so-called 'third way politics', pursued by Giddens and Leadbetter at the heart of the New Labour project, was the attempt to import elements of the Nordic model of social democracy into a UK context, drawing on its longer history of active inclusion of interest organisations in policy-making (Thorpe 2010). By 2000 deliberative modes of public engagement were already embedded in Danish science policy, particularly in the Danish Board of Technology, which was continually cited in British policy documents calling for two-way dialogue. The Danish STS scholar Maja Horst and British STS scholar Alan Irwin have situated this Danish approach to deliberation and the common good within a broader European move towards consensus politics (Horst and Irwin 2010). They argue that the move towards consensus was an important institution- and nation-building strategy (ibid.), which again indicates that such moves transcend the influence of the field of STS and its allies.

This decidedly deliberative participatory democratic imaginary of both public dialogue and the broader politics of the time was reflected in the work of many British STS scholars. While public understanding and opinion surveys remained a popular methodology, deliberative processes were increasingly adopted in order to gain a more in-depth understanding of public values and concerns – either as a complement to surveys or instead of them. Much published STS work from this time either uses these methodologies to generate arguments about the governance of science and technology and lay knowledges, or reports on and evaluates deliberative processes orchestrated by policy-makers, museums and other actors. The criticism of the Public Understanding of Science project (e.g., Wynne 1991) led many scholars to import ideal type models of partici-patory democracy from political theory into STS, to offer new frameworks for democratising science. This coincided with deliberative and dialogic models of democracy becoming a predominant democratic imagination in parts of STS (de Vries 2007; Marres and Lezaun 2011). For example, this was reflected in the large uptake of Rowe and Frewer's (2000) paper on evaluating public par-ticipation processes, which at the time of writing remains the most frequently cited paper ever published in the foundational STS journal *Science, Technology and Human Values*. Beyond STS work which dealt primarily with questions of public and democratic engagement, this deliberative participatory democratic imaginary was evident more broadly in that deliberative methods became the default recommendation for a much wider group of scholars when making argu-ments about how to better account for public values and concerns in science and technology governance.

BEYOND PUBLIC DIALOGUE

However, even by 2010 there was recognition among many working in and around the Sciencewise programme that the standardisation of the model of public dialogue might have some negative consequences. The 2010 programme evaluation states:

concerns are raised in the study about the rigidity of the way the model has been delivered and suggestions made for greater flexibility to allow for more creative dialogue that allows for greater collaborative working between the public, policy makers and expertise (Warburton 2010).

In a 2009 interview, one academic social scientist involved in the Sciencewise programme noted the danger of ignoring other forms of public engagement in policy processes and decisions, such as the open-source movement and other more informal citizen engagements around science, as 'I think science itself is a moving target in some of these areas'. The interviewee also noted that the emphasis placed on engaging innocent and disinterested citizens in public dialogue processes could be problematic, because '[what] you're going to find is more and more special interest groups getting involved in science, whether we ask them to or not and you see this with patient groups getting involved in medical research, you see it with the synthetic biology community who are trying to do the same thing, you see it [...] in computing with Open Source'. This social scientist concluded that the continual exclusion of such groups due to 'the constant desire to search for the disinterested public [...] could be quite harmful'.

During the 2012–2015 phase of the Sciencewise programme the British Science Association (BSA) and the 'think and do tank' Involve were brought in to help with the day-to-day running of the programme. Both organisations had longstanding engagement with STS scholarship and scholars, particularly through their directors at the time, Sir Roland Jackson and Simon Burall respectively. Through his work at the BSA and the Nuffield Foundation, Jackson had long been an important interlocutor and figurehead for the arguments put forward by British STS. The involvement of these organisations and individuals in the running of the programme promoted greater engagement with STS scholars, including commissioning leadership work from the STS community and allowing one of the present authors (Pallett) to carry out her PhD research on the programme.

During this period the definition and practice of public dialogue became considerably more flexible, and there were signs that Sciencewise and its partners were more open to experimenting with alternative approaches to public engagement or testing variations to the public dialogue model. A good example of this is the Bioenergy Distributed Dialogue, carried out in 2013, led by the Biotechnology and Biological Sciences Research Council (BBSRC) with Sciencewise support, and building on many earlier collaborations. Like earlier public dialogues the project was organised around a policy-relevant topic and aimed to bring together experts and lay publics. However, the BBSRC wanted to create a more flexible model for this dialogue so that it could be taken up by scientists or community groups in a more DIY fashion, so that the dialogue resources could be periodically updated with new research findings and the outputs of the dialogues in turn feed into the strategic direction of the BBSRC (see Pallett 2018). This required some compromises to be made against the 'gold standard' of public dialogue, as the workshop sessions were made shorter so as to be more accessible, the resources were distilled into a card deck so that baseline information about bioenergy could be easily understood without expert interlocutors, and some of the sessions were carried out without expert facilitators. These changes met with some resistance, but the dialogue project was eventually held up as an important innovation and a Sciencewise success story.

Following a year-long reflective process for the programme using a 'theory of change' framework, in 2014 actors involved in running the Sciencewise programme reformulated its stated aim from increasing the effectiveness and use of public dialogue in government – as it had been since the 2006 relaunch – to the ambition that all decision-making involving science and technology should take public voices into account (see Pallett 2018). This can be seen as the symbolic culmination of moves to transcend the standardised model of public dialogue.

A participation practitioner from the Sciencewise programme also pointed to developments outside the programme as an important stimulus for the opening up of the model of public dialogue after 2012, stating:

> we've got lots of new approaches coming in and new, much more marketing focused, investing in data mining kind of approaches ... really interesting, very, very new and different stuff. The dialogue community, we've been quite reactionary to that I think and quite protective of what we do ... Head Shift, they're looking at data mining techniques to understand where people have

natural deliberative conversations on the internet and getting information from there, rather than having to start a new event. So I think there's things like that, that are moving the field on and thinking about it from a different perspective.

This emergence of novel social media and data mining-based approaches to synthesise public perspectives can be seen as part of the unsettling of the more STS-infused public dialogue approach. The new approaches promised to be both quicker and cheaper whilst also resting on deep-seated assumptions about the neutrality of numerical and machine-based approaches (see Porter 1995). Other prominent social science approaches used in policy-making which, like public dialogue, had emerged in the 2000s such as 'nudge' behavioural economics (see Pallett and Chilvers 2013) were arguably better-suited to accommodate these technological developments.

At this time there were also broader constitutional shifts afoot which threatened the dominance of a deliberative consensual model of engagement. 2010 marked a change of government and the start of a period of austerity governance, justified as a response to the financial crisis. This led to the dissolution of many government-funded arms-length bodies, though the Sciencewise programme was allowed to continue. However, there was a general sense that economic logics were being reasserted as the main drivers behind government decision-making, including science policy, de-emphasising the democratic mandate. Within the Cabinet Office, inspired by open data and open government initiatives across the world – themselves enabled by the rapid development of digital technologies – Francis Maude (then Minister for the Cabinet Office) spearheaded a new initiative for 'open policy' which drew in resources and personnel from the design profession (HM Government 2012). This ill-defined concept of open policy nonetheless suggested a shift away from third way consensus politics, to a 'user engagement' style of policy-making (see Pallett 2015).

Within the field of STS this period saw many scholars begin to engage more critically with models of deliberative democracy. Some did so by taking democracy and participation themselves as objects of study (e.g., Irwin 2006; Chilvers 2008). This work brought attention to the institutional architectures and political economies underlying approaches to public engagement and uncovered the partiality and normativities of deliberative models. There has been increasing recognition of the constructions and exclusions inherent in all forms of participation and of the diverse forms and normativities of democracy that exist (e.g., Wynne 2007; Chilvers and Kearnes 2016). STS scholars have become interested in alternative models of democracy, from agonism to social movements and digital engagement (e.g., Birkbak 2013). Significant interventions in challenging deliberative democratic imaginaries in STS during this period also came from STS scholars who were deeply engaged with emerging digital methods and approaches that necessitated a different working imaginary of democracy (e.g., Marres 2007). STS scholars at this time also began paying greater attention to market tools and economic expertise (e.g., Callon et al. 2007), although this was not translated into a credible call for democratic engagement around these instruments and decisions. Conversations about the structure of STS as a field were also being renewed during this period, in recognition of the powerful influence of developments in Western European and North American contexts over other parts of the world such as Southeast Asia or South America – where the field has also been institutionalised to an extent. These discussions drew attention to the situatedness of many of the 'off-the-shelf' models of democratic politics which have been uncritically imported into STS from other disciplines.

STS AND DEMOCRACY CO-PRODUCED

This story of the co-production of British democratic politics, participatory procedures and the democratic imaginary of parts of the field of STS is one of many potential illustrations of broader processes of co-production between STS and democracy. We have deliberately focused on this particular British story in order to demonstrate, illustrate and empirically qualify our wider argument in a situated and contextual way. It has been noted (e.g., Felt 2016) that Britain has been viewed by other countries as a 'centre' or forerunner in the global development of deliberative approaches to public engagement with science and technology, both in practice and in STS studies of these practices.

Given its widespread influence in and beyond STS, we therefore suggest that Britain is an interesting setting and important site to explore the co-production of STS and democracy through the particular technology of public dialogue. However, it would be possible to narrate similar stories encompassing many other democratic situations, for example the development of technology-oriented frameworks for responsible research and innovation in the US (see Laurent 2017). Recent developments in Japanese science policy and STS offer another illustrative example.

The aftermath of the Fukushima earthquake, tsunami and nuclear accident in 2011 has led to renewed concern in the Japanese government and work by Japanese STS scholars (and others) about public trust in science policy-making. In a number of collaborative programmes, government actors and academics in Japan have explicitly drawn upon lessons from the UK, including Sciencewise's principles for public dialogue, in order to inform the funding and governance of science in Japan and help restore public trust (Arimoto and Sato 2012). Interestingly though, in the Japanese context these principles for deliberative and dialogic engagement have been translated into guidelines for better procedures for science advice and greater transparency (Arimoto and Sato 2012), rather than a programme of work fcussed around deliberative public engagement. Thus, an apparently similar crisis of trust in governance and expertise – even drawing on some of the same work by STS scholars – has played out and been translated in a markedly different way.

Reflecting on the co-production of STS and democracy in this way also allows us to question the dominant, often tacit, democratic imaginations which feature across the interdisciplinary field of STS (see Ezrahi 2012). In particular, our analysis reveals that very specific models and understandings of democracy from political theory have tended to be adopted when STS scholars turn to questions of democracy and participation. We do not take issue with these particular deliberative and dialogic models of democracy *per se*, which build on work by Jürgen Habermas and other critical theorists, but rather point out that a particular normativity of participatory democracy for a time became prevalent in parts of STS to the exclusion of others, often without sufficient reflexive awareness or exploration of the consequences. Of course, there are many examples of engagement by STS scholars with alternative models of democracy, evoking for example Chantal Mouffe's agonism, social movements and feminist approaches, and alternative readings of Dewey (Marres 2007; Wynne 2007). However, we argue that a deliberative democratic imagination is enduring and becomes particularly prominent in interventionist-oriented STS, where scholars seek to intervene in democratising technoscience and democratic processes.

Our brief story has shown that British democracy and STS scholarship pertaining to democracy and participation have been strongly co-produced in the context of science policy over the last two decades. This has been driven in a number of ways through the channelling of science funding into work on public communication and engagement (especially around controversial new technologies), through flagship government participation processes such as 'GM Nation'? and the '2050 pathways' exercise, and more theoretically informed responses to these developments in practice.

Funding for STS scholars in Britain over the last two decades has been closely linked to developments in science and technology. In particular, funding has often been linked to a framing of the need for public acceptance of controversial new technologies and scientific developments, such as genetically modified organisms, nanotechnology, synthetic biology, nuclear power and renewable energy. While it has been gradually acknowledged that public engagement, rather than just public understanding and communication, is a firmer foundation on which to build such acceptance, public acceptance of science and technology has remained the dominant framing of government departments and funders. As a result, STS scholars interested in democracy and participation have predominantly been funded as part of interdisciplinary teams with scientists, in order to do the engagement, communication or responsible innovation work of the proposed project. Alternatively, they have found funding from the government, research councils or market research companies in order to carry out, evaluate or review forms of public engagement around emerging science and technology. The science policy imperative of public acceptance has therefore shaped the progress of British STS in a very meaningful way, which at least in part explains the eruption since the early 2000s of papers on deliberative public engagement.

However, the funding landscape does not tell the full story, as it is possible to trace the ways in which British STS scholars have responded to particular events and controversies, as well as to developments in practice. The controversy around and government dismissal of the *'GM Nation'?* deliberative process which took place 2003–2004 was a key rallying point for many British STS scholars to argue for the value of deliberative public engagement, and for the relevance of the process's key findings and outcomes, though they failed to endorse the Government's pro-GM policy (Rowe et al. 2005). The move towards a more deliberative and dialogic attitude to public engagement around science within the UK government was also seen by many STS scholars as a positive step away from the 'deficit-model' style of public understanding of science schemes which had been pursued in the past. Since the creation of Sciencewise and the emergence of public dialogue as a prominent technology of British democracy, British STS scholars have responded again to the apparent institutionalisation of deliberative participation (e.g., Irwin 2006; Pallett and Chilvers 2013; Wynne 2006). This has redirected attention in STS towards the institutional and national contexts of participation, following a period of intense focus on specific discrete instances of participation (Chilvers and Kearnes 2016).

This recent interest in exploring and theorising systems of participation or deliberation in STS can again be read as an example of STS scholars responding to broader constitutional shifts. In this emerging work, STS scholars are responding in part to funders' desires for more systemic and nexus-based approaches to addressing 'grand challenges' like climate change, energy and emerging technologies, and to the increasing application of digital technologies and platforms in government, democratic and market research contexts to engage citizens and voices across a given system. This has emerged in parallel with more distributed understandings of participation and the development of new methodologies for mapping these engagements (e.g., Marres 2015; Chilvers et al. 2018; Pallett et al. 2019). The rise of the internet and social media platforms as a medium of democratic engagement has been accompanied by a burgeoning interest in digital methods in British and northern European STS (Marres 2017; Rogers 2015). The growing adoption of often more instrumental mapping techniques to understand public opinions or 'sentiments' both by the British government and the private sector, is also an object of emerging critical engagement from STS scholars.

In this chapter we have not only taken democracy and participation as objects of study in their own right, but we have taken one step further to experiment with treating STS's own democratic imagination as an object of study as well. This has implications for where STS scholars take their focus of study and intervention, opening up a potentially fruitful set of a sites where STS and democratic situations meet and are co-produced. We hope this has shown the value of turning the tools and approaches of STS back on themselves in order to closely examine the structure and power relations of the field, and its assumptions and broader governing imaginations. This approach can lead to a challenging of closely held ideals and assumptions – in this case the strong attachment of parts of the field to theories of deliberative democracy – and stimulate us to look further afield for our inspiration and conceptual resources.

The framework set out in the section linking the study of technologies of participation with constitutional developments and STS's own democratic imagination allows us to break somewhat with the now common narrative of the linear take-off model of public engagement in STS, which holds that STS scholars have helped to move approaches away from the deficit model and towards dialogue, and then, more recently, towards more upstream public engagement. Implicit in this model is a view that some countries, in terms of their policy approaches and STS scholars, are seen as being leaders or 'ahead' of others. By questioning this model and offering an alternative narrative we hope to contribute to opening up the potential for an approach that is much more receptive to cosmopolitan diversities of participatory democratic arrangements across cultures. Through this we may find new conceptual and methodological resources for work on participation and democracy in STS.

CONCLUSION

We have advanced two main arguments in this chapter. The first was to demonstrate the intimate co-productive relationship between STS and democracy, which has been ongoing for a number of decades. The second was to offer an example of an in-depth situated study of a particular technology of participation in a particular constitutional context, in order to support the broader argument of this book: that more STS scholars should engage with situated democracies in the making as key objects of study and intervention in themselves. We have aimed to show the value of this way of engaging with democratic situations through the insights it offers into the case of Sciencewise and the technology of public dialogue, as initially quite a standardised practice of democratic politics which gained prominence in a UK context and has more recently diversified into a broader set of democratic practices. Furthermore, we have turned the microscope onto STS's participatory democratic imagination itself and suggested that this should also be an important object of enquiry. We hope that projects like this volume will promote a greater diversity of approaches to studying democracy in STS and prompt a more critical approach to the models and definitions of democracy which are adopted.

ENDNOTES

1 Here we take a broad definition of co-productionist work in STS that encompasses arguments about the mutual construction and co-constitution of science and social order (e.g., Jasanoff 2004; Latour 1987; Nowotny et al. 2001). This idiom is increasingly adopted to explore the co-production of democracy and social orders (Chilvers and Kearnes 2016; Laurent 2017; and as mapped out in Birkbak and Papazu, this volume).
2 Many of the features we attribute to a single time period are often evident in others (see Pieckza and Escobar 2013). However, we hope to capture in this narrative the evolution of *dominant* participatory democratic imaginaries in STS in relation to the technology journey of public dialogue and significant constitutional shifts.

REFERENCES

Barry, A., 'Technological Zones', *European Journal of Social Theory*, 9 (2006), 239–253.
Bickerstaff, K. et al., 'Locating Scientific Citizenship: The Institutional Contexts and Cultures of Public Engagement', *Science Technology & Human Values*, 35 (2010), 474–500.

Birkbak, A., and I. Papazu, 'Introducing Democratic Situations', in A. Birkbak and I. Papazu, eds, *Democratic Situations* (Manchester, UK: Mattering Press, 2022).

Callon, M., Y. Millo, and F. Muniesa, *Market Devices*. The Sociological Review, 55 (Oxford: Wiley-Blackwell, 2007).

Callon, M., P. Lascoumbes, and Y. Barthe, *Acting in an Uncertain World: An Essay on Technical Democracy* (Cambridge MA: The MIT Press, 2009).

Chilvers, J., H. Pallett, and T. Hargreaves, 'Ecologies of Participation in Socio-Technical Change: The Case of Energy System Transitions', *Energy Research and Social Science*, 42 (2018), 199–210.

Chilvers J., 'Expertise, Professionalization and Reflexivity in Mediating Public Participation: Perspectives from STS and British Science and Democracy', in L. Bherer, M. Gauthier, and L. Simard, eds, *The Professionalization of Public Participation* (Abingdon: Routledge, 2017), pp. 115–138.

——, 'Reflexive Engagement? Actors, Learning, and Reflexivity in Public Dialogue on Science and Technology', *Science Communication*, 35 (2013), 283–310.

——, *Sustainable Participation? Mapping out and Reflecting on the Field of Public Dialogue on Science and Technology* (Harwell: Sciencewise Expert Resource Centre, 2010).

——, 'Environmental Risk, Uncertainty, and Participation: Mapping an Emergent Epistemic Community', *Environment and Planning A*, 40 (2008), 2990–3008.

Chilvers, J., and M. Kearnes, 2016. 'Remaking Participation: Towards Reflexive Engagement', in J. Chilvers and M. Kearnes, eds, *Remaking Participation: Science, Environment and Emergent Publics* (London: Routledge, 2016), pp. 261–288.

Chilvers, J., and P. Macnaghten, *The Future of Science Governance: A Review of Public Concerns, Governance and Institutional Response* (Harwell: Sciencewise Expert Resource Centre, 2011).

Cohn, C., 'Nuclear Language and How We Learned to Pat the Bomb', *Bulletin of the Atomic Scientists*, 43 (1987), 17–24.

De Vries, G., 'What Is Political in Sub-Politics? How Aristotle Might Help STS', *Social Studies of Science*, 37 (2007), 781–809.

Doubleday, R., and B. Wynne, 'Despotism and Democracy in the UK: Experiments in Reframing Relations between the State, Science and Citizens', in S. Jasanoff, ed., *Reframing Rights: Bioconstitutionalism in the Genetic Age* (Cambridge, MA: The MIT Press, 2011), pp. 239–261.

Elam, M., L. Reynolds, L. Soneryd, G. Sundqvist, and B. Szerszynski, *Mediators of Issues and Mediators of Process: A Theoretical Framework* (Göteborg: Göteborg University, 2007).

Ezrahi, Y., *Imagined Democracies: Necessary Political Fictions* (Cambridge: Cambridge University Press, 2012).

——, *The Descent of Icarus: Science and the Transformation of Contemporary Democracy* (Cambridge. MA: Harvard University Press, 1990).

Felt, U., 'The Temporal Choreographies of Participation: Thinking Innovation and Society from a Time-Sensitive Perspective', in J. Chilvers, J. and M. Kearnes, eds, *Remaking Participation: Science, Environment and Emergent Publics* (London: Routledge, 2016), pp. 178–198.

Grolin, J., 'Corporate Legitimacy in Risk Society: The Case of Brent Spar', *Business Strategy and the Environment*, 7 (1999), 213–222.

H M Government, *The Civil Service Reform Plan* (London, 2012).

Horst, M., and A. Irwin, 'Nations at Ease with Radical Knowledge On Consensus, Consensusing and False Consensusness', *Social Studies of Science*, 40 (2010), 105–126.

Irwin, A., 'Constructing the Scientific Citizen: Science and Democracy in the Biosciences', *Public Understanding of Science*, 10 (2001), 1–18.

——, 'The Politics of Talk: Coming to Terms with the "New" Scientific Governance', *Social Studies of Science*, 36 (2006), 299–320.

Irwin, A., T. E. Jensen, and K. E. Jones, 'The Good, the Bad and the Perfect: Criticizing Engagement Practice', *Social Studies of Science*, 43 (2013), 118–125.

Jasanoff, S., 'Constitutional Moments in Governing Science and Technology', *Science and Engineering Ethics*, 17 (2011), 621–638.

——, *Designs on Nature: Science and Democracy in Europe and the United States* (Princeton, NJ: Princeton University Press, 2005).

——, *States of Knowledge: The Co-production of Science and Social Order* (London: Routledge, 2004).

Kearnes, M., P. Macnaghten, and J. Wilsdon, *Governing at the Nanoscale: People, Policies and Emerging* Technologies (London: Demos, 2006).

Latour, B., *We Have Never Been Modern* (Cambridge, MA: Harvard University Press, 1993).

——, *Science in Action: How to Follow Scientists and Engineers through Society* (Cambridge, MA: Harvard University Press, 1987).

Laurent, B., 'Technologies of Democracy: Experiments and Demonstrations', *Science and Engineering Ethics*, 17 (2011), 649–666.

Lezaun, J., 'A Market of Opinions: The Political Epistemology of Focus Groups', *Sociological Review*, 55 (2007), pp.130–151.

Lezaun, J., and L. Soneryd, 'Consulting Citizens: Technologies of Elicitation and the Mobility of Publics', *Public Understanding of Science*, 16 (2007), 279–297.

Lezaun, J., N. Marres, and M. Tironi, 'Experiments in Participation', in U. Felt, R. Fouché, C. A. Miller, and L. Smith-Doerr, eds, *The Handbook of Science and Technology Studies*, Fourth Edition (Cambridge, MA: The MIT Press, 2016), pp. 195–221.

Marres, N., and J. Lezaun, 'Materials and Devices of the Public: An Introduction', *Economy and Society*, 40 (2011), 489–509.

Marres, N., *Digital Sociology* (Cambridge: Polity Press, 2017).

Marres, N., 'Why Map Issues? On Controversy Analysis as a Digital Method', *Science, Technology & Human Values*, 40 (2015), 655–686.

Marres, N., *Material Participation: Technology, the Environment and Everyday Publics* (Basingstoke: Palgrave Macmillan, 2012).

——, 'The Issues Deserve More Credit: Pragmatist Contributions to the Study of Public Involvement in Controversy', *Social Studies of Science*, 37 (2007), 759–780.

Miller, S., 'Public Understanding of Science at the Crossroads', *Public Understanding of Science*, 10 (2001), 115–120.

Nowotny, H., P. Scott, and M. Gibbons, *Re-Thinking Science: Knowledge and the Public in an Age of Uncertainty* (Cambridge: Polity Press, 2001).

Pallett, H., 'Situating Organisational Learning and Public Participation: Stories, Spaces and Connections', *Transactions of the Institute of British Geographers*, 43 (2018), 215–229.

——, 'Public Participation Organizations and Open Policy: A Constitutional Moment for British Democracy?', *Science Communication*, 37 (2015), 769–794.

Pallett, H., and J. Chilvers, 'A decade of Learning about Publics, Participation and Climate Change: Institutionalising Reflexivity?', *Environment and Planning A*, 45 (2013), 1162–1183.

Pallett, H., J. Chilvers, and T. Hargreaves, 'Mapping Participation: A Systematic Analysis of Diverse Public Participation in the UK Energy System', *Environment and Planning E*. 2 (2019), 590–616.

Pieczka, M., and O. Escobar, 'Dialogue and Science: Innovation in Policy-Making and the Discourse of Public Engagement in the UK', *Science and Public Policy*, 40 (2013), 113–126.

Porter, T. M., *Trust in Numbers: The Pursuit of Objectivity in Science and Public Life* (Princeton, NJ: Princeton University Press, 1995).

Rogers, R., 'Digital Methods for Web Research', *Emerging Trends in the Behavioral and Social Sciences*, (2015), pp. 1–22.

Rowe, G., and L. Frewer, 'Public Participation Methods: A Framework for Evaluation', *Science, Technology & Human Values*, 25 (2000), 3–29.

Rowe, G., T. Horlick-Jones, J. Walls, and N. Pidgeon, 'Difficulties in Evaluating Public Engagement Initiatives: Reflections on an Evaluation of the UK GM Nation? Public Debate about Transgenic Crops', *Public Understanding of Science*, 14 (2005), 331–352.

Soneryd, L., 'Technologies of Participation and the Making of Technologised Futures', in J. Chilvers and M. Kearnes, eds, *Remaking Participation: Science, Environment and Emergent Publics* (London: Routledge, 2016), pp. 144–161.

Thorpe, C., 'Participation as Post-Fordist Politics: Demos, New Labour, and Science Policy', *Minerva*, 48 (2010), 389–411.

Voß, J.-P., and N. Amelung, 'Innovating Public Participation Methods: Techno-scientization and Reflexive Engagement', *Social Studies of Science*, 46.5 (2016), 749–772.

Voß, J.-P., and R. Freeman, eds, *Knowing Governance* (Basingstoke: Palgrave, 2016).

Wilsdon, J., and R. Willis, *See-Through Science: Why Public Engagement Needs to Move Upstream* (London: Demos, 2004).

Wynne, B., 'Public Participation in Science and Technology: Performing and Obscuring a Political–Conceptual Category Mistake', *East Asian Science, Technology and Society: An International Journal*, 1 (2007), 99–110.

——, 'Public Engagement as a Means of Restoring Public Trust in Science: Hitting the Notes, but Missing the Music?', *Community Genetics*, 9 (2006), 211–220.

——, 'Knowledges in Context', *Science, Technology & Human Values*, 16 (1991), 111–121.

7

A DEMOCRATIC INQUIRY LAUNCHED AND LOST: THE DUTCH NATIONAL SOCIETAL DIALOGUE ON NANOTECHNOLOGY

Lotte Krabbenborg

IN 2009, THE DUTCH GOVERNMENT AIMED TO OPEN UP ITS POLICY-MAKING process on newly emerging nanotechnology to bottom-up input from civil society.[1] However, the issues that were articulated during the so-called Dutch societal dialogue did not become connected to decision-making processes within research and policy institutions. In order to find out what contributed to this 'missed opportunity', this chapter offers an analysis of the actions and considerations of the Dutch government and the committee that was appointed by the government to design and orchestrate the societal dialogue. I show that when the societal dialogue took place, the committee relied on a 'deficit model' of communication. The committee formulated restrictions with regards to 1) who could participate, 2) the kind of participation that was considered legitimate, and 3) the type of outcomes that could be produced. Consequently, what happened during the Dutch societal dialogue is that 'awareness raising' and 'reaching as many people as possible' were prioritised over further enquiry into and articulation of ethical and societal issues with the help of civil society actors, which was the original aim. I will conclude by providing some pointers on how to move forward if the aim is to have more two-way interactions between science and society on newly emerging issues of science and technology.

As already noted in Krabbenborg and Mulder (2015: 12), 'societal dialogues are ambitious attempts, initiated by government agencies, to create large scale, in-depth, and often longer-term interactions among citizens, science and technology developers and other stakeholders to inform policymakers'. Societal dialogues can be seen as democratic situations where citizens are stimulated to actively participate in policy-making processes regarding new scientific and technological developments. However, *how* a societal dialogue is actually designed and orchestrated influences the way(s) citizens are expected to participate and the extent to which their issues and concerns are or can be taken up in policy processes. Thus, to learn about democracy as a situated practice, in particular with regard to citizen participation in the governance of new science and technology, it is worthwhile to empirically study the design and outcomes of societal dialogues.

The aim of the dialogue was to identify the ethical and societal issues pertaining to nanotechnology that had not yet been taken up by existing institutions (Ministerial Resolution 2009). Civil society actors, in this respect, were positioned by the Dutch government as dialogue partners for scientists and other stakeholders and as capable of voicing issues that were deemed valuable for the further development of nanotechnology.

The fact that citizens are positioned as actual dialogue partners by the Dutch government can be seen as an example of dialogical science communication (Horst and Davies 2016). In the traditional deficit model of science communication, the public is pictured as consisting of lay persons with a cognitive deficit that makes it difficult for them to understand new science and technology properly (e.g., Irwin and Wynne 1996; Horst and Davies 2016; Shaping 1990). In the more recent dialogical model of science communication, the public is positioned as having intrinsic knowledge that could be beneficial to the scientific process (e.g., Wynne 1992). As such, the public is positioned as being capable of 'speaking back' to science (e.g., Gibbens 1999), which assumption is also reflected in the above quote of the Dutch government. In turn, science and technology developers are expected to become more responsive to the needs and concerns of society and to take up these issues in their ongoing decision-making processes (e.g., Wilsdon and Willis 2004; MacNaughten, Kearnes and Wynne 2005). However, as I will show in this chapter, in practice the opportunities created for civil society to 'speak back' to science were not fully exploited, neither by the project leaders, the Committee nor the Dutch government.

Multiple actors were involved in designing the Dutch societal dialogue. Possible topics for discussion mentioned by the government were the integrity of the human body in relation to the development of new nano-enabled medical devices, and the risk that nanosciences and nanotechnologies might increase the gap between rich and poor countries, as not every country is able to invest in emerging sciences and technologies (Parliamentary Documents 2008). The actual organisation of the societal dialogue was delegated to a committee appointed by the Dutch government. The mandate of the committee was to produce a midterm and final report about the progress and results of the societal dialogue. These reports were used by the government as a resource to further develop its policies on nanotechnology (Ministerial Resolution 2009). The committee itself was not a partner in the actual discussions on nanotechnology, but it enabled a variety of public engagement activities by funding project proposals. In practice, proposals tended to be submitted mainly by intermediaries with a professional background in bridging technology and society, either as science communicators, educators or STS researchers.

DATA COLLECTION AND HISTORICAL BACKGROUND

The story of this chapter is based on interviews with policymakers involved in the societal dialogue, in addition to participant observation at four committee meetings and four public meetings organised by the committee. I also analysed Dutch policy documents on the governance of nanotechnology produced between 2006 and 2011. By combining these materials with an analysis of publicly available progress reports, I gained insight into how the committee took up its mandate and negotiated what was at stake and what should be done, as well as how the committee aggregated results from the individual projects in its midterm and final reports. Moreover, I was a project leader myself and as such had to complete bimonthly progress reports produced by the committee, which gave me a participant's insight into what the committee found important with regard to monitoring the societal dialogue and how it wanted to operationalise its mandate for organising a societal dialogue on 'pressing ethical and societal issues' (Ministerial Resolution 2009). As such, one could argue that I had a double role as analyst and participant. However, while a participant observer will always influence the researched just by the fact of being present and asking questions (Råheim et al. 2016), I was not formally part of the deliberation or negotiation with regard to the design, set-up and evaluation of the societal dialogue.

To understand the design of the Societal Dialogue on Nanotechnology, we need to consider the Dutch history of organising large societal dialogues on new sciences and technologies (Krabbenborg and Mulder 2015), as well as the broader governance approach in the Netherlands on how to deal with newly emerging nanotechnology. In the mid-1980s, the Dutch government organised a long-term societal dialogue on nuclear energy, and in the early 2000s, a societal dialogue on biotechnology and food was organised. In both cases, the Dutch government encountered criticism from non-governmental organisations and (social) scientists (Krabbenborg and Mulder 2015). In the case of the dialogue on nuclear energy, for example, the government was criticised for not acting on the outcomes (Hajer and Houterman 1985). With regard to the dialogue on biotechnology and food, the government was blamed for framing the process too much in favour of genetically modified food (Hanssen 2009).

At the beginning of 2000, there was concern in the Netherlands (like else-where in the world) that nanotechnology, with its potential to create novel and unpredictable impacts on society,[2] would reach the same impasse as genetically modified organisms (GMOs) due to public resistance (Joly and Kaufman 2008). This convinced Dutch government agencies to do things differently and better in the case of nanotechnology (Parliamentary Documents 2006).[3] After early initiatives by the Rathenau Institute (Van Est, Malsh, and Rip 2004), the Dutch government asked for advice about the risk of nanotechnology from the Health Council of the Netherlands (2006), and about policy on nanotechnology gener-ally from the Royal Netherlands Academy of Arts and Sciences (2004). Based on these inputs, the Dutch government recognised that

only providing information and education on nanotechnology is not enough
to gain societal acceptance. [In fact], the opinion of Dutch citizens matters
[…] Societal acceptance can only be established when input from citizens
is used to shape R&D trajectories and risk evaluations. (Parliamentary
Document 2006: 28, 29)

Accordingly, the Dutch government proposed a twofold strategy to address
nanotechnology in society. The proposal was to approach risk and safety issues
(for example, the toxicity of synthetic nanoparticles) and 'broader ethical and
societal issues' in different ways. To identify risks to human health and environment, a sounding board with representatives from industry, science and
environmental organisations was set up. In order to identify and assess 'broader
ethical and societal issues', a societal dialogue with citizens and stakeholders
was proposed. Thus, while it was not made explicit, one can recognise the
idea(1) of deliberative democracy (see Habermas 1989) underlying the Societal
Dialogue on Nanotechnology. In this case, the public at large, scientists and
'other stakeholders' were expected to identify and assess the broader ethical
and societal issues related to the development of nanotechnology by sharing
their concerns and arguments.

THE WORK OF THE COMMITTEE

Given the criticism that it displayed too many biases during the societal dialogue on biotechnology and food, the Dutch government decided not to play
an active role in the Societal Dialogue on Nanotechnology. It delegated the
design and orchestration of the societal dialogue to an independent committee. The nine members appointed by a temporary interdepartmental working
group to form the committee had backgrounds in nanoscience and technology, bioethics, STS, toxicology and health policy. The chair of the committee
had no formal background in (development and/or governance of) emerging technologies but worked in the domain of economics and had been the
president of a national research funding agency. To organise and evaluate the
Societal Dialogue, the committee was assisted by a secretariat. This secretariat

consisted of three people working for a consultancy group within science, technology and innovation.

The committee opted for distributed activities and launched a call for project proposals. In this call, the committee refined and concretised the societal dialogue by focusing on five application areas of nanotechnology and articulated possible associated ethical and societal issues. The five areas were 'wellbeing, food and healthcare', 'environment and sustainability', 'safety and privacy', 'international relations' and 'sustainable economic growth'. Possible ethical and societal issues for discussion that were identified by the committee included, amongst others, 'Who or what institution can be held liable in the event of nanotechnology and nanoparticles causing harm to human health?', 'What kind of information does the consumer need and how should information be provided to consumers?', and 'How can nanotechnology provide alternatives to animal testing?' (CIEMD 2009: 8; Krabbenborg 2013; Krabbenborg and Mulder 2015). However, as I will show below, in developing its monitoring and evaluation criteria and in writing its official reports, the committee moved away from the specific questions and issues mentioned in the call for proposals, towards more generic questions about nanotechnology and project management.

As the relevant STS literature (Wynne 2001; Rogers-Hayden 2010; Pidgeon and Rogers-Hayden 2007) shows, engaging publics to discuss a newly emerging science and technology like nanotechnology is not at all easy. Citizens are typically not aware of new technological developments, as the technologies do not yet play a role in people's daily lives. Therefore, there are very few, if any, lived experiences that people can draw on in such planned interactions. What forms the technology will take, how it will materialise in society and what the societal impacts might be remains uncertain. Furthermore, the dimensions by which new technologies can be assessed are indeterminate. Therefore, making newly emerging science and technology a topic for societal deliberation is not straightforward (Krabbenborg 2013).

The committee took up this challenge by developing a two-stage approach. The first phase of the societal dialogue would focus on providing information and raising awareness about nanotechnology and related ethical and societal issues with the help of TV programmes, brochures and websites. In the second phase, a dialogue would be initiated based on insights from phase one (CIEMD 2009; Krabbenborg and Mulder 2015: 14). The activities proposed in the second phase were, amongst others, science cafés, panel discussions, one-on-one interviews and theatre performances followed by discussion sessions.

Salient in the call for proposals was the committee's focus on the citizen as a lay person who needs to become acquainted with nanotechnology, rather than on stakeholders, as had been the suggestion of the Dutch government. Actors such as companies, research institutes and government agencies were mentioned in the call for proposals, but they were positioned by the committee as actors who could take up the *outcomes* of the societal dialogue (CIEMD 2009: 5), not as active dialogue partners for civil society during actual interaction events (Krabbenborg and Mulder 2015). The choice to focus on citizens as 'lay persons' is intriguing. As Irwin (2001) and Goven (2003) argue, when scientists and technology developers do not participate as active dialogue partners during public engagement activities, it is more difficult for citizens to actively participate and problematise the underlying assumptions, worldviews and justifications, as there is no opportunity for citizens to interrogate scientists and technology developers. As I will show, this is what happened in the Dutch societal dialogue, as most projects turned out to be designed within the deficit model of communication, in which nanoscientists were offered a stage to provide information ('factual knowledge') about what nanotechnology 'is' (the inverted commas are used because the technology is still evolving). The public, in this case so-called lay citizens, was positioned as a listening, passive audience.

Any Dutch citizen and organisation could, in principle, develop a project proposal. The committee, however, explicitly encouraged civil society organisations (CSOs) to submit proposals and participate in the dialogue (CIEMD 2011: 28). However, CSOs could not just propose any kind of project. For example, one Dutch environmental organisation proposed to identify the possible risks of nanoparticles in cosmetics. According to this CSO, risk and safety issues did not receive enough attention in current policymaking on nanotechnology. In order to attract the attention of policymakers (and the media), their initial proposal was to have naked women carrying nanocosmetics at the Binnenhof in The Hague, where the Dutch parliament is seated. The committee members rejected this proposal, as explained by one member:

> There was a consensus, at least with eight of us, that the best way to proceed with the Societal Dialogue is to refrain from public displays that might be too controversial. The committee clearly preferred reasoned discussions over heated debates. (Interview with committee member 09-03-2010, Krabbenborg 2013)

During the first round, the proposals of CSOs (which were few) were not funded because they were all evaluated as being of 'lesser quality' than other proposals, mainly because they failed to present a 'balanced view' of the pros and cons of nanotechnology. The committee and its secretariat were nevertheless still eager to have CSOs on board. The committee approached CSOs and offered guidelines on how to submit 'good' proposals for the second round of funding ('good' implied proposals that represented both positive and negative aspects). The committee and secretariat did not approach scientists and companies proactively to prompt them to submit proposals. It was their expectation that 'scientists would be approached by project leaders to join activities'.

While the committee's desire to avoid public upheaval is understandable, for civil society organisations this demarcation of what can and cannot be done might be perceived as a form of muzzling that could be in tension with their right to free speech. Safeguarding freedom of speech and maintaining independence is essential for civil society organisations in order to fulfil their role as a 'watch-dog for society' (Bauer and Schmitz 2012; Krabbenborg, 2020). The tensions that can occur between, on the one hand, stimulating bottom-up input from civil society, and on the other hand, setting restrictions on who can participate and what kind of participation is desirable or legitimate is not unique to the Netherlands. In the UK, the organisers of *GM Nation?* had concerns about the predictability of the contributions and held entrenched ideas about CSOs and therefore excluded them from the debate, looking instead for the 'silent majority' of unengaged citizens with apparently 'no fixed position on GM' (Lezaun and Soneryd 2007: 290). In France, a group of citizens called Pièces et Main d'Oeuvre (PMO), concerned with the close connections between scientific research, industrial development and political interests, did not want to engage in the national dialogue on nanotechnology as an official participant (Laurent 2016). Instead, PMO used the dialogue as an entry point to spread their message via banners, counter-meetings organised in parallel to official ones, and websites in which PMO described how to contest the French national debate (Laurent 2016: 780, 781).

DEVELOPING SELECTION AND EVALUATION CRITERIA

As noted, the Dutch societal dialogue committee started with a two-stage approach of first providing information and raising awareness on nanotechnology and its broader ethical and societal issues, and then, in a second phase, stimulating an informed dialogue. Over time this strategy shifted, as providing information and building awareness, operationalised as 'outreach', became the main priority, even if not all committee members were happy with this move (Krabbenborg and Mulder 2015). The chair of the committee positioned himself as the 'process manager' of the societal dialogue and strongly advocated this focus. In an interview for ObservatoryNANO (Malsch 2011), the chair described what the aim of the societal dialogue should be and what his role and responsibility was:

> Government, but also other stakeholders, including industry, should be kept at quite some distance. The debate itself, but also the contents of the dialogue, should be determined by society. No-one should hold the steering wheel, except society itself (...) I had to play a passive role and not express an opinion on nano. I was just a process manager. (ObservatoryNANO 2011: 2, 8)

This positioning of the chair is striking. While it may sound democratic to let 'society' decide on the content of the societal dialogue, when newly emerging science and technology is the topic for debate, such a strategy is problematic. Of course, considering the aim of the Dutch government to establish a participatory interactive policy-making process on nanotechnology with the involvement of civil society, it is wise not to let industry and science predetermine the agenda. However, as has already been pointed out, newly emerging science and technology is still in process. In order for civil society actors to develop an opinion and determine topics for debate, information must be provided by scientists and industrialists about their considerations, assumptions and concrete lines of action with regard to the development of nanotechnology. So, instead of positioning 'stakeholders, including industry, at a distance', as the chair suggests, it would be wiser to actively involve them.

Moreover, 'no expression of an opinion' on the side of the committee is not the same as being passive. On the contrary, as I will show below, the committee, including the chair, was very active in many ways, and its focus on 'process management' in fact led to several restrictions with regard to civil society participation. As already showed in Krabbenborg (2013), some committee members tried to challenge this focus on outreach and knowledge transfer, in particular the participating STS scholar. They wanted to pursue a more reflexive approach in the societal dialogue, as, according to them, the main challenge was to define a meaningful societal dialogue to begin with. During a discussion among committee members about how to visualise outreach efforts, the STS scholar stated:

> The focus on numbers makes me feel uncomfortable. We should be more creative; what do we intend to have by 2011? For me, it should be more than tables and graphs. I do not want to say that it is easy, but I do want to show that a public dialogue cannot be captured in numbers and tables only. [Translation by the author]

The focus on outreach rather than debate and contestation became particularly visible during the selection and monitoring of the individual projects. In total, the committee received around 120 proposals. Seventy submissions were asked to send in full proposals. In the final stage, 35 projects were funded. The committee had two important selection criteria: the distribution of selected proposals over the five themes identified in the call for proposals, and a sufficient outreach for each project, with the aim of reaching as many people as possible with every project (CIEMD 2011; see also Krabbenborg and Mulder 2015). This shift to an emphasis on outreach was also visible in the monitoring and evaluation criteria, as project leaders had to indicate the outreach of their projects in bi-monthly progress reports, that is, how many people had been reached and how much media attention had the projects received.[4]

THE INDIVIDUAL PROJECTS

A variety of projects were organised to stimulate discussion on nanotechnology and its ethical and societal issues. Eighteen of the thirty-five projects were designed to raise awareness and stimulate dialogue by providing resources such as educational materials, vignettes (short stories) and scenarios, TV programmes and brochures (Krabbenborg 2013). The majority of these projects were designed within the deficit model of communication, focusing on providing information from the world of nanotechnology to society, highlighting the promises as well as possible risks and safety issues.

There were also projects that facilitated a more dialogic model of science communication through the production of materials; for example, by creating websites that offered an opportunity for visitors to gain insight into different and sometimes conflicting stakes and opinions present in society in relation to the development of nanosciences and nanotechnologies, as well as allowing the visitors to articulate their own visions and stakes via a special 'discussion forum' (Krabbenborg 2013). A civil society organisation, WECF (Women in Europe for a Common Future), organised a project focused on the role of retailers in managing risks related to the market introduction of nanoconsumer products for children. Their website contained short movies in which actors developing newly emerging nanotechnology, retailers, toxicologists and CSOs all articulated their visions, stakes and dilemmas with regard to health and environmental safety issues of nano-enabled products in childcare. The Dutch Society for Nature and Environment, together with the Dutch Association of Manufacturers and Importers of Cosmetics (NCV) developed a digital nano-checkpoint for cosmetics. Visitors to this website could fill in a form and check if their cosmetics contained nanoparticles and what risks this might entail. Background information on risk issues was available. The website focused on providing information and offered an opportunity for visitors to read about the positions and stakes of both the industry (NCV) and an environmental organisation.

Alongside projects developing information materials, there were others that attempted to create face-to-face or online interaction between citizens or between nanotechnology developers and citizens on the ethical and societal issues pertaining to nanotechnology. A project called Interreligious Dialogue, for instance, used the film *Gattaca* (about genetic enhancement) to stimulate discussion between people with different religious backgrounds on the question of which values or convictions behind the development of nanotechnology can be considered acceptable or not. I myself organised three interactive multi-stakeholder scenario workshops on how certain nano-enabled point-of-care devices in the healthcare sector might change the existing roles, values and responsibilities of physicians, patients and insurance companies. The aim of the workshops was to generate discussion on how to value and anticipate these changes.

SELECTIVE AGGREGATION: THE ROAD FROM INDIVIDUAL PROJECTS TO OFFICIAL REPORTS AND POLICY DOCUMENTS

As we have seen, the mandate of the committee was to produce a midterm and final report on the process and content of the Dutch societal dialogue. To do so, the committee had to decide how to aggregate experiences and articulate issues from the individual projects into outcomes that could be taken up in the reports. While ethical and societal issues were articulated in some of the individual projects, almost no ethical and societal issues were mentioned in the official reports produced by the committee. For example, in the final report, called *Responsibly onwards with nanotechnology* (CIEMD 2011), the main conclusions were: 'the knowledge of Dutch citizens increased by ten percent between 2009 and 2010', 'Dutch citizens see opportunities, but also risks, especially within the field of nanotechnology and food', and 'Dutch citizens think transparency of information is more important than precaution' (CIEMD 2011).

While some reduction of complexity is necessary to enable decision-making, in this case there is some irony involved in how this was done. Enquiries took place, and broader ethical and societal issues were articulated in a number of projects. However, in evaluating and monitoring the projects, the committee relied on a more traditional deficit model of science communication, in which the focus is on outreach, media attention and increased knowledge (Simis 2016). Therefore, the ethical and societal issues that were articulated in individual projects could not be sufficiently captured by the evaluation forms of the committee. As a result, these issues were not given visibility in the reports. Consequently, the issues did not become part of policy considerations within government, as the government had already decided prior to the start of the dialogue that it would only use the summative progress reports as a resource in its decision-making process. What remained were very general conclusions and recommendations which are difficult for policy makers to utilise in concrete policy-making processes (see also Pidgeon and Rogers-Hayden 2007).

Selective aggregation of items discussed in dedicated public engagement events into official outcomes is not unique to the Netherlands. Goven (2003, 2006), for example, analysed (large-scale) dialogue processes between science and society on genetically modified plants in New Zealand. She showed that citizens' concerns that did not fit hegemonic, in this case neoliberal, values of economic growth, commercial incentives and private property rights (e.g., the right to patent DNA sequences) were filtered out and/or rephrased in official outcomes and reports. For example, concerns about the accountability of scientists, transparency (e.g., with regard to labelling GM products), and the public's right to know were transformed by the organisers into a problem of public misunderstanding of science and ineffective science communication (Goven 2003: 431–432).

DISCUSSION

I have shown that, despite a promising design and good intentions, the Dutch Societal Dialogue on Nanotechnology did not realise its full democratic potential in the sense of issue articulation and interactive policy-making, because it relied on the deficit model of communication in setting up and evaluating the outcomes of the dialogue. The Dutch societal dialogue has, however, been partly successful on its own terms, for instance in raising awareness and providing information on nanotechnology. While this is important in itself, the process failed to meet its aim 'to identify and categorise themes and issues, in particular pressing ethical and societal issues pertaining to nanotechnology, that had not yet been taken up by other institutions in the Netherlands' (Dutch Government 2008).

How could this happen? Was the focus on outreach and the eventual backgrounding of social and ethical issues the result of the fact that organising a national societal dialogue, in the end, is a mundane practice full of contingencies? Or did it have to do with more general difficulties associated with the aim of creating an upstream dialogue between scientists, the public at large and other stakeholders on newly emerging technologies? There were definitely contingencies in the way the committee interpreted its mandate to design and evaluate the societal dialogue. The most significant contingency was that the committee, in order to write its official reports, decided to rely on the content of the progress reports that were written by the individual project leaders (Krabbenborg and Mulder 2015). With this choice, the committee made itself dependent on how much time the project leaders were willing to put into their progress reports. An alternative strategy could have been for committee members to be present as observers at concrete events organised by project leaders and/or to develop more fine-grained evaluation criteria and forms to monitor the projects in order to better capture the content of the debates within them. Furthermore, there were contingencies in terms of which committee members were available and willing to devote extra time and effort (Krabbenborg, 2013). During the process, I observed how some committee members turned out to have less time than foreseen. Moreover, as we have noted, the chair of the committee was focused on raising awareness and managing the process by gaining media attention, while he was less oriented towards the content, which was mostly left to project leaders to decide on. This choice was not without consequences, as it influenced the type of projects that were selected, and the types of outcomes were seen as legitimate.

However, there are also more general difficulties involved. As Rip and Talma (1998) have argued, there is an entrenched cultural repertoire in Western societies which is used to manage newly emerging technologies. A cultural repertoire functions as a toolkit from which actors can draw certain elements (myths, symbols, stereotypes) to make sense of particular situations and shape their actions (Swidler 1986). Risks and safety issues related to new science and technology can become a topic for deliberation between different actors relatively easily, because by now there is a cultural repertoire available for these issues on which actors can fall back. There are examples from earlier technologies that can be mobilised, and there are professional institutions that have responsibilities and mandates, for example, to study the toxicity of chemicals, including nanoparticles, and/or to monitor and inform citizens about health risks and environmental damage. For other societal issues, such as the way technology shapes how we relate to the world and to each other, and how it might change the way we value certain behaviours and norms (Boenink et al. 2010; Feenberg 1999; Swierstra and Te Molder 2012), there is much less of a repertoire available for actors to use as a toolkit. The same holds for the deficit model of communication. While the committee's reliance on the deficit model, for instance by using concepts and frames from evaluations of traditional mass media campaigns, certainly had to do with the preferences of individual committee members, the fact that tools, skills and routines from the deficit model of communication are widely available in society probably also contributed to this. Concepts and methodologies used to shape communication in a deficit model are already available and people have experience with them, making them an easily available recourse (Krabbenborg and Mulder 2015).

There is no simple solution for how to do better, and the committee should be praised for its pioneering attempt to initiate a broad societal dialogue given these contingencies. One way forward could have been to incorporate (more) moments of reflection during the societal dialogue, paying attention to questions such as: Are we still on track? Are we reaching our goals?

Another way forward is to move from awareness-building to inquiry in the sense of Dewey (1927) and Lindblom (1990): a form of deliberation and negotiation in which participants jointly try to uncover what is at stake in particular indeterminate situations by actively sharing experiences, dilemmas and concerns, and by questioning each other (Krabbenborg 2016). The notion of 'inquiry' is important because it encompasses all actors, not just the general public or lay citizens: nanotechnology is new and indeterminate for everyone, and no one has a complete overview of what is or might be at stake. Still, there is the question of sufficient information about and understanding of the socio-technical and socio-political dynamics of newly emerging technology: if information is absent, there is little basis for enquiry. The original two-phase approach of the Dutch societal dialogue did consider this, although it separated awareness-raising from inquiry, putting awareness-raising first rather than making it part of the inquiry. This separation then allowed the committee to postpone and subsequently cancel the inquiry phase altogether, because it believed that much awareness raising (meaning knowledge transfer from science to society, and outreach in the form of reaching as many people as possible) among 'ignorant citizens' still had to be done (Krabbenborg 2013). Focusing on citizens as lay persons implicitly assumes the main priority to be raising awareness about what the new technology entails from a scientific perspective. The problematisation of underlying assumptions, justifications and key political and sociotechnical choices then becomes less of a priority.

Upstream public engagement exercises are often positioned by policy makers and organisers alike as an opportunity for citizens to become a dialogue partner for science and industry and break the traditional monopoly of scientists and industrialists with regard to decision-making on technoscientific issues (Goven 2003). Yet when general publics remain conceptualised as having a knowledge deficit that must be filled with 'factual', scientific information, and when key information (and expertise) about broader socio-political dynamics is lacking, public engagement may remain a symbolic exercise. There is, however, no quick fix for how to move forward with upstream public engagement exercises such as societal dialogues. As this chapter has shown, and as already argued by Rip and Joly (2012), upstream public engagement events should not be seen as an occasion for open-ended fluidity, in the sense that everything is possible. On the contrary, the wider social, cultural and political contexts influence which strategies and interactions are easier to perform than others (Rip and Joly 2012;

Krabbenborg and Mulder 2015). While established rules and practices, such as the entrenchment of the deficit model of communication in research and policy institutes, are not easy to change, they are not static and not all-determining. It is at this point that STS scholars can play an important role (and already do; see, for example, Pallett and Chilvers in this volume). Because of their intermediary position at the science-policy-society interface (see Chilvers 2013), STS scholars can make the dynamics of the wider world visible and turn these into topics for conversation and reflection during, before, and after public engagement events (see also Macnaghthen, Kearnes, and Wynne 2005), just as this anthology aims to do.

ENDNOTES

1 Parts of the case study and analysis presented in this chapter have already appeared in earlier work. For more details, see Krabbenborg and Mulder (2015) and Krabbenborg (2012; 2013).

2 Nanotechnology refers to the observation and manipulation of matter at the nanoscale (1–100 nanometer). One of its revolutionary features is that chemicals at the nanoscale possess unique properties when compared to their macroscale equivalents (Bowman, 2017). Nanosilver particles, for example, have unique optical, electrical and thermal properties, which are now used in all sorts of (consumer) products. As such, nanotechnology is surrounded by a halo of expectations (for example, to improve healthcare). But there are also concerns, including the risks that engineered nanomaterials might pose to human health and the environment.

3 An early societal debate in the 1970s focused on recombinant DNA. Investment in biotechnology in the 1980s was accompanied by public debates (Rip and Talma 1998), which increased during the 1990s when GM food was introduced to the market. People were hesitant to buy GM products, and environmental organisations and consumer groups were concerned about potential harm to human health and consumer freedom and were also worried by the power of the GM industry (especially dominant companies such as Monsanto). As a response to the social contestation, government agencies and industry wanted to involve representatives of civil society. By the early 2000s, government agencies in the Netherlands and the UK had initiated large-scale societal debates. The assumption was that informed dialogue would lead to societal acceptance – this, however, did not happen.

4 In the bi-monthly progress reports, three questions related to project management (planning, cooperation with other projects, finance), three on outreach (direct outreach, in terms of the numbers of people reached in the project activities; indirect outreach,

through an overview of media attention; and an overview of media communication plans and ways to reach out to the general public for the next two months), and one question on 'findings relevant to the Societal Dialogue on Nanotechnology and suggestions for new or further possibilities' had to be addressed. These questions concerned the process. Questions aimed at elucidating content were not part of the progress reports.

REFERENCES

Barben, D., E. Fisher, C. Selin, and D. Guston, 'Anticipatory Governance of Nanotechnology: Foresight, Engagement and Integration', in E. Hackett, O. Amsterdamska, M. Lynch, and J. Wajcman, eds, *The Handbook of Science and Technology Studies*, 3rd edn. (Cambridge, MA: The MIT Press, 2007), pp. 979–1000.

Bauer, D., and H. P. Schmitz, 'Corporations and NGOs: When Accountability Leads to Co-Optation', *Journal of Business Ethics*, 106 (2012), 9–21.

Bickerstaff, K., I. Lorenzoni, M. Jones and N. Pidgeon, 'Locating Scientific Citizenship: The Institutional Contexts and Cultures of Public Engagement', *Science, Technology & Human Values*, 35 (2010), 474–500.

Boenink, M., T. Swierstra, and D. Stemerding, 'Anticipating the Interaction between Technology and Morality: A Scenario Study of Experimenting with Humans in Bionanotechnology', *Studies in Ethics, Law and Technology*, 42 (2010), 1–38.

Chilvers, J. 'Reflexive Engagement? Actors, Learning and Reflexivity in Public Dialogue on Science and Technology', *Science Communication*, 35 (2013), 283–310

CIEMD, *Commissie Maatschappelijke Dialoog Nanotechnologie: Naar een Maatschappelijke Agenda over Nanotechnologie*, (2009).

CIEMD, *Het giga van nano: Rapport 1-meting van de publieke opinie over nanotechnologie*. Leusden: MarketResponse, (2010).

CIEMD, *Commissie Maatschappelijke Dialoog Nanotechnologie: Verantwoord verder met nanotechnologie. Bevindingen maart 2009-januari 2011*, (2011).

Dewey, J., *The Public and its Problems* (Athens, OH: Swallow Press Books, 1927).

Feenberg, A. *Questioning Technology* (London: Routledge, 1999).

Goven, J. 'Deploying the Consensus Conference in New Zealand: Democracy and De-Problematization', *Public Understanding of Science*, 12 (2003), 423–440

Goven, J. 'Processes of Inclusion, Cultures and Calculation, Structures of Power: Scientific Citizenship and the Royal Commission on Genetic Modification', *Science, Technology & Human Values*, 31 (2006), 565–598.

Habermas, J., *The Structural Transformation of the Public Sphere: An Inquiry into a Category of Bourgeois Society* (Cambridge, MA: The MIT Press, 1989).

Hajer, M., and G. Houterman, 'Energy Policy and Democratization', *Intermediar*, 21 (1985), 19–27.

Hanssen, L., *From Transmission towards Transaction, Design Requirements for Successful Public Participation in Communication and Governance of Science and Technology* (PhD Dissertation, University of Twente, the Netherlands, 2009)

Hanssen, L., M. Langeslang, T. Vos, and B. Walhout, *Een Reflectieve Analyse van de Maatschappelijke Dialoog Nanotechnologie* (Den Haag: Rathenau Instituut, 2011).

Horst, M., and S. Davies, 'Reframing Science Communication', in U. Felt, R. Fouche, C. A. Miller, and L. Smith-Doerr, eds, *Handbook of Science and Technology Studies*, 4th edn. (Cambridge, MA: The MIT Press, 2016), pp. 881–908.

Irwin, A., and B. Wynne, *Misunderstanding Science? The Public Reconstruction of Science and Technology* (Cambridge: Cambridge University Press, 1996).

Irwin, A., 'Constructing the Scientific Citizen: Science and Democracy in the Biosciences', *Public Understanding of Science*, 10 (2001), 1–18.

Jasanoff, S., 'Science and Citizenship: A New Synergy', *Science and Public Policy*, 31 (2004), 90–94.

Krabbenborg, L., and H. A. J. Mulder, 'Upstream Public Engagement in Nanotechnology: Constraints and Opportunities', *Science Communication*, 37 (2015), 452–484.

Krabbenborg, L., *Involvement of Civil Society Actors in Nanotechnology: Creating Productive Spaces for Interaction*, (PhD thesis, University of Groningen, 2013).

——, 'The Potential of National Public Engagement Exercises: Evaluating the Case of the Recent Dutch Societal Dialogue on Nanotechnology', *Australian Journal of Emerging Technologies and Society*, 10 (2012), 27–44.

Krabbenborg, L., *Deliberation on the Risks of Nanoscale Materials: Learning from the Partnership between the Environmental NGO EDF and the Company DuPont* (Policy Studies, 2020).

Laurent, B., 'Political Experiments That Matter: Ordering Democracy from Experimental Sites', *Social Studies of Science*, 46 (2016), 773–794.

Lezaun, J., and L. Soneryd, 'Consulting Citizens: Technologies of Elicitation and the Mobility of Publics', *Public Understanding of Science*, 16 (2007), 279–297.

Lindblom, C. E., *Inquiry and Change. The Troubled Attempt to Understand and Shape Society*, (New Haven, CT: Yale University Press, 1990).

Macnaghten, P., M. Kearnes, and B. Wynne, 'Nanotechnology, Governance and Public Deliberation: What Role for the Social Sciences?', *Science Communication*, 27 (2005), 268–291.

Malsch, I., 'Onwards Responsibly with Nanotechnology', ObservatoryNano, 2011.

Ministerial Resolution, 'Instellingsbesluit Commissie maatschappelijke dialoog nanotechnologie', 61, (2009), <http://wetten.overheid.nl/BWBR0025574/geldigheidsdatum_31-12-2010> [accessed 8 April 2020]

Parliamentary Documents, 'Vision Document: Nanotechnologieën: Van Klein naar Groots', 29 338 (54). (The Hague, the Netherlands, 2006).

Parliamentary Documents, *Action Plan for Nanotechnology* (The Hague, the Netherlands, 2008).

Pidgeon, N., and T. Rogers-Hayden, 'Opening up Nanotechnology Dialogue with the Publics: Risk Communication or "Upstream Engagement"?', *Health, Risk & Society*, 9 (2007), 191.

Råheim. M., L. H. Magnussen, et al., 'Researcher–Researched Relationship in Qualitative Research: Shifts in Positions and Researcher Vulnerability', *International Journal of Qualitative Studies on Health and Well-Being*, 11 (2016), 30996.

Rip, A., and P. Benoit-Joly, 'Emerging Spaces and Governance'. Theme Paper for the *EU-SPRI Workshop*, Paris, 2-3 July 2012.

Rip, A., and A. S. Talma, 'Antagonistic Patterns and New Technologies', in C. Disco and B. van der Meulen, eds, *Getting New Technologies Together* (Berlin: Walter de Gruyter, 1998), pp. 299–323.

Rogers-Hayden, T., 'Upstream Engagement', *Encyclopedia of Science and Technology Communication*, 2 (2010), pp. 925–930.

Shapin, S., 'Science and the Public', in R. C. Olby, G. N. Cantor, J. R. R. Christie, and M. J. S. Hodge, eds, *Companion to the History of Modern Science* (London: Routledge, 1990), pp. 990–1007.

Simis, M. J., H. Madden, M. A. Cacciatore, and S. K. Yeo, 'The Lure of Rationality: Why Does the Deficit Model Persist in Science Communication?', *Public Understanding of Science*, 25 (2016), 400–414.

Stirling, A., 'Risk, Precaution and Science: Towards a More Constructive Policy Debate. Talking Point on the Precautionary Principle', *Embo Reports, Science & Society Series on Convergence Research*, 8 (2007), 309–315.

——, '"Opening Up" and "Closing Down": Power, Participation, and Pluralism in the Social Appraisal of Technology', *Science, Technology & Human Values*, 33 (2008), 262–294.

Swierstra, T., and A. Rip, 'Nano-ethics as NEST-ethics: Patterns of Moral Argumentation about New and Emerging Science and Technology', *Nanoethics*, 1 (2007), 3–20.

Wilsdon, J., and R. Willis, *See-through science: Why Public Engagement Needs to Move Upstream* (London: Demos, 2004).

Wynne, B., 'Misunderstood Misunderstanding: Social Identities and Public Uptake of Science', *Public Understanding of Science*, 1 (1992), 281–304.

——, 'Creating Public Alienation: Expert Cultures of Risk and Ethics on GMOs', *Science as Culture*, 10 (2001), 445–481.

8

CONVENE, REPRESENT, DELIBERATE? REASONING THE DEMOCRATIC IN EMBRYONIC STEM CELL RESEARCH OVERSIGHT COMMITTEES

Rachel Douglas-Jones

> In addition to experts in biology and stem cell research, ESCRO committees should include legal and ethical experts as well as representatives of the public (National Academies of Science, 26 April 2005).

> STS research has been more effective in showing how people build scientific instruments, medical standards or large technological systems than legal rules, ethical principles or regimes of administrative rationality (Jasanoff 2012: 7).

THIS CHAPTER IS CONCERNED WITH HOW COMMITTEE MEMBERS, CHARGED with the oversight of a contentious domain of scientific research, reason with ideals of democracy in describing their work. The committee work I analyse is conducted by embryonic stem cell research ethics committees, or ESCROs[1] in the United States of America. I suggest that what makes ESCROs of particular interest within a discussion of STS and democracy is the largely tacit role that democratic ideals have within such spaces of research governance, and the contrasting conceptualisations of the 'appropriateness' of an ESCRO-type committee in stabilising and settling anxieties about controversial research.

STS scholars have long advocated for, and participated in, the participatory turns in the democratic governance of science. As recent critics have pointed out, though, by promoting participation STS scholars have imported democratic ideals into the science-society relationship, putting some of today's scholars, as Chilvers phrases it, in the 'tricky position' of shifting from a role *promoting* the 'democratisation of science' to 'critically and reflexively analys[ing] these very same practices' (Chilvers 2017: 117; see also Pallett and Chilvers, this volume). The move away from implicit theories of democracy towards an approach that considers the democratic as an emergent set of logics and practices refuses preconceived understandings of the democratic and instead examines it through its varied instantiations in bureaucracy, elections and discourse (Paley 2008). Today, researchers can map entire fields of contrasting consultative, participatory and inclusive models (Laurent 2017; Pallett et al. 2019). How decisions are made and authority is deployed across institutions has become a matter of empirical examination. Along the way, critical analyses of participation as performance also bring the recognition that models for participation are freighted with norms about what democracy is, and what it should look like. In the wake of often STS-led 'democratisations' of scientific engagement, scholars have found themselves taking the commercialisation of deliberation as an object of study and analysing consultants of the participation industry (Hendriks and Carson 2008; Bherer and Lee 2019). This reflexive turn has expanded the sites where STS scholars see questions of democracy to be at stake, and encouraged them to ask, for example, whether in particular cases democratic engagement is being done democratically. When scholars suggest 'deliberately cultivating multiple alternative atmospheres of democracy within participatory processes to open up normativities of democracy and make them a focus of experimental comparison' (Chilvers and Kearnes 2019: 12), the assumption remains that this 'cultivation' is *desired* by those responsible for the process. Once participation is viewed as constructed rather than as a normative good in its own right, how it is organised, argued for, and justified become empirical questions.

The work that happens in the settings of this chapter, ESCRO committee meetings, is not democratic in any straightforward sense: it is not cross-societal, it is not especially participatory, nor in pursuit of broad-based consensus. Meetings happen out of sight, and largely without public scrutiny. As the chapter proceeds, I make the case that a series of justificatory ideals about democracy are used – primarily by committee members – within the work of these unusual committees. What *do* institutions 'do in practice when they claim to be reasoning in the public interest' (Jasanoff 2012: 5)? Where does this reasoning take place, and through what measures? Committees have long interested me for their decision-making practices, their evaluative cultures and their negotiations over what will count as valid or authoritative knowledge (Douglas-Jones 2015; Jasanoff 2005: 250; see also Camic et al. 2011). As time-bound, topic-focused entities, they may be closed or open, present themselves as routine or extraordinary and constitute samples of various publics. More often than not, committees are brought into existence to mediate questions of concern, whether new scientific objects or technological devices. Committees exist within regimes of representation: members are often tasked with 'speaking for' others not on the committee or in the room. As such, my curiosity about their work belongs to the turn in STS towards making 'participation and democratic practice [objects] of study and intervention in their own right' (Chilvers and Kearnes 2019: 8).

As the editors of this collection suggest, STS is particularly well equipped to unpack democratic politics in its various guises, both through its close attention to practices and through conceptual developments that identify and specify not only the character of claims to knowledge but also the processes by which decisions are made. This chapter contributes an analysis of a 'mundane' committee, a social technology that I suggest produces knowledge not *on* but *in the name of* democratic participation in science. Just as it is important that STS should explore the democratic through its everyday instantiations and practices, I suggest that we must also become attentive to where ideas of democracy are made to do justificatory work for institutional or bureaucratic processes. To act in the name of someone or something does not always require – or result in – their involvement. In the case of ESCRO committees, operating within a US tradition of public bioethics, most interesting, perhaps, are the ambiguity of practices around democratic ideals as they have become contained within a model of scientific self-governance. What can analyses of invocations of the democratic show us? Let us first consider the cells that they seek to oversee, as I show why the question of democratic involvement in the governance of stem cells requires a history of their introduction into a fraught political environment.

MEETING CELLS, MEETING COMMITTEES

In 1998, researcher James Thomson at the University of Wisconsin in the United States found a way to isolate stem cells in human embryos and grow these cells in the laboratory. Stem cells were first derived from mouse embryos in the early 1980s, and their potential for medical research continues to excite scientists around the world (Taussig et al. 2013). As cells from which other more specialised cells can be derived, they can be used to model potential responses to drugs, or to explore the development of disease. 'Lines' of embryonic stem cells can be cultivated indefinitely, meaning that they are propagated in labs, but US governments through the years have differed as to whether public funds can be used to research these cells, based on moral concern for their origins in embryos (Wertz 2002, Salter and Salter 2007, Interlandi 2010, Robertson 2010). In 2001, the then US President George W. Bush instituted a moratorium on the provision of national funding for stem cell research. Calling research involving stem cells a serious matter of 'dinner table discussions' across the United States, he invoked the image of cells in laboratories, frozen, destroyed or donated. During the moratorium, reversed in 2009 by President Barack Obama, no new 'lines' of cells could be created.

During that decade, the US National Academy of Sciences took on the task of producing guidelines on stem cell research. On 26 April 2005, the National Academies of Sciences, Engineering and Medicine released the outcome of their discussions. In the press release, the co-chair of the committee producing the guidelines, Jonathan D. Moreno, argued that '[h]eightened oversight is essential to assure the public that stem cell research is being carried out in an ethical manner [...] set[ting] a higher standard than required by existing laws or regulations' (Kearney and Petty 2005: np). While he admitted to hesitation over 'another bureaucratic oversight entity', Moreno stated that the burden was 'justified, given the novel and controversial nature of embryonic stem cell research' (Kearney and Petty 2005: np). In their recommendations, the specific form of 'heightened oversight' recommended by the US National Academy of Sciences borrowed from the by-then well settled model of the Institutional Review Board (Friesen et al. 2018). ESCROs, described in some detail in the NAS document, were given procedural tasks such as monitoring the procurement of and provenance of stem cell lines, and reviewing the derivation and banking of hESC lines (with the 'h' standing for Human; see also Hinterberger 2018). They were also given responsibility for 'local initiatives' (Chapman 2015), such as educating stem cell researchers to understand ethical issues and meeting regularly to evaluate research proposals for their scientific and ethical dimensions. In short, ESCROs can be seen as a device which drew on certain familiarities of committee work to settle and stabilise compromise around the turbulent political scene in US American research politics (Robertson 2010, Johnston 2005, Streiffer 2005), where the impacts of scientific mistrust are now widely seen (Dillon et al. 2017). While the politically charged context for their introduction cannot be overlooked, the scope of their remit shifted over time due to changing mechanisms[2] of 'deriving' cells useful to research (see Douglas-Jones 2022).

Researchers across STS and the critical social sciences have taken considerable interest in the way stem cells become the site of intense negotiation across contrasting scientific, legal and social worlds (Bharadwaj 2018; Raval et al. 2008; Hogle 2010, 2018; Franklin 2018, Sleeboom-Faulkner et al. 2018; Sleeboom-Faulkner 2013; Landecker 2007; Svendsen 2011; Thompson 2013). This is not surprising – following the contortions of stem cell policies – 'spectacle(s) ripe for anthropological analysis' (Hogle 2005: 24–25) – scholars have gone as far as to call stem cells 'theory machines' (Bharadwaj 2012: 304; see also Jent 2018). Bioethicists have approached stem cells as a different kind of machine: one of professional advance. In his recent overview of the history of professionalising public bioethics in the United States, Ben Hurlburt explores various bioethics bodies struggling with the problem of how they could 'represent' or 'stand in' for a wider public (2017: 14), turning debates about stem cells into debates over how scientific knowledge should figure in public bioethical deliberation and thus over the right relationship between science's epistemic authority and democracy's modes of collective moral sense-making' (2017: 8). By titling his book *Experiments in Democracy* and drawing our attention to how public reasoning might take place, Hurlburt argues that 'bioethical authorities drew upon the authority of science in constructing accounts of what forms of public reasoning were appropriate' (2017: 14) in their work of 'segregating reasonable disagreement – the lifeblood of democracy – from unacceptable ontological (and thus moral) confusion' (2017: 9). The question facing all involved, he suggests, was normative: how should a 'democratic polity reason together about morally and technically complex problems that touch upon the most fundamental dimensions of human life – through what institutional mechanisms, guided by what forms of authority, in what language, and subject to what political norms and limitations?' (Hurlbut 2017: 2).

How, indeed? Timothy Caulfield, a Canadian health law professor, describes stem cell research overall as a 'natural experiment that spans the globe' (Caulfield et al. 2009). Accordingly, its mode of governance is 'one of the great applied bioethics experiments of our time – the creation, through voluntary, nongovernmental action, of a special ethics review process for *one particular kind of research*' (Greely 2013:52, emphasis added). The committees at the centre of this chapter are 'experimental' because they are not a federally mandated form of review. Their introduction by the NAS meant that they were taken up as an 'entirely voluntary' form of oversight, written into requirements only in the states of California and Connecticut.[3] This voluntary oversight continued quietly for eight years.

In 2013, eight years after National Academy of Science's 2005 guidelines were published, and three years after they were updated, the American Journal of Bioethics dedicated its 100th issue to the topic of stem cell governance. A collection of papers dedicated to ESCROs appeared, provoked by California-based bioethicist Hank Greely's proposal that it was time to 'begin moving toward a world without ESCROs, at least as we have known them' (2013: 52). Calling the work done by ESCROs a 'special ethics review process' Greely's proposal invited responses reflecting on what ESCROs had contributed, and what it would mean to move toward the world Greely envisaged (Devereaux and Kalichman 2013).

I took the 2013 moment of potential dissolution of ESCRO committees as my starting point for the interviews that followed later that year. Using the proposal of an end to their work as a point of departure, I asked committee members what they thought about the work they did. We discussed the kinds of research they review and the processes involved, as well as broad questions (who is the committee for?) and more personal ones (what did they themselves do on the committee?). Some discussions covered the kind of work that committees do in 'sorting new entities (and sometimes old ones) into ethically manageable categories' (Jasanoff 2011: 77): in other words, ascertaining whether or not a researcher's stem cell proposal details the kind of thing that warrants ethical concern. This sorting, which Jasanoff refers to as 'ontological surgery', is part of the boundary- drawing that states institutions and experts do around what will constitute life and non-life, human and nonhuman, person and property (Jasanoff 2012, Pottage and Mundy 2004). A full analysis of ontological surgery in practice would have required observation access to deliberations and minutes, which I did not gain. However, during the course of the three-month study on which the following analysis is based, the eighteen stem cell or ethics committee members[4] across three committees in three different US states spoke with me at length about the purpose and role of the committees. The transcribed dialogues of 22 hours of conversation gave me an overview for coding themes. Institutions conducting stem cell research in the United States vary considerably, and state-specific rules apply. Site 1 is a private, research-intensive university on the east coast, Site 2 a large Midwestern university, and Site 3 a public university in the south-west. Each 'choreographs' its committee work differently, resulting in modes of reasoning that build local versions of systems to oversee research.

If the overall argument of this collection is that democratic practice can, through the techniques of STS, be seen as a series of situated events, then my contribution is the thesis that studying ESCRO work closely allows us to see how ideas and ideals of *the democratic* are brought by committee members into their practice. Each of the following sections works through a different facet of the way committees imagine and enact their role within this non-mandatory oversight regime of stem cell work. I draw out their sense of the necessity or appropriateness of public participation in committee work. As we shall see, many committee members felt their work should be open – in multiple senses of the term – but this was not the practice they lived with.

OPENNESS

Inspired by the detailed observations of decision making emerging from STS collections (Camic et al. 2011), my initial research design rested on observational access to committee meetings. I wanted to see how committees sorted ethically challenging cells from familiar ones, and how different disciplines managed risk and uncertainty in new spheres of stem cell research. Seeking access, as is often the case, became a revelatory probe, allowing me to regard the attempt as part of my study (Stryker and González 2014). Whether a researcher could observe committee practices raised many questions for committees themselves and prompted discussion of a longstanding question around the degree to which their activities should be 'open'. Consequently, openness became my starting point for how the idea of the public figures in the way the committee thinks about itself.

My first meeting with the committee at Site 1 began with Maria, the full-time administrator employed by the ESCRO to process applications, make decisions about what issues demanded full board attention and convene meetings. Physical access to the administrative buildings was guarded by uniformed officers, who checked me against a clip board and tested my ID card at the gate. Satisfied with my pre-arranged appointment, they handed me a visitor tag, let me through the turnstile and allowed me to call a lift that would take me up ten floors. Beyond Maria's name and job title, I knew little about what and who I would be encountering. My searches online had yielded remarkably little: no composition of the committee, no names of current or past members. Once settled in her office, I asked Maria if she could tell me why there had been so little available online to help me prepare. Had I missed something? Maria confirmed that they did not publish members' names:

It was before my time, but I think there were concerns at the beginning about… well. There were death threats or something, so with the concern about protecting members, we decided not to publish their names online (BL 1.4).

Traces of prior controversy around stem cells – what they are and what should or should not be done with them – thus haunt bureaucratic practice. Maria's committee was not unique in its wariness. The committee at Site 2 similarly withheld the names of its members for a long time. While names are now published online, their administrator told me that worries remain. In my meeting with Site 2's committee administrator, she was at pains to show me how she makes public how many *kinds* of stem cell protocols Site 2 receives, and the 'lay descriptions' that are published of the research proposal. Taking our interview as an opportunity to reflect, one member of the committee at Site 2 explained his desire that information about the committee be published 'so people have a realistic sense of what's going on'. Yet this nonspecific 'people' was followed with an anxiety in the same breath: the publishing of even anonymised work might, he fretted, make it possible to figure out which lab or researcher was involved in research that had been through the committee. It felt right to this interviewee to make the protocols under review 'open' in some way, yet the conditions of openness left him uneasy. Moments such as this characterised the unsettled nature of openness across my interviews, with committees ultimately still uncertain of the scrutiny they remained under. When I asked whether there was any 'external' interest in the committee's meetings, a member of Site 2's committee was dismissive:

I don't know if they know that we exist. I mean, I think that the broader community doesn't realise, necessarily, that these different committees are separate. So, I don't know that they know a lot about us (BL 2.4).

The 'they' of this sentence, my interviewee clarified, is both the university's own research community and beyond it. The committee, despite now quietly publishing its membership and bothering to create non-specialist summaries, does not know whether its work is known about by those external others. Site 3 does not have an ESCRO but uses a mix of Institutional Review Boards (IRBs), Institutional Animal Care and Use Committees (IACUC) and Biosafety committees. If stem cell research does happen, what might be considered worthy of review would fall to one of these three established oversight entities. James, a member of the IACUC during our interview, reflected more broadly on this issue of committee openness:

> These committees [referring to IRBs, IACUCs, Biosafety] are set up in such a way that we *say* they're open to the public, we say they're accessible, but try finding it. Try finding minutes from meetings. It's not easy. And uh, I would prefer, all institutions to be more transparent in how they do their work but I also recognise there may be a security risk in doing that (BL: 3.2).

James is pointing to the collective entity of the university – 'we say [the committees are] open to the public, we say they're accessible', and expressing a personal preference for more transparency *in general*. However, he knows it would be very difficult for someone to gain that access. From his position on the Animal Care and Use Committee, he also acknowledges that ideas of 'security' play into how information is made available – or not. Initially concerned in our interview that I might be interviewing him on the basis of animal protection activism, the openness that James would imagine as desirable involves digital searchability, published minutes. Yet as each interviewee indicates a way they would like the committee to be, they admit (and point to) how this is not what is currently practised. From references to a controversial past to worries about 'security', the act of making public who is on a committee or providing access to minutes is not seen as possible.

Committee members carry these concerns about the openness of the committee into how open they feel they can be about their committee work. A legal member of the committee at Site 1, who classified herself as 'non-scientific' (but not 'lay', either, as she saw herself as bringing specific legal expertise to bear), was particularly displeased with internal committee-agreed restrictions on her ability to speak about what the committee talked about beyond the committee itself:

To me, we [committee members] have to be free to talk to students, write papers, talk to the press in extreme cases about the very.... these issues, isn't that why you put some of the non-scientists on this committee? To at least give the appearance that this is a regulatory body that's going to protect the public against scary things happening, and yet you're trying to tell us you want us to be bound by confidentiality so that if scary things *are* happening, we can't talk about it? (BL: 1.5)

This interviewee is pointing to a contradiction. Non-scientists are appointed to the committee to provide a non-scientific view. Yet by having strict limits placed on their capacity to act upon what they see on the committee they are granted access to a predominantly scientific world only to remain within it: they cannot speak outside its walls. James and Maria admitted that the committee was hard to locate physically and digitally, inaccessible in content and illegible in membership. Members revealed the continued enclosure of their debates against a backdrop where their work was deemed too dangerous to be done in public view. On whose behalf, then, are committees operating? While a valued relationship of openness had been built between the committee and the scientific community it served, the committee also constituted the enclosure of debates within a forum composed of people at least some of whom nevertheless carry openness as an ideal.

DOING REPRESENTATION

If it is difficult to access the membership and materials of ESCRO work, this is not to say that publics are not brought in. As Jasanoff notes in the context of committee work, representation is a legitimising function (2011: 74). So, who sits on ESCROs? Some background to the *recommended* composition is useful here. When the National Academy of Sciences drew up its first guidelines in 2005, the expert knowledge deemed relevant included that of developmental biologists and immunologists or reproductive biologists, alongside a layperson, and other 'non-scientific' members such as lawyers. Since ESCROs borrow from the model of the Institutional Review Board, they inherited the expert/

layperson dichotomy common to Euro-American framings of engagement. Participants not identified as a particular form of expert are described as 'at least one member from the community', shifting later in the 2007 clarifications to 'independent representatives of the lay public'.

In this, the authors of the NAS guidelines borrow from a longer tradition of the 'layperson', who takes on the role of standing in for a national public. The layperson is a well-established figure in Euro-American discourses of public engagement with science, borrowing from particular forms of both institutional and scientific authority. Maranta et al. argue that this figure is 'not a sociologi-cally comprehensive representation of lay persons but rather an action in the knowledge production which ascribes epistemic and functional competences to lay persons' (2003: 154). Recognisable renditions of laypersons are distin-guished by their medical ignorance, and in standing in contrast to the medical members of the committee, they assist in creating the latter as experts (Strathern 2004; Michael 1996).

Since the formation of ESCROs is not mandatory, the guidelines merely advisory and the membership not routinely published, it is not easy to find out how committees are composed in practice. In 2007 the philosopher and chair of the University of Connecticut's ESCRO, Anne Hiskes, and a PhD student in the Department of Sociology, Krysten Brown, conducted a national survey for the National Academy of Sciences Eastern Regional Meeting (Brown and Hiskes 2007). Their aim was to obtain a national snapshot of the state of stem cell research oversight, and they approached 118 different institutions across the United States. Amongst a range of questions, they asked about the membership of these committees.

Hiskes and Brown found that only four of the thirty participants answered the question about whether they had 'a layperson': half of those who answered said yes, and half said no (Brown and Hiskes 2007). So, two declared laypersons. Despite their scarcity in survey data, laypersons capture imaginations as a key site of 'representation' for publics. They circumvent the problem of making a committee itself 'representative', which is essentially the impossibility of creating a committee as a miniature of the entirety societal diversity. North American committees, with pragmatist considerations, sense limits to the number of possible perspectives a committee can feasibly contain. Nonetheless, they tie representation deeply to the legitimacy of their declarations, and if the committee itself is not designed to be 'representative', then the weight of this can be carried by the layperson.

In this research I spoke to nearly every member about their role, and the role of others on the committee, but I spoke to only one self-described layperson. This was John, who had served on the committee at Site 1 for six years. John told me that he had initially wondered whether his having qualifications from the university where he was being invited to serve on the ESCRO might impede his membership:

> On the one hand, I have 2 degrees from [Site 1 University], so I am not a 'community resident sitting out in [named suburbs]' that kind of thing, that was OK. It might have been different if I had had scientific credentials, which I don't (BL: 1.1).

John differentiated himself as a specific *kind* of layperson: not a 'community resident' of the town's suburb, but someone already familiar with the university, albeit not one in possession of *scientific* knowledge. As we spoke, he recalled how the invitation had come through a friend, and the introductory proposition put to him: 'if you have reservations about stem cell research', he was told, 'the going-in proposition is, within bounds, it's allowable. So, let's talk about the bounds'. The 'going-in proposition' asked him to accept that stem cell research was happening and should happen as a starting point. John's reservations were welcome *provided* they were channelled into a discussion about 'the bounds' in which research already going forward would take place. That is the conversation he has been a part of ever since.

This framing of the layperson's role as facilitatory resonates with the concluding remarks in the 2005 NAS guidelines, where the authors state the starting 'presumption that the work is important for human welfare, that it will be done, and that it should be conducted in a framework that addresses scientific, ethical, medical and social concerns' (NAS 2005: 28). John was careful to emphasise the limits of his knowledge in addressing *scientific* concerns. Yet, in the spirit of the guidelines, he emphasised that his perspective mattered for the validity of the committee. It mattered that he was there:

> I've always understood the purpose of having those diverse perspectives as, I guess, in the end, bringing some balance. To judgements about the propriety of research (BL: 1.1).

John's concern with propriety is fascinating in this setting. The sense of suitability or appropriateness carried with the term invokes the social acceptability he is there to embody. While committee members generally agreed it was 'good' to have a committee member who was not involved in 'the science', nobody except the layperson himself actually challenged the adequacy of representation through having a single layperson on the committee. Initially siding with the benefits of pluralistic 'interdisciplinarity' and commending the thoughtfulness of his colleagues, John said

> The things that aren't good, probably, if you were to think about really good oversight, there's little … no opportunity for community input, even within the community, let alone …. we aren't doing sessions at churches and clubs to say, 'hey what do you guys think about this research'? Which I suppose in an ideal process would be a part of it (BL: 1.1).

This quote makes evident that there are ways of engaging publics that committee members are aware of but which are not pursued under the remit of ESCRO work. John knows who that 'public' is out there 'in churches and clubs'. As he summons the imagined public, he also summons a process through which ESCROs would be ideally engaged. As literature from STS demonstrates, traditions of participatory decision-making emphasise the kind of thing John is describing: roundtables, open fora and consensus events 'intended to involve the lay public in decisions' (Weingart 2008: 141; see also Maranta et al. 2003; Joss and Durant 1995; Flear 2009). This is also where John's imagination goes. Yet, this may not be where the committee wants John to take his role. Reflecting on her own involvement in the ESCRO committee at Berkley, STS scholar and anthropologist Charis Thompson succinctly states that: 'putting [NAS] regulations into action, then, is first and foremost about enabling research in an environment of ethical controversy, and not about ethical inquiry' (2013: 64). Similarly, in her research into human-animal hybrids and the status of chimeric lifeforms, Amy Hinterberger, one of a few STS scholars to examine the mechanisms by which scientists engage with how their research is governed, has argued that 'ESCRO committee deliberations are oriented toward providing a space for research to happen, not about questioning the basis of legal and ethical categories' (Hinterberger 2016: 15). John's imagined events in 'churches and clubs' would worry some committee members, who see their primary purpose as ensuring that the university avoids newspaper headlines. In the words of one committee member, 'There is also a lot of emphasis on "it's our job to protect the scientists and to keep things from going public"'. In what follows, I set the protective role the committee plays against an imagined public.

IMAGINING OTHERS: ON SERIOUSNESS AND WATCHERS

Having looked at questions of representation through presence, let me now turn to the way publics are brought in through the imaginations of committee members. This requires moving from who is physically present in the room to who is brought into the room when committee members think of themselves as representing others 'out there'. The first step in having discussions about ethical questions around stem cells on behalf of others is to consider what those non-specific others might perceive to be ethical issues. The second step is for the committee to evaluate whether those perceived issues warrant their attention. Throughout my interview notes, committee members imagine viewers into the room. I found these imagined concerns particularly interesting, given the lack of openness about discussion and decision. Viewers are external observers, watching the committee's work. As such, committee members repeatedly returned to what – in the view of these external viewers – would constitute the committee's 'trustworthy behaviour'.

Susan, a committee member at Site 2 introduced me to the idea of 'trustworthy behaviour' during our interview on how to handle consent and re-consent issues around donated embryos. Susan's committee was facing a series of questions about the question of what should happen to embryos donated for research. If, for whatever reason, these embryos were not going to be used, could they be destroyed without permission from the donors? If they were going to be used for something other than the originally described research, what was the responsibility of the researcher towards the donors? Susan said she had asked herself what would look like trustworthy behaviour from the point of view of the donors? Bringing this concern into the discussion, Susan said the committee asked itself:

> Have we, or anybody else at the institution where they originally agreed to donate for research, have we made some kind of promise that would be violated if we did X or Y? (BL: 2.4)

In this framing, the trustworthiness of the committee is baked into checking what promises had been made – by them *or* by others at the institution. Some researchers would want to do right by 'their own sense of personal integrity', or their relationship to the donors, Susan said. But the sense of 'if this were to be seen by others' went beyond specific donors, being tied materially to donated embryos and their fates. A fellow committee member of Susan's at Site 2 brought up the way that this larger sense of imagined others was present to him in his role:

> The question that sits in my mind, and literally the question has come up: if somebody was a voter in upstate [State] and they were *watching* this delibera-tion, would this look like a serious deliberation that is addressing the things that are of concern to them, that they would think we should address? (BL: 2.3, emphasis added)

Would this look like a serious deliberation? Does it address the things that are of concern to them? While John's proposal to take the question to the residents of his town was out of the question, committee members nonetheless spent time pondering how their processes would look from the outside. The phrasing shows the influence of both 'directions': the imagined, generic 'voter' coming into the committee room, and the committee member projecting herself into that upstate voter's shoes to look back at the committee's discussion in order to evaluate its 'seriousness'. Generating seriousness is no minor matter, and its importance to committee members should not be underestimated, as this interviewee reflected:

> I feel that there's a strong desire to have good oversight systems in place and to have a sense of accountability to the public, so the public knows that you have strong oversight systems in place, so that you could credibly say – this is a process that we went through, these are the things we took into consideration, so even if someone disagreed with you, they could at least feel that people were taking very seriously these concerns (BL: 1.2).

This worry, repeated across committees, about generating a *sense* that people were taking the concerns seriously, bears on Marres' argument that STS approaches allow us to see the 'mobilization of socio-ontological associations that mediate actors' involvement in the issues at stake' (2007: 776). In contrast to focusing solely on what is said in these interviews, we bear in mind how the committee, composed of people sitting in a room together, shapes what counts as an issue, and is itself a reflection of an established, 'appropriate' form of managing a controversial topic. By the time we arrive at this final quote, the particular views or perspectives of those *on whose behalf* the discussions were taking place have faded, and what virtue there is in the discussion, in the appearance of seriousness and trustworthiness, has become a *process*. Here, in one of the few interviews to speak directly about public accountability, the credibility of the committee's work rests on the committee itself becoming a machine of seriousness. Long into a discussion about the 2005 formation of committees, conducted with an interviewee who had been involved in the National Academies of Sciences consultation process, he reflected on why the committees had been introduced at all:

> ... what the ESCROs were trying to do, was to give the public some confidence that scientists are not off on their own doing all sorts of ethically challenging work, without some kind of oversight. So, the idea is to *comfort*

the public that there is some restraint and consideration of ethical issues (BL1.5, emphasis added).

CONCLUSION

Neither the institutions of scientific work nor democratic processes are stable over time. ESCROs were introduced during a turbulent moment in stem cell research, and these interviews with ESCRO members were undertaken in the shadow of their proposed dissolution. Committee members' reflections offer us insight into how voluntary mechanisms of oversight persist in the aftermath of political heat. Stem cell research itself continues, with new developments in the creation of synthetic embryos prompting reflections from ESCRO committees and ethicists alike (Troug and Lopez 2018; Aach et al. 2017). Neither the National Academies of Science nor the International Society for Stem Cell Research address synthetic embryos, and researchers are advised to ensure that their work is 'overseen and authorized by a special committee capable of evaluating the ethical and scientific justification of proposed research' until new guidelines are produced in 2021 (ISSCR 2020).

For a collection on STS and democracy, the committees' longevity demonstrates their quiet utility, revelatory of logics by which 'adequate governance' is constructed in the US context. Adequacy is participatory, yet in conditions of controversy, it is participation at a remove. A committee where no ideal of participation was invoked would not be adequate to the task, yet John's 'churches and clubs' would be insufficiently removed for the committees to 'work'. Interviewees reveal the negotiated detail of democratic themes in contentious, potential-filled research spaces. From the 'upstate voter' to the open list of names, democratic ideals of transparency and accountability fill my notes on the way that ESCRO committee members conceptualise their roles and responsibilities. The ideals largely remain ideals. Arguably, the existence of ESCROs, rather than their actions, provides a placeholder for broader, more difficult societal disagreements.

Turning the analytic eye of STS towards democracy as practice, enacted and constructed in specific moments and encounters, means meeting the gaze of researchers in other disciplines: empirical political scientists (Weeden 2010), ethnographers of democracy (Paley 2002; Ellison 2018), bioethicists and historians, all of whom grapple with describing, analysing and perhaps re-prescribing how normative decisions are made. The contribution that STS scholars can make to these debates occurs not only through their ethnographic sensitivities to how artefacts, materials and technologies play a role in constructing the conditions of possibility for engagement and debate, but also through their critical engagement with the entanglement of expertise and authority within the knowledge traditions of science. STS orientations to democratic situations allow us to recognise that the *doing* of authoritative knowledge may entail the deployment or manipulation of tropes that have long since seeped into institutions and bureaucratic structures. For the members of ESCROs in this chapter, a lens attentive to the form of authoritative knowledge makes evident that despite explicit discussion of democratic ideals and principles of participation, committee practices remain at a remove from participatory engagement. If we are indeed to open up normativities of democracy (Bellamy, Lezaun and Palmer 2017) then we must also become attuned to the cultivation of 'democratic atmospheres' that remain atmospheric rather than substantive, where stories that include 'representatives of the public' result in public reasoning taking place behind closed doors (Jasanoff 2011: 84). Operating in a comparative mode, STS scholars can explore the social and material life of ideals such as 'democracy', to reveal the complex negotiations, compromises and contradictions that make up their institutional life.

ENDNOTES

1 As research using *embryonic* stem cells become one of several options for working with stem cells, some committees dropped the 'E' and became known as SCROs instead. For further discussion of this change, see Hinterberger (2018).

2 In 2006, four genes were introduced to adult stem cells, reprogramming them to work like embryonic stem cells (Takahashi and Yamanaka 2006). These became known as 'induced pluripotent stem cells' or iPSCs for short, and they are reported to vary in terms of what they can become. See Meskus 2018.

3 Yet as King and Perrin (2014:3) note '[m]any research institutions have created ESCROs or 'SCROs' to review hESC and iPSC research; others rely on their institutional review boards or their animal care and use committees or both'.

4 As with many expert groups, committee members are very busy people, serving on the committee in addition to their existing academic work, teaching and service. Opportunities to speak about their committee work seemed few, and several welcomed the chance to reflect on what they do, and what the role of the committee is.

ACKNOWLEDGMENTS

This work was supported by the *Biology and the Law* research grant, funded by the Faraday Institute and hosted at the Kennedy School of Government, Harvard University (PI, Sheila Jasanoff). I thank project PI Sheila Jasanoff, co-investigators Ben Hurlburt and Kris Saha, and project collaborator Amy Hinterberger for their support during the design and analysis of this fieldwork. This work received feedback at Uppsala University as part of the 'Medicine at the Borders of Life' project, and my thanks go to Helena Tinnerholm Ljungberg, Francis Lee and Morag Ramsey, as well as to the workshop participants. Irina Papazu and Andreas Birkbak have lent their editorial skills throughout. Thanks are also due to Laurie Waller and the anonymous reviewers whose perceptive suggestions led to the clarification and improvement of the chapter.

REFERENCES

Aach, J., J. Lunshof, E. Iyer, and G. M. Church, 'Addressing the Ethical Issues Raised by Synthetic Human Entities with Embryo Like Features', *eLife* 6 (2017): e20674.

Bellamy, R., J. Lezaun, and J. Palmer, 'Public Perceptions of Geoengineering Research Governance: An Experimental Deliberative Approach', *Global Environmental Change*, 45 (2017): 194–202.

Bharadwaj, A., 'Anthropology, Substance and Science of Stem Cells', *Annual Review of Anthropology*, 41 (2012), 303–17.

Bherer, L., and C. W. Lee, 'Consultants: The Emerging Participation Industry' in S. Elstub and O. Escobar, eds, *Handbook of Democratic Innovation and Governance* (Cheltenham: Edward Elgar Publishing, 2019), pp. 196–208.

Brown, A., and K. Hiskes, 'A National Survey of Embryonic Stem Cell Research Oversight (ESCRO) Committees', Paper Presented at Stem Conn07, Hartford Connecticut, 2007.

Camic, C., et al., eds, *Social Knowledge in the Making* (Chicago, IL: University of Chicago Press, 2011).

Caulfield, T., A. Zarzeczny, and J. McCormick, et al., 'International Stem Cell Environments: A World of Difference', *Nature Reports Stem Cells*, 16 April 2009.

Chapman, A. R., 'Induced Pluripotent Cells: Ethical Answer or a Source of Continuing Ethical Dilemmas?', in J-T Schantz and D. W. Hutmacher, eds, *Advanced Therapies in Regenerative Medicine* (Singapore: World Scientific Publishing, 2015).

Chilvers, J., 'Expertise, Professionalization, and Reflexivity in Mediating Public Participation: Perspectives from STS and British Science and Democracy', in L. Bherer, M. Gauthier, and L. Simard, eds, *The Professionalization of Public Participation* (Oxford: Routledge, 2017), pp. 115–138.

Chilvers, J., and M. Kearnes, 'Remaking Participation in Science and Democracy', *Science, Technology & Human Values*, 45 (2019), 347–380.

Devereaux, M., and M. Kalichman, 'ESCRO Committees – Not Dead Yet', *American Journal of Bioethics*, 13 (2013), 59–60.

Dillon, L., D. Walker, N. Shapiro, et al., 'Environmental Data Justice and the Trump Administration: Reflections from the Environmental Data and Governance Initiative', *Environmental Justice*, 10 (2017), 182–192.

Douglas-Jones, R., 'A "Good" Ethical Review: Audit and Professionalism in Research Ethics', *Social Anthropology*, 23 (2015), 53–67.

——, 'Committee Work: Stem Cell Governance in the United States', in M. Højer Bruun, A. Wahlberg, K. Hoeyer, R. Douglas-Jones, C. Hasse, D. Brogaard Kristensen, and B. Ross Winthereik, eds, *The Handbook of the Anthropology of Technology* (New York: Palgrave Macmillan, forthcoming).

Ellison, S., *Domesticating Democracy? The Politics of Conflict Resolution in Bolivia* (Durham, NC: Duke University Press, 2018).

Flear, M. L., 'The EU's Biopolitical Governance of Advanced Therapy Medicinal Products', *Maastricht Journal*, 16 (2009), 113–137.

Franklin, S., 'Somewhere Over the Rainbow, Cells Do Fly', in A. Bharadwaj, ed., *Global Perspectives on Stem Cell Technologies* (New York: Palgrave Macmillan, 2018), pp. 27–49.

Friesen, P., B. Redman and A. Caplan, 'Of Straws, Camels, Research Regulation and IRBs' *Therapeutic Innovation and Regulatory Science*, 53 (2018), 546–534.

Gottweis, H., B. Salter and C. Waldby, eds, *The Global Politics of Human Embryonic Stem Cell Science: Regenerative Medicine in Transition* (New York: Palgrave MacMillan, 2009).

Greely, H., 'Assessing ESCROs: Yesterday and Tomorrow', *The American Journal of Bioethics*, 13 (2013), 44–52.

Hendriks, C., and L. Carson, 'Can the Market Help the Forum? Negotiating the Commercialization of Deliberative Democracy', *Policy Sciences,* 41 (2008), 293–313.

Hinterberger, A., 'Regulating Estrangement: Human-Animal Chimeras in Postgenomic Biology', *Science, Technology & Human Values,* 45 (2016), 1065–1068.

——, 'Marked H for Human: Chimeric Life and the Politics of the Human', *BioSocieties* 13 (2018), 453–469.

Hogle, L., 'Stem Cell Policy as Spectacle Ripe for Anthropological Analysis', *Anthropology News,* October 2005, 24–25.

——, 'Characterizing Human Embryonic Stem Cells: Biological and Social Markers of Identity', *Medical Anthropology Quarterly,* 24.1 (2010): 433–450.

——, 'Intersections of Technological and Regulatory Zones in Regenerative Medicine', in A. Bharadwaj, ed., *Global Perspectives on Stem Cell Technologies* (New York: Palgrave Macmillan, 2018), pp.51–84.

Hurlbut, B., *Experiments in Democracy: The Human Embryo Research and the Politics of Bioethics* (New York: Columbia University Press, 2010).

Hurlbut, J., and J. Robert, 'Good Governance Connects Science and Society', *Journal of Policy Analysis and Management,* 31 (2012), 722–726.

Interlandi, J., 'Getting It Right on Stem Cells', *Scientific American,* 1 November 2010. https://www.scientificamerican.com/article/getting-it-right-on-stem-cells/ [Accessed 18 August 2021].

Interstate Alliance on Stem Cell Research., '2011 Survey of ESCRO Committees', https://nas-sites.org/iascr/files/2013/08/ESCRO2011.pdf [Accessed 25 June 2021].

International Society for Stem Cell Research., 'ISSCR Statement on Ethical Standards for Stem Cell-based Embryo Models', 16 January 2020, https://www.isscr.org/news-publicationsss/isscr-news-articles/article-listing/2020/01/16/isscr-statement-on-ethical-standards-for-stem-cell-based-embryo-models [Accessed 25 June 2021].

Irwin, A., 'The Politics of Talk: Coming to Terms with the "New" Scientific Governance', *Social Studies of Science,* 36 (2006), 299–320.

Jasanoff, S., *Designs on Nature: Science and Democracy in Europe and the United States,* (Princeton, NJ: Princeton University Press, 2005).

——, 'Making the Facts of Life', in S. Jasanoff, ed., *Reframing Rights: Bioconstitutionalism in the Genetic Age* (Cambridge, MA: The MIT Press, 2011), pp. 59–84.

——, *Biology and the Law* Research Application: The Faraday Institute for Science and Religion, Uses and Abuses of Biology Program. St Edmund's College, Cambridge.

——, *Science and Public Reason* (London: Routledge, 2012).

Jasanoff, S., B. Hurlbut, and K. Saha, 'CRISPR Democracy: Gene Editing and the Need for Inclusive Deliberation', *Issues in Science and Technology,* 32 (2015), 25–32.

Jent, K., 'Stem Cell Niches', *Fieldsights*, 25 April 2019. https://culanth.org/fieldsights/stem-cell-niches [Accessed 25 June 2021]

Johnston, J., 'Stem Cell Protocols: The NAS Guidelines Are a Useful Start', *Hastings Centre Report*, 35 (2005), 16–17.

Joss, S., and J. Durant, eds, *Public Participation in Science: The Role of Consensus Conferences in Europe* (London: Science Museum, 1995).

Kearney, B., and M. Petty, 'Guidelines Released for Embryonic Stem Cell Research' National Academies of Science. http://www8.nationalacademies.org/onpinews/newsitem.aspx?RecordID=11278, [accessed 25 June 2021].

King, N. M., and J. Perrin, 'Ethical Issues in Stem Cell Research and Therapy', *Stem Cell Research & Therapy*, 5 (2014), 85.

Landecker, H., *Culturing Life: How Cells became Technologies* (Cambridge, MA.: Harvard University Press, 2007).

Laurent, B., *Democratic Experiments: Problematizing Nanotechnology and Democracy in Europe and the United States* (Cambridge, MA: The MIT Press, 2017).

Lezaun, J., N. Marres, and M. Tironi, 'Experiments in Participation', in U. Felt, R., Fouché, C. Miller, and L. Smith-Doerr, eds, *The Handbook of Science and Technology Studies: Fourth Edition* (Cambridge MA: The MIT Press, 2017), pp. 195–221.

Maranta, A., M. Guggenheim, P. Gisler, and C. Pohl, 'The Reality of Experts and the Imagined Lay Person', *Acta Sociologica*, 46 (2003), 150–165.

Marres, N., 'The Issues Deserve More Credit: Pragmatist Contributions to the Study of Public Involvement in Controversy. *Social Studies of Science*, 37 (2007), 759–780.

Meskus, M., *Craft in Biomedical Research: The iPS Cell Technology and the Future of Stem Cell Science*, (New York: Palgrave Macmillan, 2018).

Michael, M., 'Ignoring Science: Discourses of Ignorance in the Public Understanding of Science', in A. Irwin and B. Wynne, eds, *Misunderstanding Science* (Cambridge: Cambridge University Press, 1996), pp. 107–125.

National Academies of Sciences, 'Guidelines for Human Embryonic Stem Cell Research', (Washington DC: National Academies Press 2005), https://www.nap.edu/catalog/11278/guidelines-for-human-embryonic-stem-cell-research [Accessed 25 June 2021].

——, 'Press Release: Guidelines Released for Embryonic Stem Cell Research. Office of News and Public Information https://www8. Nationalacademies.org/onpinews/newsitem.aspx?RecordID=11278 [Accessed 25 June 2021].

——, '2007 Amendments to the National Academies' Guidelines for Human Embryonic Stem Cell Research' (Washington DC: National Academies Press, 2007) https://www.nap.edu/catalog/11871/2007-amendments-to-the-national-academies-guidelines-for-human-embryonic-stem-cell-research [Accessed 25 June 2021].

Paley, J., 'Toward an Anthropology of Democracy', *Annual Review of Anthropology*, 31 (2002), 469–496.

——, ed., *Democracy: Anthropological Approaches* (Santa Fe, NM: School for Advanced Research Press, 2008).

Pallett, H., J. Chilvers, and T. Hargreaves, 'Mapping Participation: A Systematic Analysis of Diverse Public Participation in the UK Energy System', *Environment and Planning E: Nature and Space*, 2 (2019), 590–616.

Pottage, A., and M. Mundy, *Law, Anthropology and the Constitution of the Social: Making Persons and Things* (Cambridge, UK: Cambridge University Press, 2004).

Raval, A., T. Kamp, and L. Hogle, 'Cellular Therapies for Heart Disease: Unveiling the Ethical and Public Policy Challenges', *Journal of Molecular Cellular Cardiology*, 45 (2008), 593–601.

Robertson, J. A., 'Embryo Stem Cell Research: Ten Years of Controversy', *The Journal of Law, Medicine and Ethics*, 38 (2010),191–203.

Salter, B., and C. Salter, 'Bioethics and the Global Moral Economy: The Cultural Politics of Human Embryonic Stem Cell Science, *Science, Technology & Human Values*, 32 (2007), 554–581.

Sleeboom-Faulkner, M., 'Regulating 'Respect' for the Embryo: Social Mindscapes and Human Embryonic Stem Cell Research in Japan', *Science, Technology and Society*, 18 (2013), 361–377.

Sleeboom-Faulkner, M., H. Chen, and A. Rosemann, 'Regulatory Capacity Building and the Governance of Clinical Stem Cell Research in China', *Science and Public Policy*, 45 (2018), 416–427.

Stark, L., 'Meetings by the Minute(s): How Documents Create Decisions for Institutional Review Boards', in C. Camic, N. Gross and M. Lamont, eds, *Social Knowledge in the Making* (Chicago, IL: Chicago University Press, 2011), pp. 233–256.

——, *Behind Closed Doors: IRBs and the Making of Ethical Research* (Chicago, IL: Chicago University Press, 2012).

Strathern, M., *Commons and Borderlands* (Oxford: Sean Kingston Publishing, 2004).

Streiffer, R., 'At the Edge of Humanity: Human Stem Cells, Chimeras and Moral Status', *Kennedy Institute of Ethics Journal*, 15 (2005), 347–370.

Stryker, R., and R. González, eds, *Up, Down, and Sideways: Anthropologists Trace the Pathways of Power* (Oxford: Berghahn Press, 2014).

Svendsen, M. N., 'Articulating Potentiality: Notes on the Delineation of the Blank Figure in Human Embryonic Stem Cell Research', *Cultural Anthropology*, 26 (2011), 414–437.

Takahashi, K., and S. Yamanaka, 'Induction of Pluripotent Stem Cells from Mouse Embryonic and Adult Fibroblast Cultures by Defined Factors', *Cell* 126 (2006), 663–676.

Taussig, K. S., K. Hoeyer, and S. Helmreich, 'The Anthropology of Potentiality in Biomedicine', *Current Anthropology*, 54 (2013), S3–S14.

Thompson, C., *Good Science: The Ethical Choreography of Stem Cell Research* (Cambridge, MA: The MIT Press, 2013).

Troug, R., and M. J. Lopez, 'Report: Ethical Issues Related to the Creation of Synthetic Human Embryos, 2018', The Petrie-Flom Centre for Law Policy, Biotechnology and Bioethics at Harvard Law School, https://petrieflom.law.harvard.edu/ resources/article/ethical-issues-related-to-the-creation-of-synthetic-human-embryo [Accessed 25 June 2021].

Weeden, L., 'Reflections on Ethnographic Work in Political Science', *Annual Review of Political Science*, 13 (2010), 255–272.

Weingart, P., 'How Robust is "Socially Robust Knowledge"?', in M. Carrier, D. Howard and J. Kournay, eds, *The Challenge of the Social and the Pressure of Practice: Science and Values Revisited* (Pittsburgh: University of Pittsburgh Press, 2008), pp. 131–145.

Wertz, D. C., 'Embryo and Stem Cell Research in the USA: A Political History', *Trends in Molecular Medicine* 8 (2002), 143–146.

9

THE DARK SIDE OF CARE? WAYWARD PARTICIPANTS IN SAMSØ'S RENEWABLE ENERGY TRANSITION

Irina Papazu

INTRODUCTION

I ONLY EVER SAW HIM IN OVERALLS AND CLOGS, BUT THE SAMSØ FARMER named Henrik[1] is a rich man. As the Danish island of Samsø's renewable energy transition took shape between 1997 and 2007, Henrik invested in one 1-megawatt land-based wind turbine out of a total of eleven such turbines established on Samsø. He also owns half of a 2.3-megawatt offshore turbine. In fact, Henrik was a key player in the establishment of Samsø's offshore wind farm of ten turbines, which is a central brick in Samsø's path toward becoming 'CO$_2$-negative' by 2007. He was the chairman of the project, and together with a few other locals whose experience with large wind energy projects was also limited, he raised and managed the many millions the wind turbines cost and, as the chairman, bore the responsibility in case the project failed. He lived with the risks of the project. 'I had red wine running in my veins in those years', he told me. 'I suffered from stress, couldn't remember names or anything, it was terrible' (interview, November 2013).

For over ten years now, Samsø has been 'Denmark's Renewable Energy Island' (REI), and the on- and offshore wind turbines are still spinning and making money; some for farmers like Henrik, others for Samsø Municipality, which bought five offshore turbines, thus running the risk of bankrupting the island due to the uncertainty of the investment (interview with the mayor at the time, Nov 2013). Still others are owned by cooperatives of islanders who invested from as little as one thousand Danish kroner up to hundreds of thousands to become co-owners of a wind turbine and a formal part of the island's transition. I studied this transition ethnographically from 2013 to 2015. For six months, I was located at the Samsø Energy Academy, a local organisation pursuing renewable energy projects on Samsø and beyond. In the remainder of the period, I visited Samsø regularly to participate in and observe different events organised by the Energy Academy (see Watts 2019 for another ethnographic retelling of an island-based RE project).

Despite his central role in Samsø's biggest project to date, Henrik, the wind farmer, is not used to being the protagonist of stories about Samsø's RE transition. The 'hero' (Time Magazine 2008) of Samsø's transition is, to most people as well as to the press, Søren Hermansen, the master communicator of the REI project and current CEO of Samsø Energy Academy. The main narrative of Samsø's transition is one of 'energy democracy' (see Chilvers and Pallett 2018; Mitchell 2011; Watts, Winthereik and Maguire 2021 for other academic engagements with this concept). According to this narrative, when the islanders realised they stood on the 'burning platform' (fieldnotes, Hermansen, Nov 2013) of a deteriorating, increasingly marginalised rural community, they embarked on a collaborative effort to save their community through the daunting project of making Samsø self-sufficient with renewable energy over the course of ten years. The official narrative prioritises community organising and emphasises public acceptance of RE technologies over the technical-material efforts related to the project. As the daily manager of the aforementioned Energy Academy explained to me:

> Our visitors don't come to see the world's newest, fanciest plant. Our offshore wind farm may have been among the largest in the world when we built it, but today it's probably the smallest. That's not how we sell tickets. Instead, it's about 'how on earth we got people to accept it'? It's about the social processes, not the technologies (fieldnotes, September 2013).

This quote is telling of two important tendencies I want to highlight with regard to how Samsø's RE transition is represented to the island's spectators and visitors eager to learn from and copy the islanders' experiences. First, the technical (including legal and financial) dimensions and challenges of the project have been downplayed at the expense of 'the social processes', which according to the Academy manager constitute a better, more interesting story about the transition. It is not for nothing that the public 'hero' of the story is the *communicator*, Hermansen. In reality, Hermansen led the REI project together with the engineer Aage Johnsen, whose name few people remember today.

The story, as it is usually told, stresses the importance of good communication for the successful realisation of the RE transition. You often see locals opposing new RE installations (the so-called 'not in my backyard', or NIMBY, reaction), but, according to the narrative, on Samsø, everyone chipped in and participated in the comprehensive RE transition (see Papazu 2016a). This supports a distinctly Danish ideal of democracy, which centres around consensus (Horst and Irwin 2010). In contrast, the major local investors, the farmers and the local landlord, have not been granted central roles in the stories about the transition. Apparently, they do not have much to offer the Energy Academy's narrative about energy democracy – a story that, despite the fact that only three out of 21 wind turbines are collaboratively owned, centres on communally owned energy infrastructures (Papazu 2017b).

This last point brings us to the second tendency worth highlighting in relation to the above quote, namely that Samsø's transition story has been made a story about 'participatory democracy'. As Hermansen told me, the most important lesson he learned when faced with the challenge of fundamentally transforming the island's energy systems had nothing to do with technicalities or technologies. It was, rather, that 'we had to establish a quorum of citizens willing to take responsibility for their community; we had to learn how to cooperate. "What we can agree on" became our mantra' (Hermansen, interview, Nov 2013).

This preference for the social and participatory dimensions of the project is not exclusive to the Energy Academy actors. Some of my own renderings of the REI project display the same tendency to focus on the 'social' aspects of the project: communication, collaboration and participation (Papazu 2016a,

2017a). This tendency, I believe, has its origins in the field of STS. First, I was 'following the actors' (Latour 2005a) and letting them make their own theories about their actions and activities. As part of tracing these associations in the field, I reconstructed and extended the stories I encountered, rather than challenging them. Secondly, while in STS there is a strong scholarly concern with participation as an uncertain, empirically traceable and materially composed practice (Barry 2013; Marres 2012; Papazu 2016b), the notion of participation is often deployed normatively. As articulated by Moore, a 'participatory paradigm' has been prevalent in STS as 'the principal heuristic guiding analyses' (Moore 2010: 798; see also Soneryd and Sundqvist, this volume). I will therefore take my cue from Irwin, Elgaard and Jones, who contend that 'the (often implicit) evocation of the highest principles that engagement might ideally fulfil can make it difficult to acknowledge and pay serious attention to the varieties of engagement that are very much less than perfect but still somehow "good"' (2012: 120).

In the remainder of this chapter, I will turn my attention to Henrik, the farmer whose part in the story at first sight fits rather poorly with the participatory paradigm of the Samsø narrative, as well as that of some STS approaches. As a big private investor and a wilful capitalist made rich by the REI project, he may seem to represent the problem rather than the solution. It is easy to present Henrik in a critical light, and he is often portrayed as a dominating, disruptive figure by other actors in my fieldwork. In my interview with him, he even seems to intentionally present himself in a negative light, as I will detail in the following. Indeed, I had first written off my interview with him as failed or, at least, unsuccessful. It was not until I came upon the STS concept of care that Henrik became visible to me. Applying the lens of care made me aware of Henrik's central position in the REI project, as this lens allows the actors' affects and passions, together with their socio-material investments, to guide the researcher's attention (Puig de la Bellacasa 2011). By encouraging an 'ethos of care' (Puig de la Bellacasa, 2011: 85) – even if such an ethos cannot be uncritically extended but must be considered as at least potentially exclusionary in itself (see Murphy 2015) – I will attempt to reinsert the farmer into Samsø's transition story – a place that I believe he earned through his undervalued care practices. This also involves attempting to add some nuance to the Samsø narrative, and thus tell a more down-to-earth story about this democratic situation, through a shift in focus away from the 'social processes' towards the more technical aspects that become visible when questions of financing, risk, legality and responsibility enter the stage to complicate, but not replace (see Winthereik and Verran 2012), hitherto prioritised stories about participatory processes and practices.

INTERVIEW WITH A FARMER

It is difficult to care about Henrik. Not only is he a proud, successful capitalist, a big investor who insists on 'the business case' of his involvement in the REI project; that there was not an ounce of green idealism in his RE investments and that he, in fact, does not really care about climate change: 'A poor bugger doesn't invest 20 million DKR for the sake of idealism' (interview, Nov 2013)! Some of the stories he tells me on this chilly November afternoon, as the sun sets over his newly built house overlooking his fields with the land-based wind turbines, ooze bitterness and cynicism, despite being recounted with a touch of humour. In one of the anecdotes that has stayed with me, during the building of his house, a builder working for him pointed at one of his turbines that had for some reason stopped spinning and gleefully exclaimed: 'Ha, Henrik, you're not making any money today'! To this Henrik replied, dryly: 'I had to turn it off because my bank account is full'. Recounting this incident to me, Henrik still seems angry: this man had been employed by Henrik; who was he to take pleasure in the fact that there was a problem with one of Henrik's turbines? With a bitter smirk, he adds, 'I usually say that I only get to keep 46% of the value produced by the turbines, the rest is taxes. Taxes also benefit my neighbours, so actually everyone should be happy when my windmills are spinning'.

Henrik's tendency to boast about his wealth and complain about other people's envy has been the cause of some bad media experiences. He complains to me about how, while he has been interviewed by international TV stations '34 times', the Danish media interest has been limited. One of the rare headlines in a Danish newspaper read: 'I'm laughing all the way to the bank'. After that, he and his wife, who also attended the interview, agreed that he would stop making that kind of statement – humorous, but bitter – to the press. On the afternoon of my visit, his wife, who he had met seven years earlier on the dating site *Farmer Dating*, worked hard to moderate his crude presence and statements and create a pleasant atmosphere, serving biscuits and tea in the spacious open-plan kitchen with wall-to-ceiling windows, and rolling her eyes or interjecting small objections to signal to me when Henrik's responses became too obstinate, that – as she later explained – 'I had caught him on the wrong day'.

When I asked Henrik who the central actors in the REI project had been, he responded 'no one', followed by a long silence during which his wife sent him several annoyed glances, trying to alert me to the fact that he is not always *that* uncooperative. I tried to probe him further about the trajectory of the REI project as he remembered it but did not get much out of him. 'Hermansen', the communicator and main coordinator of the project, 'did nothing. I also don't recall *any* public meetings. But Aage Johnsen', the engineer of the REI project, '*he* worked hard'. Henrik also names other farmers who took upon themselves the responsibility to coordinate projects. These men, he admits, were central to the REI project.

In the thirty-something formal interviews I conducted on Samsø, I heard Hermansen's name mentioned and emphasised over and over again when I asked my interviewees to sketch the REI project network as they saw it. But Henrik challenges this network, just as he denies the significance of the participatory processes – the 'energy democracy' that the popular Samsø story is based on. My first reaction to Henrik's remarks and his wayward attitude was to disregard him. A moody farmer, yet powerful and well-known on Samsø, his stubborn conduct and rejection of the version of the Samsø story that nearly everyone else was conveying to me made him seem irrelevant, a distraction or outlier. On closer examination, however, the interview data did convey something more; something that perhaps should not be ignored. Three things in particular puzzled me, as they did not fit with the image Henrik was trying to convey of himself as a contrarian loner.

First, Henrik claimed not to be planning any new green investments ('I don't wanna be part of something that probably won't pay off'), but after the interview, when I was alone with his wife, she corrected his answer, adding that he was in fact planning to buy an electric car. This was not a very profitable investment in Denmark in 2013, but Samsø was at the time very focused on extending the use of electric vehicles, and Henrik apparently wanted to support that agenda. 'But he says that I'm the one who should drive it, because it looks so politically correct'. Henrik, it seems, works hard to portray himself as an outsider when in practice he might be more of an active fellow player.[2]

Second, Henrik's reluctance to provide elaborate answers to my questions, and his demeanour bordering on unfriendliness, were counterbalanced by his eagerness to help me when it turned out, just as I was leaving, that my bike lock was stuck. You might imagine my dismay, caught in the early evening between an unfriendly farmer and the dark November road. It would have taken me at least 45 minutes to walk home along unlit roads, leaving my bike chained to a place I was not planning to return to. But Henrik immediately offered to drive back to his farm on the other side of the island to get the angle grinder he needed to open my lock. Meanwhile I was asked to keep his wife company grocery shopping. This was not the Henrik he had worked hard to convey to me during the interview. Something changed in our relation when I concluded the interview, put away my recorder and became just a regular visitor chatting with him and his friendly wife.

Third, there were a few emotional outbursts during the interview, especially when I asked about the offshore windfarm for which he, as the chairman of the project, had had the main responsibility.

> Whether the offshore windfarm was risky? Hell yes! We simply couldn't cope with it, so we had a lawyer draw up a document with all the risks associated with the project. It was two pages long; no one had the guts to read it, we all just signed. That lifted some of the responsibility from my shoulders. Sometimes, when it all became too much and I thought I couldn't handle it anymore, I had a beer with Ole, Arne and Erik [fellow businessmen and farmers]. Then things would fall back into place.

In these three instances, Henrik discloses that he cares. About the environment and the community in the first instance, about me in the second, and about the offshore wind project in the third instance.

WHAT SORT OF CARE?

The concept of care in STS is associated with Annemarie Mol and her colleagues' studies of medical practices (Mol 2008; Mol, Moser and Pols 2010). In Mol's 'logic of care', care describes a practice of 'persistent tinkering in a world full of complex ambivalence and shifting tensions' (Mol, Moser and Pols 2010: 14). Mol and others' concept of care aims to be 'attentive to tinkering practices and technologies' (Martin et al. 2015, 626); a deliberately flexible concept fit for studying empirical cases not strictly limited to those of the nursing home or hospital (see, for example, Birkbak 2016). This concept of care does, however, lean toward the empirical fields in which the concept was developed, and in which care figures (or should figure) as a key part of care practices, that is, in 'clinics, homes and farms' (Mol, Moser and Pols 2010). While this work aims to 'revis[e] and revalue mundane practices of tinkering and experimentation as characteristic of *good care*' (Gill, Singleton and Waterton 2017: 8; emphasis added), later developments in feminist technoscience studies have attempted to foreground the political dimensions of care, 'privileging themes of power in specific on-the-ground sites of care' (Martin 2015: 626) – an approach that can be termed *critical care* (Gill, Singleton and Waterton 2017, 9). Critical questions formulated on this basis do not just ask 'how and for whom to care?', as Mol and others might, but also, more critically, '"Who cares?" "What for?" "Why do 'we' care?"' (Puig de la Bellacasa 2011: 96). These studies of care, moreover, tend to veer further from the classic arenas of care to explore, for instance, empirical sites of late industrialism (Puig de la Bellacasa 2015), modern warfare (Suchman 2015) and new technologies of sustainability (Arora et al. 2020).

Puig de la Bellacasa contrasts Latour's concept 'matters of concern' – by which Latour turned what used to be 'matters of fact' into open, empirical questions about the intricate agencies and entanglements of humans and non-humans (2004, 2005a) – with the notion of 'matters of care' (2011). Puig de la Bellacasa argues that concern 'call[s] upon our ability to *respect* each other's issues'. Matters of concern 'translates the political life of things into a language compatible with contemporary majoritarian democracies dealing with "issues" of "public concern"' (2011: 88). She hereby implies that, compared to care, the notion of concern contains an element of distance: 'Understood as affective states, concern and care are [...] related. Care, however, has stronger affective and ethical connotations. We can think of the difference between affirming: "I am concerned" and "I care". The first denotes worry and thoughtfulness about an issue [...]; the second adds a strong sense of attachment and commitment to something' (2011: 89–90). Puig de la Bellacasa's concept helps foreground the concerns of the less articulate actors in my field, thereby enhancing my own capacity for intervention, understood as the difference I can make *in* and *on* the world with my storytelling (Law and Singleton 2013; see also Winthereik and Verran 2012). The concept of matters of care prompted me to reconsider my data – to reanalyse interviews I had first written off as failed or, at least, unsuccessful.

For Puig de la Bellacasa, to care signifies 'an affective state, a material vital doing, and an ethico-political obligation' (2011: 89_90). To apply care as an analytical lens is to become aware that for Hermansen, the REI project communicator, the project was a matter of concern. He was concerned with 'selling' the project to the islanders (interview, Nov 2013). The project was his job; one that he was and still is deeply engaged in. It is also to become aware of the farmer, Henrik's, attachments, his worries and care: remember how he described his 'terrible' feelings of stress and the sense of having red wine running in his veins. What he describes can be interpreted as 'an affective state, a material vital doing, and an ethico-political obligation'; he is invested in the project with his whole being. To apply the lens of care rather than that of concern is to become aware of Henrik's central position in the REI project, as this lens allows the actors' affects and passions, together with their socio-material investments, to guide the researcher's attention (Puig de la Bellacasa 2011). This lens, in turn, brings out a competing version of the REI project network to the one that places participatory methods and communication at the heart of the project – a version that renders the local workers and investors visible by finally bringing them into focus. The analytical task here becomes to assemble 'oft-neglected voices, objects, and interests, while staying accountable to the politics, power, and privilege involved in such work' (Martin et al. 2015: 630).

In this view, the recalcitrant farmer, Henrik, displays an 'ethico-political obligation' (Puig de la Bellacasa 2011: 90) that tied him to the project despite the risks and that he attempted to cope with both through legal means and, simply, by drinking and sharing the burden with friends. 'An affective state' and 'a material vital doing', Henrik's care for the project became a practice sustained over several years, involving a range of different activities: meetings (friendly as well as formal), planning, drinking. Viewed as such, the sociotechnical challenge of establishing Samsø's offshore windfarm becomes a 'matter of care' (93) rather than a dry planning exercise, and Henrik's position in the project, hitherto overlooked, comes into view in a new way through the lens of care.

Hermansen arranged public meetings, he discussed the RE projects with the islanders and managed to create an atmosphere of support rather than opposition, but he was not the one to bear the responsibility and concrete risks involved in the different RE projects. From Henrik's point of view, because of this, Hermansen did not *do* anything; he just talked. If we instead try to see the REI project from Henrik's perspective, we can 'approach the ethicality involved in sociotechnical assemblages in an ordinary and pragmatic way' (Puig de la Bellacasa 2011: 100). A surprising alignment with domestic work, 'the devalued ordinary labors that are crucial for getting us through the day' (ibid: 93), arises, reminding us of the feminist origins of the concept of care. Henrik's personal implication in the project alerts us to 'the hidden labours' of the local RE transition – the hard work and personal engagement of the people implementing the RE projects in practice. This work has been largely overlooked, as the success of the REI project was translated into an accomplishment of masterful communication, of well-timed and -executed public meetings, of gathering people around 'the burning platform' and managing the different politics, interests and goals of the relevant local actors, including Henrik (Hermansen, fieldnotes Nov 2013). If Hermansen's relation to the project was one of *concern*, managing 'the troubled and unsettled ways… by which a gathering… is constructed and holds together' (Puig de la Bellacasa 2011: 88), Henrik's was one of care, which, with its 'stronger affective and ethical connotations', 'adds a strong sense of attachment and commitment' (ibid: 89–90) to the project.

But it is difficult to care about Henrik, and he is painfully aware of this. He knows that the role he plays in the popularised Samsø story is disproportionate to the attachments and commitment he feels toward the project, the investments he has made and the risks he has accepted. He is not just a farmer who struck gold and got rich, as the Danish press tends to portray him. But by feeding the unflattering image ('I'm laughing all the way to the bank') and giving people – the press, researchers, local islanders – good reason to discount his efforts, he displays the 'darker side' of his care (Martin et al. 2015; Gill, Singleton and Waterton 2017: 10).

GENERATING CARE

> The point is not only to expose or reveal invisible labours of care, but also to generate care… [G]enerating care means counting in participants and issues who have not managed or are not likely to succeed in articulating their concerns, or whose modes of articulation indicate a politics that is 'imperceptible' within prevalent ways of understanding (Puig de la Bellacasa 2011: 94–95).

Henrik is not the prototypical marginalised voice, and he is certainly not over-looked, in the straightforward sense of the term, by other actors in my data. He is treated as someone with power, whose presence at meetings has to be skilfully handled – something an inexperienced municipal planner did not manage to do in the situation described in this quote by Hermansen: 'A guy like Henrik must be kept on a tight leash, otherwise he'll act like a loose bull without direction. I can control him, but the planner definitely can't! Henrik can destroy a meeting in seven seconds'! (Hermansen, fieldnotes Oct 2013). Despite (or rather because of) his central position and reputation as one of the 'tough boys' or 'chiefs' on the island (fieldnotes Oct 2013), Henrik is generally not referred to in a respectful tone. He is described as 'an opportunist who only talks about money' (fieldnotes May 2014) and as someone 'whose mind is only open to his own world' (fieldnotes Oct 2013). A local environmentalist and retired politician told me about her resistance to a new wind project off the preserved northern coast of the island, the Mejlflak project, which Henrik was involved in: 'I'm PRO renewable energy for nature's sake, and AGAINST the Mejlflak turbines for the same reason – for nature's sake. They can't be allowed to come here from the outside, just because Henrik wants to make more money. That's his only aspiration, and he makes no secret of it' (interview, Nov 2013).

Henrik is not an easily likeable person, and due to his position as a man of money and power on the island, his fellow islanders feel free to discuss him in critical phrases. But, as I have attempted to demonstrate above, Henrik does care. However, he experiences that his engagement, his personal investments and the risks he has taken – for the island, the REI project and also, certainly, for himself – are being discounted. His care has taken on a wounded, self-willed expression, which Henrik shows by discounting the efforts of the collective (if they do not acknowledge his efforts, why should he acknowledge theirs?) and instead boasting about his bank account. As Puig de la Bellacasa formulates it in the above quote, he has not managed to articulate his concerns; his 'modes of articulation indicate a politics that is "imperceptible" within prevalent ways of understanding' (2011: 94–95). Having exposed the ways in which Henrik cares, my desired intervention is to go one step further and attempt to 'generate care' for Henrik.

Generating care takes us down the path of what Martin et al. have termed 'care's darker side: its lack of innocence and the violence committed in its name' (2015: 627). As Martin et al. continue, 'care is a selective mode of attention: it circumscribes and cherishes some things, lives, or phenomena as its objects. In the process, it excludes others. Practices of care are always shot through with asymmetrical power relations: who has the power to care? Who has the power to define what counts as care and how it should be administered'? (2015: 627). On Samsø, as indicated in the critical remarks about Henrik, care can take certain shapes and not others. Caring for nature is, for instance, a legitimate type of care in this local context. The Energy Academy actors' care tends to be directed, further, towards the local community and the participatory practices of 'energy democracy' related to and developed through the REI project: co-ownership, citizen meetings, etc. But in practice, these forms of caring have become, as formulated by Martin et al., selective and exclusionary modes of attention.

They leave no room for an actor like Henrik who, as he himself puts it, 'doesn't want to be part of something that might not pay off' – someone who is open about his motivations for joining the REI project being financial rather than environmental or social. The locally dominant modes of caring end up condoning the exclusion of certain actors whose cares are not recognised ('I'm so sick of him', an Energy Academy project manager casually states (fieldnotes, May 2014)). And they make his contributions and labour invisible, which leads to the construction of a dominant narrative about the REI project which neglects more complicated, legal-technical – and personal – forms of accomplishment and attachment.

WHICH, AND WHOSE, VERSION OF 'ENERGY DEMOCRACY'?

In what remains of this chapter, I want to dwell on the problems related to this exclusion and the invisibility of Henrik's hard work and contributions to the REI project. I understand these as problems of democratic politics. In the introduction of his book about climate change politics, Anthony Giddens states that '[t]he book is a prolonged enquiry into a single question: why does anyone, anyone at all, for even a single day longer, continue to drive an SUV? For their drivers have to be aware that they are contributing to a crisis of epic proportions concerning the world's climate' (Giddens 2009: 1). According to Puig de la Bellacasa, Latour also addresses the SUV driver, but caringly rather than critically, as he states that we need to 'love our monsters', the technologies of our own making – even those as *Frankensteinian* as the SUV (and their drivers) (for a discussion of Latour's argument, see Puig de la Bellacasa 2011: 90).

While by no means oblivious to the climate crisis, Latour argues that blind criticism and exclusion of the SUV driver renders the rest of us irresponsible. What we ought to do is engage in a dialogue by which we take on the ethical obligation of caring for the becoming of this hybrid – the driver and his SUV (which also means that Giddens is mistaken when he focuses all his attention on the driver, ignoring the politics of the socio-material world guiding and framing his choices). Where Giddens demonises and writes off SUV drivers (in Giddens' depiction, specific individuals who are 'aware' of the climate crisis and thus act contrary to their knowledge, in bad faith), Latour seeks to include them. If we do not manage to include those with whom we disagree, we run the risk of relegating our own concerns to the margins, 'a bunch of activists' agreeing only among ourselves, unable to formulate our cares as the 'major problem[s] of contemporary participatory democracies' (Puig de la Bellacasa 2011: 91). This type of political problem formulation requires a collective broad enough to encompass the voices we do not agree with. As Puig de la Bellacasa puts it, 'to effectively care for a thing we cannot cut off those with whom we disagree from the thing's political ecology. [...] Here, care is mobilised to serve a gathering purpose: to hold together the thing. This has political consequences' (2011: 90). By choosing an attitude of care as an alternative form of criticism, you avoid creating 'fundamentalist oppositions'; oppositions that would exclude actors with certain cares from having 'a say in an assembly of representative democracy' (2011: 91).

In the Samsø story, Henrik plays the role of the SUV driver. This particular hybrid – the farmer and his lucrative wind turbine – has been generated by the people responsible for the Renewable Energy Island project. Keeping the RE technologies in local hands by encouraging local investors to purchase them and making a strong case for 'what's in it for you' to sell them the idea, has led to the creation of the type of wind farmer (I am reluctant to write 'the type of monster'), which the same REI storytellers are now trying to dissociate themselves from. It is through the promotion of care for Henrik and his attachments, whether we like them or not, that we may manage 'to replace excessive critique and the suspicion of socio-political interests with a balanced articulation of the involved concerns' (Puig de la Bellacasa 2011: 91). As long as Henrik's cares and attachments are discounted and ridiculed, his major personal investments and achievements in the REI project will go unacknowledged. The emphasis on the participatory and democratic dimensions of the REI project, the weighting of participatory ideals and co-ownership of individual investments, seems, paradoxically, to have made the project *less* participatory, in the sense of less inclusive.

CONCLUSION

In this chapter, I have tried to turn Samsø's renewable energy transition into a matter of care (Puig de la Bellacasa 2011: 93). Applying the lens of care has turned the Samsø project into more of a *sociotechnical* issue than is perhaps commonly recognised. Recall the Energy Academy manager's comment that 'it's about the social processes, not the technologies' (fieldnotes, September 2013). I argue that this is only half the picture. Examining Henrik's role can inform a shift in focus from communication and participation to hitherto devalued labours of care relating to issues of legality, financing, and the heavy burden of personal responsibility of lay islanders suddenly deeply involved in the REI project. Whether this involvement is fuelled by environmental convictions, concerns for the local community's viability or a desire to boost one's bank account does not change the experience or the vulnerable position of that person finding himself suddenly responsible for central elements of the island's transition process.

Samsø is known for its 'energy democracy' (see, e.g., Kando, 2014), but this version of democracy suffers – like to some extent the field of STS, as argued earlier – from a participatory bias leading to a blindness to modes of engagement that are more problematic, less innocent, that make for less compelling narratives, but which are, nonetheless, 'still somehow "good"' (Irwin et al. 2012: 120). Taking on Puig de la Bellacasa's reconceptualisation of care means installing an analytical hesitation as to which activities should be considered relevant or valuable. As we have seen, the slightly altered view that this analytical lens produces may challenge some of the STS researcher's implicit theories and go against the grain of some 'truths' of the field, such as the valuation of certain types of participation over others. As such, the figure of the wayward farmer may teach us not just to 'slow down' (Stengers 2005) but also to critically interrogate our own reasoning and to be open to where the analysis may take us, even if the new terrain might seem at first unfamiliar and uncomfortable to navigate.

Does Henrik's kind belong to the past? Not necessarily. Would Samsø's RE transition – or any community-based energy transition in the future, for that matter – have been possible without financially strong, bullish actors willing to risk it all and sacrifice their sleep for several years straight? Probably not. Would they be willing to do it were it not for a solid 'what's in it for me' argument built into the process? Not likely. There is a need for more realistic transition narratives and for promoting a fuller, more inclusive, but also more problematic story and trajectory for the future.

ENDNOTES

1 While anonymisation is nearly impossible when writing about a case well-known to the public with a limited number of central actors, I have changed the protagonist's name in this chapter.
2 The wayward demeanour of Michel Callon and Vololona Rabeharisoa's interviewee, Gino, comes to mind here as a parallel in the STS literature (2010).

REFERENCES

Arora, S., B. van Dyck, D. Sharma, and A. Stirling, 'Control, Care, and Conviviality in the Politics of Technology for Sustainability', *Sustainability: Science, Practice and Policy*, 16 (2020), 247–262.

Barry, A., *Material Politics: Disputes along the pipeline*, (West Sussex: Wiley-Blackwell, 2013).

Birkbak, A., 'Caring for Publics' (PhD thesis, Aalborg University, 2016).

Callon, M., and V. Rabeharisoa, 'Gino's Lesson on Humanity: Genetics, Mutual Entanglements and the Sociologist's role', *Economy and Society*, 33 (2004), 1–27.

Chilvers, J., and H. Pallett, H., 'Energy Democracies and Publics in the Making: A Relational Agenda for Research and Practice', *Frontiers in Communication* 3 (2018), 1–16.

Giddens, A., *The Politics of Climate Change* (Malden, MA: Polity Press, 2009).

Horst, M., and A. Irwin, 'Nations at Ease with Radical Knowledge. On Consensus, Consensusing and False Consensusness', *Social Studies of Science*, 40 (2010), 105-126.

Irwin, A., T. Elgaard Jensen, and K. E. Jones, 'The good, the bad and the perfect: Criticizing engagement practice', *Social Studies of Science*, 43 (2012), 118–135.

Kando, A., 'The Energy-Democracy Connection', *The New Maine Times*, 18 March 2014. http://www.newmainetimes.org/articles/2014/03/18/energy-democracy-connection/ [accessed February 2019].

Latour, B., *Reassembling the Social. An introduction to Actor-Network Theory* (Oxford: Oxford University Press, 2005)

——, 'Why Has Critique Run out of Steam? From Matters of Fact to Matters of Concern', *Critical Inquiry*, 30 (2004), 225–248.

Law, J., and V. Singleton, 'ANT and Politics: Working in and on the World', *Qualitative Sociology*, 36 (2013), 485–502.

Marres, N., *Material Participation: Technology, the Environment and Everyday Publics* (Basingstoke: Palgrave Macmillan, 2012).

Marres, N., and J. Lezaun, 'Materials and Devices of the Public: An Introduction', *Economy and Society*, 40 (2011), 489–509.

Martin, A., N. Myers, and A. Viseu, 'The Politics of Care in Technoscience', *Social Studies of Science*, 45 (2015), 625–641.

Mitchell, T., *Carbon Democracy. Political Power in the Age of Oil* (London, New York: Verso, 2011).

Mol, A., I. Moser, and J. Pols, 'Care: Putting Practice into Theory', in A. Mol, I. Moser, and J. Pols, eds, *Care in Practice: On Tinkering, Homes and Farms* (Bielefeld: Transcript Verlag, 2010), pp. 7–26.

Mol, A., *The Logic of Care: Health and the Problem of Patient Choice* (New York: Routledge, 2008).

Moore, A., 'Review: Beyond Participation: Opening up Political Theory in STS', *Social Studies of Science*, 40 (2010), 793–799.

Murphy, M., (2015) 'Unsettling Care: Troubling Transnational Itineraries of Care in Feminist Health Practices', *Social Studies of Science*, 45 (2015), 717–737.

Papazu, I., 'Authoring Participation', *Nordic Journal of Science and Technology* 4 (2016a), 17–31.

——, 'Management through Hope: An Ethnography of Denmark's Renewable Energy Island', *Journal of Organizational Ethnography*, 5 (2016b), 184–200.

——, 'Nearshore Wind Resistance on Denmark's Renewable Energy Island: Not Another NIMBY Story', *Science and Technology Studies*, 30 (2017a), 4–24.

——, 'Storifying Samsø's Renewable Energy Transition', *Science as Culture*, 26 (2017b), 198–220.

Puig de la Bellacasa, M., 'Matters of Care in Technoscience: Assembling Neglected Things', *Social Studies of Science*, 41 (2011), 85–106.

——, 'Making Time for Soil: Technoscientific Futurity and the Pace of Care', *Social Studies of Science*, 45 (2015), 691–716.

Stengers, I., 'The Cosmopolitical Proposal', in B. Latour, and P. Weibel, eds, *Making*

Things Public: Atmospheres of Democracy (Cambridge, MA: The MIT Press, 2005), pp. 994–1003.

——, 'Comparison as a Matter of Concern', *Common Knowledge*, 17 (2011), 48–63.

Suchman, L., 'Situational Awareness: Deadly Bioconvergence at the Boundaries of Bodies and Machines', *MediaTropes*, 5 (2015), 1–24.

Walsh, B., 'Heroes of the Environment 2008. Soren Hermansen', *Time Magazine*, 24 September 2008. http://content.time.com/time/specials/packages/article/0,28804,1841778_1841782_1841789,00.html [accessed February 2019].

Watts, L., *Energy at the End of the World: An Orkney Islands Saga* (Cambridge, MA: The MIT Press, 2019).

Watts, L., B. R. Winthereik, and J. Maguire, eds, *Energy Worlds in Experiment* (Manchester: Mattering Press, 2021).

Winthereik, B., and H. Verran, 'Ethnographic Stories as Generalizations that Intervene', *Science Studies*, 25 (2012), 37–51.

PART III

RECONFIGURING DEMOCRATIC POLITICS WITH NEW NONHUMAN ACTORS

10

ENLISTING THE BODY POLITIC: GOVERNMENTALISED TECHNOLOGIES OF PARTICIPATION IN DIGITAL DIPLOMACY

Alexei Tsinovoi

INTRODUCTION

THE EMERGENCE OF SOCIAL MEDIA PLATFORMS WAS DRIVEN BY THE PARTICI-patory ideals of the Web 2.0 business model,[1] and aimed to solicit and facilitate the production and dissemination of user-generated content (O'Reilly 2009). In political theory, as well as in STS, public participation has traditionally been conceived as the essence of democratic situations (see Habermas 1987; Mouffe 2009; Irwin 1995; Jasanoff 2003), and many academics and practitioners initially associated social media with its apparently inherent democratic potentialities (see Kelty 2019). It was argued that these technologies afford new forms of public participation that allow previously marginalised voices to be heard, thus pluralising and reinvigorating democratic politics (see, for example, Shirky 2008, 2011; Bakardjieva 2009; Dahlberg 2011; Papacharissi 2015). In the realm of international politics, influential practitioners and academics began to argue that foreign policy can no longer remain the domain of a few elites, because these participatory technologies enable lay citizens to take a bigger part in matters of foreign affairs by speaking directly with their peers abroad, articulating issues of common concern and building reconciliatory bridges across entrenched political divides (Sifry 2009; Viner 2009; Seib 2012; see also Bjola 2015). As this chapter will illustrate, however, the ideals that associate digitally mediated participatory practices with inherent democratic potentialities often fall short in practice, which emphasises the need to problematise and explore 'in action' (Latour 1987) the political role of social media technologies in the enactment of digitally mediated public participation.

Combining elements of digital ethnography involving immersion in digital environments and 'walkthroughs' of digital interfaces (see Light et al. 2018), expert interviews with public relations and public diplomacy practitioners, government reports and media sources, I discuss three examples of Israeli digital diplomacy[2] initiatives where governmental agencies attempt to spark, mobilise and then steer civic participation in issues of foreign affairs using new media technologies. I invoke Latour's (1987) concept of 'action at a distance', and its adoption by Foucault-inspired enquiries into modes of governmentality, as a way to highlight the 'governability' of public participation in the so-called digital age. Contributing to the ongoing conversation in STS about 'issue-oriented' politics (Marres 2007) and the 'participatory turn' (Irwin 1995; Jasanoff 2003; Wynne 2006), the chapter highlights how the material specificities of new media technologies not only play a central role in the public articulation of issues online (Marres 2017; Rogers 2013), but are also pivotal to the multiplication of new governable surfaces through which public participation can be acted on and steered from remote 'centres of calculation' (Latour 1987: 215).

Specifically, I illustrate how the different components of social media, such as profiles, social buttons, threads and data streams afford the flattening and fragmentation of participation into a multitude of micro-performances that can be enlisted into broader networks of governance and steered, even automated, with unprecedented precision and continuity. As such, as social media become governmentalised – that is, enlisted into broader networks through which the authorities steer the movements of the body politic – the new affordances of digitally-mediated participation may not only be insufficient for democratic situations to emerge, but can even play a role in prohibiting them. The analysis in the chapter thus moves away from conceptualising participation as an *a priori* democratic ideal towards discussing it as a contingent empirical phenomenon which should be scrutinised by studying the multiplicity of everyday practices in which it is performed, in the context of specific political situations (Barry 2012).

REMEDIATING ISRAEL'S ESTRANGEMENT: A TALE ABOUT IMAGINAL POLITICS

Articulating international misrecognition as an unresolved public issue

Israel's former foreign minister and, later, President Shimon Peres 'held the opinion that if a country has good policies, it does not need PR, and if the policy is bad, the best PR in the world will not help' (Gilboa 2006: 735), reflecting the prevailing approach of Israeli policy makers over the years to the issue of international image and reputation. However, in the last two decades, as various indicators[3] began to point out that 'Israel's reputation abroad has dramatically deteriorated' (Gilboa 2006: 715) following the halt of the peace process and a series of controversial policies towards Palestinians, the issue of the country's international image and reputation emerged as a prime matter of political and public concern. According to the predominant narrative, articulated in Israel at the time by central political actors, official reports, strategy think tanks, communications experts and others, this shift in global public opinion has less to do with Israel's ongoing policies than with the way in which the state is represented abroad.[4] Central to this narrative was the idea that 'there is a very big gap, created over the years, between the image of Israel and who we really are' (Livni cited in Walla News 2007). For example,[5] practitioners and communications experts frequently claimed that the foreign press covering the Israeli-Palestinian conflict 'exaggerate, lie, and reproduce stereotypes' (interview, Jerusalem, 3 January 2016), thereby creating 'distorted, inaccurate, misleading and biased' representations (Gilboa 2006: 726) that have 'consequences for the millions of people trying to comprehend current events, including policy-makers' (Friedman 2014). Moreover, the activities of non-state actors, such as the BDS movement,[6] which utilise social media platforms as new public spheres for resistance politics contesting the Israeli self-image (Aouragh 2008, 2011; Siapera 2014; Hitchcock 2016) were increasingly presented as a potential 'strategic threat' (The Reut Institute 2010: 77) and countered by new legislation (Olesker 2013) and new digital governmental initiatives (Blau 2017).

While such claims of misrecognition were frequently contested both in Israel and abroad – illustrating the fragility and political character of this discursive formation,[7] – concern over the purported misrepresentation of events and identity narratives was becoming a central issue in Israel's foreign policy, and expert reports and academic publications started to associate the deterioration of Israel's international reputation with the lack of managerial attention to public diplomacy,[8] commonly referred to in Israel as *Hasbara* (loosely translated from Hebrew as 'the activity of explanation'). Specifically, it was argued that *Hasbara* efforts, intended to 'present and clarify' Israel's position both abroad and at home (State Comptroller 2002: 9), are intertwined with innovations in new media technologies because today 'war takes place simultaneously on two fronts – the battlefield and "on screen" [...] over the shaping of images and favorable public opinion' (State Comptroller 2007: 457; Gilboa 2006; Naveh 2007; The Reut Institute 2010; see also Greenfield 2012). Communications experts suggested that *Hasbara* activities needed to take advantage of the networked structure of new media technologies, invest more funds in training professionals, and involve civil society organisations in trying to better 'utilise the Internet to counter attacks by its [Israel's] enemies and to promote a favourable e-image' (Gilboa 2006: 740). Specifically, it was argued that 'it takes a network to fight a network' (The Reut Institute 2010: 68), and public participation was considered essential in its development.

Enlisting the body politic

For this purpose, the Israeli government decided on a series of reforms in order to create a more 'credible, uniform and consistent Hasbara policy' (Prime Minister's Office 2007). Cooperation with civil society organisations was to be deepened in order to 'leverage their activities as an auxiliary tool in the state of Israel's Hasbara efforts', and special attention was to be allocated to new media, in order to 'significantly expand' the voluntary *Hasbara* activities performed on the Internet by the Israeli population (Prime Minister's Office 2007). In such efforts, the primary strategic imperative seems to have been to increase the credibility and reach of government messages. As explained by the former minister of Public Diplomacy and Diaspora Affairs (MPDDA), Yuli Edelstein, 'in our world those with a suit and a tie and an official title are usually less credible as an information source' (The Committee for Immigration, Absorption and Diaspora Affairs 2012). Instead, 'the truth catches on better if it is not spread by someone with a tie and a title of a minister and or ambassador [...] but a student, someone that you can have a beer with, a Facebook friend' (Edelstein 2012). In this logic, '[t]he governments that can harness the communication potential of their citizens will be the ones to conduct effective public diplomacy offensives' (Attias 2012: 474). The ability to influence foreign publics – captured both by benign terms like public diplomacy and soft power, as well as by more pejorative terms like propaganda – has always been central to diplomacy, and credibility is considered central in that regard (Nye 2008).[9] From the perspective of the authorities, public participation has less to do with democratic plurality in this political situation and more with strategic utility as a resource that can be mobilised.

Illustrating this approach, as elaborated elsewhere (Adler-Nissen and Tsinovoi 2019), in 2010 the MPDDA launched a nation-wide campaign involving video clips that encourage Israeli citizens travelling abroad to try and correct misconceptions about the state. For example, in one of the promotional videos a reporter misrepresents the state by depicting the camel as 'the typical Israeli animal', and then a voiceover declares: 'Are you tired of seeing how we are represented in the world? You can change the image. Visit the website and receive information about the correct [way to do] *Hasbara*' (Masbirim's channel, 2010). According to focus groups, such videos were seen as an 'effective call to action', and between 2010 and 2012 over three million people visited the campaign website (Attias, 2012: 477). The website displayed information that aimed to correct alleged misconceptions about the state and carried detailed suggestions on how to do so. For example, a section of the website called 'Myth vs. Reality' blended the rebuttal of trivial Orientalist 'myths'[10] – such as 'Israel is a desert and they all ride camels', instead emphasising Israeli democracy and scientific and technological progress – with trivialising controversial and complex issues by claiming, for example, that it is a 'myth' that '[t]here's no peace because of the settlements' (Ministry of Public Diplomacy & Diaspora Affairs 2010a). Another section entitled 'Tips for the Novice Public Diplomat' provides detailed instructions as to how these narratives should be mediated by the participating citizens, including advice such as: 'first listen, then talk', 'body language is just as important as verbal content', and 'Tell [your] own personal story' (Ministry of Public Diplomacy & Diaspora Affairs 2010b).

While the campaign was widely criticised both in Israel and abroad,[11] practitioners considered it exceptionally successful (interview, Jerusalem, 3 January 2016), and the political technique it employed, which attempts to spark and then steer public participation toward predefined governmental goals, became central to Israel's *Hasbara* efforts. However, while the campaign enlisted the bodies and personal stories of Israeli citizens travelling abroad into carrying state-endorsed narratives, it was argued that 'in the future the project will seek to involve Israelis […] connected to foreigners through social media networks' (Attias 2012: 482). According to a former official, social media technologies were indeed becoming pivotal to Israel's new approach to *Hasbara*. In an interview, the former official argues that it was not until 'the advent of the technologies [that] citizens today could reach out much better than the government, much quicker and with more credibility', thus constituting 'a game changer', where 'the involvement of the public [through new media technologies] creates the multiplier effect that we are looking for […] This is where the future lies' (Interview, Jerusalem, 3 January 2016).

Enlisting digital extensions[12]

Tapping into a popular sentiment of suspicion towards the representation of the Israeli-Palestinian conflict online (Kuntsman and Stein 2015),[13] one of the first attempts to mobilise civic participation through new media technologies was through so-called advocacy 'war rooms'[14] that aimed to organise and coordinate the activities of volunteers on social media during Israeli military operations (interview, Petah Tikva, 7 January 2016). Satisfied with the outcome, government officials kept searching for more continuous, and at times covert, ways to mobilise participation through social media technologies and 'orchestrate this from above' in the 'struggle for hearts and minds' (interview, Jerusalem, 3 January 2016; see also Ravid 2013). These attempts peaked in 2015 with the establishment of the Ministry of Strategic Affairs and Public Diplomacy (MSAPD). Entrusted with leading the struggle against the BDS movement in order to secure a positive representation of Israel abroad (Blau 2017), the MSAPD operates in partnership with an unknown number of private citizens and NGOs in the attempt to form a pro-Israel network with the ministry as a central node. As explained by the ministry's director: 'We are fighting against a network, [and] only a network can act against a network. Not individuals… not embassies, not consulates… Only a network in which all parts act together in synergy' (The Special Committee for the Transparency and Accessibility of Government Information 2017: 29).[15] For this purpose, the ministry adopted a 'no-logo policy' that aimed to conceal its involvement with the organisations forming this network, arguing that publicity would harm effective cooperation (The Special Committee for the Transparency and Accessibility of Government Information 2017: 23). Despite the covert mode of operations, some of the committee's activities are nonetheless public, providing ample illustration of how parts of this heterogenous pro-Israel *Hasbara* network operate in practice.

In 2017, in cooperation with several civil society organisations, the MSAPD launched a public campaign called *4IL*, which, similarly to its predecessor, first staged various instances of misrepresentation as an unresolved political issue, and then proposed a solution to the citizens willing to participate. In one of the main videos of the campaign, a millennial who is frustrated with 'fake news' decides 'to tell the whole world the real truth about Israel' and thus help 'protect' the state. The video then seems to ridicule how hard it is to do that, which, according to the video, includes participating in offline political and cultural events and posting the pictures on social media, suggesting 'the easy way' as an alternative: 'Want to defend Israel? Log on to 4IL, download

the app and share the truth'. (4IL 2017b). On the main page of the *4IL* website, visitors are greeted with an embedded loop from the previous video
and another call to action: 'EVERY TWO MINUTES A NEW LIE ABOUT
ISRAEL IS SHARED ONLINE. You can put an end to this. Influence the
conversation'! (4IL 2017a). For this purpose, the website provides various
content, such as articles, videos and political cartoons. These items were meant
to be disseminated on social media platforms through embedded social buttons, thus, similarly to the 2010 campaign, inducing government-sanctioned
content with the credibility typically associated with the subjective everyday
experiences of individual users. The smartphone app ACT.IL, which the users
were encouraged to download while visiting the website, took this logic one
step further.

Despite actually being the focal point of the website, the app was described
as a 'a student initiative' (4IL 2017a) that was launched, according to a ministry-
sponsored publication, by students with previous experience with advocacy
'war rooms' as 'a civilian project ... dedicated entirely to waging Israel's battle
of Hasbara online', emphasising that it is 'not government-supported and has
no political affiliations' (Weiss 2017). Explaining the purpose of the app, one
of the students argues: 'Companies, such as Facebook, remove content following reports from the community [...] As soon as content inciting against Israel
is posted online, we send a message through the app, and all of its subscribers
immediately report it' (Weiss 2017). In order to understand how this new digital
mode of participation functions, I downloaded the app – as prompted by the
nation-wide campaign – and explored its interface.[16] The app's home tab included
a profile, with a space for username, score, access to messages, and so on. Below,
several 'missions' were presented, with bonus points for completion, which
enabled unlocking new missions and competing with other users. For example,
in order to report a Facebook page, a detailed description of how reporting is
done was provided, and the user was then directed via a hyperlink to the page
in question in order to complete the 'mission'. In another instance, an article was
described as 'misleading', and readers were encouraged to endorse this judgement
via 'like' and comment functions. Other missions included a wide range of other
digitally mediated actions, such as retweeting, liking, commenting, sharing and

reporting content across social media platforms, including signing petitions and filing complaints on various websites. To foster a sense of community, a news feed was kept by the app, informing users about the missions accomplished by others. Moreover, the application sent push notifications several times a day in order to update users about new available missions.

Unlike the 2010 MPDDA campaign, where public participation involved talking to foreigners face-to-face, enabling a wide range of complex and nuanced subjective experiences to become part of the mediation process, participation in the *4IL* campaign is preconditioned by the scripts of social media platforms.[17] In comparison to the 2010 campaign, the app thus enables higher thematic granularity and precision in its steering of civic participation towards specific political performances, such as reacting to a specific comment within a thread in relation to a specific news item within the platforms' data stream. Moreover, the app has facilitated a new kind of temporal continuity in these steering efforts, where participation is not limited to occasional encounters with alterity but can be systematically integrated into the everyday life of the citizens and performed easily and frequently with the assistance of push notifications and links to social buttons. This very process, however, simultaneously seems also to diminish the political agency of the participating citizens. Instead of reflecting the ambiguous and subjective experiences of individual citizens, participation is flattened and fragmented into a multitude of homogenous digitally mediated micro-performances, which aim to increase the visibility of pro-Israeli content while attempting to make counter-narratives invisible.[18] To use Latour's terms, the app reduces public participation from a 'mediator' of governmental messages, which can 'transform, translate, distort, and modify the meaning or the elements they are supposed to carry', to an 'intermediary' which 'transports meaning or force without transformation' (Latour 2005: 39); a form of 'Double Click' participation which 'tries to avoid all opportunities for metamorphosis' (Latour 2013: 200).

While the ACT.IL app still requires some user discretion in going through with each of these micro-performances, a small-scale Twitter app experiment – apparently set up by the Israeli Ministry of Foreign Affairs (IMFA) – illustrates that, in principle, even that might become redundant in some digitally mediated participatory practices, thus taking the 'Double Click' logic to its technologically afforded extreme consequence. While the IMFA traditionally had a more conservative approach to *Hasbara*, digital communication technologies have become increasingly central also to their activities, marked by the establishment of the digital diplomacy department in 2011 (State Comptroller report 2016: 835). As noted by the IMFA director general, 'we are in the middle of a revolution. The Digital Revolution [...] is profoundly relevant to diplomacy [and] requires us to rethink how we work, how we preserve and enhance our ability to impact on the world around us' (Rotem 2017). Specifically, in interviews, officials expressed concerns with being 'in competition for attention', which requires being more 'creative [...], daring [...], innovative' (interview, Jerusalem, 26 July 2016). Though no details about these initiatives were provided, a few months after the interviews, after following a few Twitter accounts related to the ministry, I received a Twitter message which might shed some light on how some aspects of this new digital diplomacy may unfold in practice.

The message appeared to be automatically generated, based on my assumed interest in Israel, extending an invitation to join a 'digital task force'. By clicking on the provided link, I was directed to the webpage of an initiative where a new type of call to action was extended. The call claimed that due to 'echo chambers and fake news, factual information about Israel is rapidly becoming victim to "alternative truths"'. In order to help 'counter this alarming reality', the webpage invited the user to join 'an online community of information spreaders which retweets [...] important information about Israel automatically [...] and makes sure the truth about Israel is loud and clear'. After pressing the 'JOIN IN' button, I was taken to a page related to Twitter's API and asked to authorise the application to use my Twitter account. The logo and description indicated that this Twitter application was developed by the IMFA, to 'enable daily automatic retweets of facts about Israel, curated by the Israeli Ministry of Foreign Affairs'. This authorisation enabled the application to see my timeline, who I follow, follow new accounts on my behalf, update my user profile, post tweets from my account and access my private messages (Author's field notes).

In order to examine how this mode of enlistment operates in practice, I decided with a modicum of trepidation to provide the application with the requested authorisation. In the following weeks, several tweets appeared on the timeline of my account that to all intents and purposes looked as if they were in fact retweeted by me. The tweets did not appear to have any politically controversial content, focusing instead on positive representations of Israel in relation to technology, tourism and coexistence. Moreover, this experiment clearly seemed to have a limited scope. Each of the tweets was retweeted at most a few hundred times, and after a few weeks they stopped appearing altogether (Author's field notes). Such retweet apps and bots, including other forms of automation, were in common use on Twitter by both commercial and political actors until 2018, when the platform decided to significantly limit the ability of users to engage in coordination and automation of tweets and retweets (see Roth 2018). Nonetheless, this experimental Twitter app illustrates how the technological affordances of digital mediation in the present media environment enable the transformation of digitally mediated participation from a transformative *mediator* into a passive *intermediary*, where besides the initial API authorisation participation no longer seems to require any input by the participant. Especially noteworthy is the desire of government authorities to enlist these new technological affordances into their everyday political practices. If the 2010 campaign attempted to mobilise the bodies of the citizens into participatory diplomatic practices, with new media technologies simply providing state-endorsed information, what was mobilised into participation just a few years later was already a certain hybrid between a knowing subject with subjective everyday experiences and a knowable data-object, consisting of a social media profile which can be conveniently enlisted for specific purposes and steered with increasing precision and (potential) reach. Through these seamless and increasingly automatised participatory processes, a certain paradoxical dynamic begins to emerge, where the technological affordances of social media which aim to facilitate participation go hand in hand with increasing the *governability* of the participants.

DIGITALLY MEDIATED ACTION AT A DISTANCE AND WHY PARTICIPATION IS NOT ENOUGH

In *Science in Action*, Latour uses examples such as the mapping of Sakhalin and innovations in Portuguese ship building technologies[19] to illustrate that it is possible 'to act at a distance on unfamiliar events, places, and people [...] by *somehow* bringing home these events, places, and people [...] By inventing means that (a) render them *mobile* [...] (b) keep them *stable* [...] and (c) are *combinable*' (Latour 1987: 223). If such 'immutable and combinable mobiles' (Latour 1987: 227) can be found, mobilised and retrieved from faraway places, through for example cartography, collections of artefacts and plants, scientific charts and tables, and so on, and then used in new expeditions, then a marginal point can become a centre which dominates others 'at a distance'. Encouraging us to forsake *a priori* analytical distinctions between technology, politics, science and so on, understanding such processes, according to Latour (1987: 222), requires tracing 'the unique movement that makes all of these domains conspire towards the same goal: a cycle of accumulation that allows a point to become a *centre* by acting at a distance on many other points'.

The movement which carries 'action at a distance' from one point to another is enacted through a heterogeneous actor-network, or an assemblage, and it is clearly relevant today not only to technoscience but also to governance and public participation in politics (or technopolitics, if you wish). Latour's concept of 'action at a distance' was indeed a central inspiration for governmentality studies, which applied Foucault's (2002, 2008) genealogies of the Western state in examining contemporary – and often neoliberal – modes of government. These studies invoked the concept of 'governing at a distance' in order to illustrate how contemporary political power is often exercised not through a 'direct imposition... but through a delicate affiliation of a loose assemblage of agents and agencies into a functioning network' (Miller and Rose 1990: 9–10). In these assemblages, two simultaneous movements often take place, which we also observe in the cases of digital diplomacy described above. On the one hand, a certain process of *responsibilisation* extends 'a call for action' as a form of 'interpellation which constructs and assumes a moral agency and certain dispositions to social action that necessarily follow' (Shamir 2008: 4). Such attempts 'to activate action' (Garland 1996: 452) are accompanied by *knowledge production*, through which the behaviour of the newly sparked public can be steered 'at a distance' – that is, without direct government intervention and imposition – towards specific governmental ends (Löwenheim 2007; Tsinovoi and Adler-Nissen 2018). This way, in Latourian terms, the participating individuals can be enlisted into a movement steered at a distance by a governmental *centre of calculation*.

The aforementioned examples of participatory diplomatic initiatives provide ample illustration of such a movement of 'governing at a distance' where technological and political elements are woven together into working towards the same predefined goal through a functioning network. In line with Marres' (2007) discussion of public participation as a pragmatist response to unresolved issues in which the individuals are implicated, the articulation of misrepresentations by Israeli authorities evidently attempts to 'spark a public into being', first in reference to the foreign press and then to various digital media outlets which allegedly spread fake news. At the same time, in line with governmentality studies (Dean 2010), it is clear that these campaigns constitute very specific subject positions for the participants as morally superior and guilt-free (Adler-Nissen and Tsinovoi 2019), while also providing narrow technological scripts to channel this participation toward specific ends. This way, unlike Marres' (2007) notion of public participation as an organic and spontaneous response, participation in these examples comes into being as the result of a strategic and calculated movement. This type of action also significantly differs from the accounts of influence campaigns using paid commentators (trolls) or social bots by states such as Russia (Jensen et al 2019; McCombie et al. 2020), since it does not rely on paid labour or direct interventions, but on the freedom of the participating users to partake, or at least sign up, voluntarily.

The scripts of social media platforms afford a deepening and widening of such cycles of action at a distance. As noted by Latour (1987: 228), 'if inventions are made that transform numbers, images and texts from all over the world into the same binary code inside computers, then indeed the handling, the combination, the mobility, the conservation and the display of the traces will all be fantastically facilitated'. As I have illustrated in this chapter, these general affordances of digital mediation,[20] combined with the 'explosion of profiles' prompted and then accumulated by social media platforms (Latour 2011: 806), enable rendering individuals, or at least their digital extensions, as 'immutable and combinable mobiles' which can increasingly *intermediate* governmental messages. In the 2010 campaign, individuals were sent off 'empowered' with narratives conveyed by a static web page, which then required embodied *mediation* in face-to face encounters, involving the complex subjective everyday experiences of the individuals, which leaves a space for ambiguity and transformation. Seven years later, in alliance with the affordances of social media platforms and mobile devices, these cycles of 'government at a distance' no longer depend on embodied *mediation* but on enlisting user profiles that can *intermediate* governmental messages with a minimum of modification and involvement. By eliminating the need for embodied performances, these technological affordances not only enable steering participation at higher levels of thematic granularity and temporal continuity, but also – through API authorisation, for example – potentially eliminating the need for any individual action to be taken altogether by the participating user, leading to a new, radical mode of 'Double Click' participation in politics.

In these emerging natively digital politics – politics enacted through 'the objects, content, devices and environments that are "born" in the new [digital] medium' (Rogers 2013: 19) – the political rationality that aims to enlist the body politic into governmental movements, combined with the technological affordances of social media platforms, can in principle extend the logic of 'governing at a distance' on an unprecedented scale, due to the multiplication of surfaces through which individuals, together with their digital extensions, can be acted on from remote centres of calculation. Extending the reach of this technique is, however, not the same as increasing its impact. While data on these activities is at times difficult to trace, a recent report monitoring the activities of the MSAPD app indicates that it has a rather negligible impact on the online conversation, involving only a few hundred page views and Facebook interactions during the monitored period (@DFRLab 2019). Similarly, the IMFA tweets were retweeted only a few hundred times, suggesting a very limited user base. Despite the intentions of apps such as ACT.IL to 'recruit millions around the world for one giant powerful internet-based task force working to defend the State of Israel' (Weiss 2017), the extent to which such interventions can capture global user attention on a mass scale and then translate it into political impact is questionable. Nonetheless, what is perhaps most interesting about these examples is the evident appeal of 'Double Click' participation to governmental authorities, and the manner in which the ubiquity of digital mediation enables the extension of this technique of government into any digitally mediated domain. Perhaps what is emerging from these cases is, then, not only a story about new forms of participatory diplomacy, but also a more generalisable new mode of technopolitical 'action at a distance' that can be applied to a multiplicity of other issues

In political theory, there is a long tradition of associating democracy with open-endedness, plurality and ambiguity. From this perspective, a democratic situation must not only be participatory, but should also imply a modicum of political openness, contestability, creativity and even transgressive playfulness (Agamben 2000, 2010; Žižek 2008; Mouffe 2009; Rancière 2004).[21] In this chapter, however by tracing the associations between public discourses, governmental logics and affordances provided by digital interfaces, I have described cases where public participation was sparked strategically, retrieved into centres of calculation, fragmented into 'immutable and combinable mobiles' and then recirculated. This process increasingly reduces political participation from complex political *mediations* in favour of homogenous and governable *intermediations*; a mere *part-taking*, enlisted and absorbed into the a priori calculations of specific governmental movements. Participation is thus enacted in these examples as somewhat of a Janus-faced phenomenon, wherein that which manifests itself as democratic participation to the users is also a resource which can be mobilised strategically by the authorities in order to address the assumed credibility deficit of the state. This kind of enactment of public participation in practice, where civic participation turns into an instrumental intermediary for governmental ends, appears to be incongruent with the typical democratic tropes of plurality and openness. Instead, it illustrates the extent to which the formation of publics in natively digital politics can be easily sparked, steered and governed, and emphasises the imperative to study public participation in practice, as a situated and multi-faceted phenomenon.

For this purpose, facilitating an inclusive and continuous conversation between STS and political theory is an essential step. While this entails several challenges – particularly in the context of international politics (Barry 2013) – the ubiquity of digital mediation, which has the potential to turn political practices such as diplomacy into a loose and porous assemblage of public, private and algorithmic mediators, raises serious questions about the role of materiality and technological expert knowledge, which STS is well placed to address. At the same time, as these technologies become increasingly governmentalised – that is, enlisted into broader assemblages through which sovereign entities govern the behaviour of large populations – STS faces new questions concerning governance that fields such as political science and international relations have been addressing for many years. Indeed, if the concerns of institutional politics are increasingly conflated with the politics of science and technology, the disciplines dedicated to their respective studies should follow suit.

ENDNOTES

1 The Web 2.0 business model includes various principles such as using the web as a platform, providing services instead of products, 'harnessing collective intelligence', software 'architecture of participation', database management and so on, which characterise companies that managed to survive the 'dot-com' financial crisis in the end of the 1990s (O'Reilly 2009).

2 Digital diplomacy can be broadly defined as 'the use of social media for diplomatic purposes' (Bjola 2015, 4).

3 For example, the 2003 Eurobarometer survey indicated that Israel was perceived as the biggest threat to world peace (European Commission 2003, 78), and the 2007 and 2012 BBC surveys indicated that Israel has had one of the worst influences on world politics (Knesset Research and Information 2010).

4 For a discussion see Adler (2013) and Adler-Nissen and Tsinovoi (2019).

5 From here on, all sources originally in Hebrew, such as interviews, documents, news items, and so on, were translated by the author.

6 The Boycott, Disinvestment and Sanctions movement (BDS) is a coalition of civil society organisations claiming to represent Palestinian interests by appealing to the international community to put pressure on Israel through academic and cultural boycotts, economic divestment, and governmental sanctions (Ananth 2013; BDS 2017).

7 See Endnote 11 for examples.

8 While diplomacy is typically understood as a government-to-government form of communication, public diplomacy refers to a state attempt at 'direct communication with foreign peoples, with the aim of affecting their thinking, and ultimately, that of their governments' (Malone 1985: 199).

9 For more on the conceptual distinction between public diplomacy and propaganda, see Melissen (2005) and Snow (2012).

10 As these were understood by governmental *Hasbara* experts (interview, Jerusalem, 3 January 2016).

11 For instance, critics mention the unfair depiction of foreign reports (Rabinovsky 2010), the dissociation between international critique and Israel's policies (Bronner 2010; Caspi 2010) and even the undermining of the peace process through a narrow, right-wing understanding of Israeli identity (Haaretz 2010; Ynet 2010).

12 Here I paraphrase McLuhan's (2013[1964]) famous title *Understanding Media: The Extensions of Man.*

13 Illustrating this sentiment, Kuntsman and Stein (2015) discuss the example of amateur digital forensics, where lay social media users attempt to expose possible manipulations of conflict images online and share these on social media.

14 The exact term used in the interview is Chapak (חפ"ק) which in Israeli military terminology refers to central command room.

15 As such, in Callon and Latour's (1981) terms this describes *Hasbara* in its 'unscrewed' state (see also Birkbak 2016), as a heterogenous multiplicity rather than a uniform actor.

16 The latest version of the application can be accessed at: https://apps.apple.com/us/app/act-il/id1141853455

17 On the concept of script see Akrich (1992).

18 For a more detailed review of the concept of visibility in this context see Tsinovoi (2020).

19 This specific example is based on an earlier study by John Law (1984: 235) were he associates innovation in naval technologies and maritime practices with the ability to exert 'long-distance social control' as part of the Portuguese imperial expansion in the fifteenth and sixteenth centuries.

20 For more on the general affordances of digital representations see Manovich (2001).

21 This distinction between 'politics' and 'the Political' has also been made in some STS accounts (see, for example, Barry 2001).

REFERENCES

4IL, 'Stop the Hate. Ministry of Strategic Affairs and Public Diplomacy' (2017a), <https://web.archive.org/web/20180305230400/http://www.4il.org.il/eng/> [Accessed 5 March 2018].

4IL, 'Do the Right Thing – The Easy Way!' (2017b) <https://www.youtube.com/watch?v=HxKrn8Aqa0A> [Accessed 21 August 2017].

Adler-Nissen, R., and A. Tsinovoi, 'International Misrecognition: The Politics of Humor and National Identity in Israel's Public Diplomacy', *European Journal of International Relations,* 25 (2019), 3–29.

Adler, E., *Israel in the World: Legitimacy and Exceptionalism* (London and New York: Routledge, 2013).

Akrich, M., 'The De-scription of Technical Objects', in W. E. Bijker and J. Law, eds, *Shaping Technology/Building Society. Studies in Sociotechnical Change* (Cambridge, MA: The MIT Press, 1992).

Ananth, S., 'The Politics of the Palestinian BDS Movement's Socialism and Democracy', *Socialism and Democracy,* 27 (2013), 129–143.

Aouragh, M., 'Everyday Resistance on the Internet: The Palestinian Context', *Journal of Arab and Muslim Media Research,* 1 (2008), 109–130.

——, *Palestine Online: Transnationalism, the Internet and the Construction of Identity* (London: I. B. Tauris, 2011).

Attias, S., 'Israel's New Peer-to-Peer Diplomacy', *The Hague Journal of Diplomacy,* 7 (2012), 473–482.

Barry, A., 'The Translation Zone: Between Actor-Network Theory and International Relations', *Millennium,* 41 (2013), 413–429.

—— 'Political Situations: Knowledge Controversies in Transnational Governance', *Critical Policy Studies,* 6 (2012), 324–336.

—— *Political Machines: Governing a Technological Society* (London: The Athlone Press, 2001).

Bakardjieva, M., 'Subactivism: Lifeworld and Politics in the Age of the Internet', *The Information Society,* 25 (2009), 91–104.

BDS, 'What is BDS?' (2017)<https://bdsmovement.net/what-is-bds> [Accessed 11 June 2018].

Birkbak, A., 'Unscrewing Social Media Networks, Twice', *Akademisk kvarter / Academic Quarter,* 15 (2017), 11–26.

Bjola, C., 'Introduction: Making Sense of Digital Diplomacy', in C. Bjola and M. Holmes, eds, *Digital Diplomacy: Theory and Practice* (London: Routledge, 2015).

Blau, U., 'Inside the Clandestine World of Israel's "BDS-busting" Ministry', *Haaretz,* 26 March 2017, <https://www.haaretz.com/israel-news/MAGAZINE-inside-the-clandestine-world-of-israels-bds-busting-ministry-1.5453212> [Accessed 15 June 2018].

Bronner, E., 'Positive Views of Israel, Brought to You by Israelis' (2010), <https://www.nytimes.com/2010/02/18/world/middleeast/18israel.html> [Accessed 1 July 2021].

Caspi, D., '[Explaining Israel or the Minister?]' *Ynet,* 26 February 2010 (In Hebrew), <http://www.ynet.co.il/articles/0,7340,L-3854453,00.html> [Accessed 8 December 2016].

Dahlberg, L., 'Re-constructing Digital Democracy: An Outline of Four "Positions"', *New Media & Society* 13 (2011), 855–872.

Dean, M., *Governmentality: Power and Rule in Modern Society* (London: Sage, 2010).

Edelstein, Y., '[Israeli Youth are Fighting Apartheid Week - Israeli Propaganda]', *YouTube,* 23 February 2012 (In Hebrew) [Video file], <https://www.youtube.com/watch?v=QfU6GKvCASQ> [Accessed 15 June 2018].

European Commission, *Eurobarometer: Iraq and Peace in the World* (2003), <http://ec.europa.eu/public_opinion/flash/fl151_iraq_full_report.pdf> [Accessed 12 August 2017].

Foucault, M., 'Governmentality', in J. D. Faubion, ed., *Michel Foucault, Power: Essential Works of Foucault, 1954–1984* (London: Penguin, 2002).

——, *The Birth of Biopolitics: Lectures at the College de France, 1978–1979* (Basingstoke: Palgrave Macmillan, 2008).

Friedman, M., 'What the Media Gets Wrong About Israel', *The Atlantic,* 30 November 2014, <https://www.theatlantic.com/international/archive/2014/11/how-the-media-makes-the-israel-story/383262/> [Accessed 25 February 2018].

Garland, D., 'The Limits of the Sovereign State: Strategies of Crime Control in Contemporary Society', *The British Journal of Criminology,* 36 (1996), 445–471.

Gilboa, E., 'Public Diplomacy: The Missing Component in Israel's Foreign Policy', *Israel Affairs,* 12 (2006), 715–747.

Greenfield, S., 'Israeli Hasbara: Myths and Facts', *Molad. The Center for Renewal of Israeli Democracy* (2012), <http://www.molad.org/images/upload/files/49381451033828.pdf> [Accessed 21 December 2016].

Haaretz, 'A Government Without Hope', 28 February (2010), <http://www.haaretz.com/a-government-without-hope-1.263848> [Accessed 8 December 2016].

Habermas, J., *The Theory of Communicative Action: Lifeworld and System: A Critique of Functionalist Reason,* Vol. 2 (Boston: Beacon Press, 1987).

Hitchcock, J., 'Social Media Rhetoric of the Transnational Palestinian-led Boycott, Divestment, and Sanctions Movement', *Social Media + Society*, 2 (2016), 1–12.

Irwin, A., *Citizen Science* (London: Routledge, 1995).

Jasanoff, S., 'Technologies of Humility: Citizen Participation in Governing Science', *Minerva*, 41 (2003), 223–244.

Jensen, B., B. Valeriano, and R. Maness, 'Fancy Bears and Digital Trolls: Cyber Strategy with a Russian Twist', *Journal of Strategic Studies* 42 (2019), 212–234.

Kelty, C., *The Participant* (Chicago, IL: University of Chicago Press: 2019).

Kunstman A., and R. L. Stein, *Digital Militarism: Israel's Occupation in the Social Media Age* (Stanford, CA: Stanford University Press, 2015).

Latour, B., *Science in Action: How to Follow Scientists and Engineers through Society* (Milton Keynes: Open University Press, 1987).

———, 'On Technical Mediation – Philosophy, Sociology, Genealogy', *Common Knowledge*, 3 (1994), 29–64.

———, 'Networks, Societies, Spheres: Reflections of an Actor-Network Theorist', *International Journal of Communication*, 5 (2011), 796–810.

———, *An Inquiry into Modes of Existence: An Anthropology of the Moderns* (Cambridge, MA: Harvard University Press, 2013).

Law, J., 'On the Methods of Long-Distance Control: Vessels, Navigation and the Portuguese Route to India', *The Sociological Review*, 32 (1984), 234–263.

Light, B., J. Burgess and S. Duguay, 'The Walkthrough Method: An Approach to the Study of Apps', *New Media & Society*, 20 (2018), 881–900.

Löwenheim, O., 'The Responsibility to Responsibilize: Foreign Offices and the Issuing of Travel Warnings', *International Political Sociology*, 1 (2007), 203–221.

Manovich, L., *The Language of New Media* (Cambridge, MA: The MIT Press, 2001).

Marres, N., *Digital Sociology: The Reinvention of Social Research* (Cambridge: Polity, 2017).

———, 'Issues Spark a Public into Being: A Key but Often Forgotten Point of the Lippmann-Dewey Debate', in B. Latour and P. Weibel, eds, *Making Things Public: Atmospheres of Democracy* (Cambridge, MA: The MIT Press, 2005).

Masbirim's channel, 'Masbirim 1', *Masbirim*, 17 March 2010 [Video file], <https://www.youtube.com/watch?v=qkuX4RLr0yA> [Accessed 7 December 2016].

McCombie, S., A. J. Uhlmann, and S. Morrison, 'The US 2016 Presidential Election & Russia's Troll Farms', *Intelligence and National Security* 35 (2020), 95–114.

McLuhan, M., *Understanding Media: The Extensions of Man* (Corte Madera, CA: Gingko Press, 2013[1964]).

Melissen, J., 'The New Public Diplomacy: Between Theory and Practice', in J. Melissen, ed., *The New Public Diplomacy: Soft Power in International Relations* (New York: Palgrave Macmillan, 2005).

Miller, P. and N. Rose, 'Governing Economic Life', *Economy and Society,* 19 (1990), 1–30.

Ministry of Public Diplomacy & Diaspora Affairs, 'Myth vs. Reality' (2010a), <https://web.archive.org/web/20120724085041/http://masbirim.gov.il/eng/i_myth.html> [Accessed 14 December 2016].

Ministry of Public Diplomacy & Diaspora Affairs, 'Tips' (2010b), <https://web.archive.org/web/20120724085437/http://masbirim.gov.il/eng/i_ourtips.html> [Accessed 14 December 2016].

Mouffe, C., *The Democratic Paradox.* (London: Verso, 2009).

Naveh, C., 'The Palestinian-Israeli Web War', in P. Seib, P, ed., *New Media and the New Middle East* (Basingstoke: Palgrave Macmillan, 2007).

Nye, J. S., 'Public Diplomacy and Soft Power', *The ANNALS of the American Academy of Political and Social Science,* 616 (2008), 94–109.

O'Reilly, T., 'What Is Web 2.0? Design Patterns and Business Models for the Next Generation of Software', in M. Mandiberg, ed., *The Social Media Reader* (New York, NY: New York University Press, 2012).

Olesker, R., 'Law-Making and the Securitization of the Jewish Identity in Israel', *Ethnopolitics,* 13 (2013), 105–121.

Papacharissi, Z., *Affective Publics: Sentiment, Technology, and Politics* (Oxford: Oxford University Press, 2015).

Prime Minister's Office, '[Government resolution no. 1936 from the 08.07.2007]', *Gov.il: Israel's government services and information website* (in Hebrew) (2007), <https://www.gov.il/he/departments/policies/2007_des1396> [Accessed 16 December 2020].

Rabinovsky, T., '[European reporters against the Hasbara campaign: Not Stupid.]', *Ynet* (in Hebrew.) (2010), <http://www.ynet.co.il/articles/0,7340,L-3855017,00.html> [Accessed 8 December 2016].

Ravid, B., '[The PM's office establishes shadow-units of students for covert online Hasbara]', *Haaretz.* 13 August 2013, (in Hebrew), <https://www.haaretz.co.il/news/politics/.premium-1.2095791> [Accessed 25 February 2018].

Rogers, R., *Digital Methods* (Cambridge, MA: The MIT Press, 2013).

Rotem, Y., 'Remarks from MFA director general Rotem at the 2nd international conference on digital diplomacy' (2017), <https://mfa.gov.il/MFA/AboutTheMinistry/Events/Pages/Remarks-from-MFA-Director-General-Rotem-at-2nd-Digital-Diplomacy-Conference-7-Dec-2017.aspx> [Accessed 16 December 2020].

Roth, Y., 'Automation and the Use of Multiple Accounts', *Twitter Developer Blog* (2018).

Seib, P., *Real-Time Diplomacy: Politics and Power in the Social Media Era* (Basingstoke: Palgrave Macmillan, 2012).

Shamir, R., 'The Age of Responsibilization: On Market Embedded Morality', *Economy and Society*, 37 (2008), 1–19.

Shirky, C., 'The Political Power of Social Media: Technology, The Public Sphere, and The Political Change', *Foreign Affairs*, 90 (2011), 28–41.

Siapera, E., 'Tweeting #Palestine: Twitter and the Mediation of Palestine', *International Journal of Culture Studies*, 17 (2013), 539–555.

Sifry, M. L., 'Hillary Clinton Launches "21st Century Statecraft" Initiative by State Department', *Tech President,* 13 May 2009, <http://techpresident.com/blog-entry/hillary-clinton-launches-21st-century-statecraft-initiative-state-department> [Accessed 31 May 2018].

Snow, N., 'Public Diplomacy and Propaganda: Rethinking Diplomacy in the Age of Persuasion', *E- International Relations,* (2012), <http://www.e-ir.info/2012/12/04/public-diplomacy-andpropaganda-rethinking-diplomacy-in-the-age-of-persuasion/> [Accessed 1 December 2021].

State Comptroller, '[Annual report 53A]' (in Hebrew) (2002), <http://www.mevaker.gov.il/he/Reports/Pages/353.aspx?entity> [Accessed 12 August 2017].

——, '[Annual report 58A]' (in Hebrew) (2007), <http://www.mevaker.gov.il/he/Reports/Pages/293.aspx> [Accessed 12 August 2017].

——, '[Annual report 66C]' (in Hebrew) (2016), <http://www.mevaker.gov.il/he/Reports/Report_537/2545b606-b040-4ad8-a20f-37c1d04c1b81/217-hasbara.pdf> [Accessed 12 August 2017].

The Committee for Immigration, Absorption and Diaspora Affairs, '[Protocol 256, 16th of July]', (in Hebrew) (2012) <http://knesset.gov.il/protocols/data/rtf/alia/2012-07-16.rtf> [Accessed 12 August 2017].

The Reut Institute, '*Building a Political Firewall Against Israel's Delegitimization Conceptual Framework*' (2010) <http://reut institute.org/Data/Uploads/PDFVer/20100310%20Delegitimacy%20Eng.pdf> [Accessed 12 August 2017].

The Special Committee for the Transparency and Accessibility of Government Information, '[Protocol 101, 24 July 2017)]'. <http://main.knesset.gov.il/Activity/committees/GovInfo/Pages/CommitteeProtocols.aspx> [Accessed 12 August 2017].

Tsinovoi A., and R. Adler-Nissen, 'The Inversion of the "Duty of Care": Diplomacy and the Protection of Citizens Abroad from Pastoral Care to Neoliberal Governmentality', *The Hague Journal of Diplomacy,* 13 (2018), 211–232.

Tsinovoi, A., 'The Management of Visibility in Digital Diplomacy: Infrastructures and Techniques', *First Monday* 25 (2020).

Viner, K., 'Internet has changed foreign policy for ever, says Gordon Brown', *The Guardian,* 19 June 2009, <https://www.theguardian.com/politics/2009/jun/19/gordon-brown-internet-foreign-policy> [Accessed 2 October 2017].

Walla News '[Livni: Entering Gaza will reinforce the extremist]', *Walla News,* 14 May 2007, (in Hebrew), <https://news.walla.co.il/item/1106579> [Accessed 25 February 2018].

Weiss, R., 'A Lesson in Hasbara', *Ynet,* 27 June 2017, <https://www.ynetnews.com/articles/0,7340,L-4981081,00.html> [Accessed 25 February 2018].

Wynne, B., 'Public Participation in Science and Technology: Performing and Obscuring a Political-Conceptual Category Mistake', *East Asian Science, Technology and Society: An International Journal,* 1 (2007), 99–110.

Ynet, '*PR Website: Justifying State or Government?*', 21 February 2010. <http://www.ynetnews.com/articles/0,7340,L-3852485,00.html> [Accessed 8 December 2016].

11

DEMOCRATISING SOFTWARE? SITUATING POLITICAL CAMPAIGNING TECHNOLOGY IN THE UK'S EU REFERENDUM

Laurie Waller and David Moats

INTRODUCTION

IN 2016, IN THE WAKE OF THE UK'S EU REFERENDUM, A SERIES OF CON-
troversies emerged about the use of personal data and computational tools
by political campaigns to target their messages to potential voters.[1] These
controversies were sparked by a scandal involving the political consultancy
firm Cambridge Analytica gaining access to large volumes of social media data
and using psychological profiling to advise political campaigns in both the
UK and the US. In the UK, public inquiries have since been conducted by the
Electoral Commission (2018a, 2018b), the Information Commissioner (2018)
and the Digital, Culture, Media and Sport's Select Committee (2019) about
the harvesting of personal data from digital platforms, campaigns' spending
irregularities on social media advertising and the roles of tech companies and
political consultants in online disinformation campaigns (see also Howard and
Kollanyi 2016). Some commentators have argued that such technologies, and
the companies that run them, potentially compromise the very basis for free
and fair elections.[2]

In a blog post not long after the UK's referendum result, the director of the Vote Leave campaign, Dominic Cummings, announced the 'open-source' release of a piece of software called VICS that, he argued, played a critical role in the campaign's success.[3] He asserted that the campaign's management software enabled Vote Leave to interactively link sophisticated data analysis processes with 'on the ground' canvassing, continuously improving and testing the predictive models used by the campaign via the incorporation of 'live feedback'. Cummings argued that it was precisely this technological form of interactivity between the campaign and citizens that gave the campaign its authentic edge and enabled it to mobilise 'people who usually ignore politics'.

What are we to make of such claims about the 'democratising' or 'anti-democratic' influence of technology in relation to a political event like Brexit? The editors of this volume argue that it is no longer sufficient for STS researchers to mobilise theories of democracy in analysing technological processes, without also attending to the ways in which related ideas and notions are deployed and contested in empirical settings. The events above demonstrate that, on various sides of the Brexit debate, the democratic legitimacy of the referendum is, to varying degrees, inflected through controversies about technologies, and their roles in politics. In these controversies, actors are constantly redrawing or questioning boundaries between 'the technical' and 'the political'. Thus, some technologies are invested with political capacities, like increasing participation (see the chapters by Papazu and Pallett & Chilvers, this volume), while others fade into the background, as mundane, everyday aspects of political practice. Attending carefully to these empirical mobilisations of democratic ideals may be particularly important, we argue, in situations like the UK's EU referendum, where technologies are linked to practices some deem to be anti-democratic, such as misinforming the electorate or attacking experts and the judiciary, and political rhetoric conflating popular sovereignty with isolationist and, at times, explicitly xenophobic nationalism. Indeed, in the case of the Vote Leave campaign, claims about participation and freedom seemed often to coexist with a reactionary, almost Schmittian, understanding of democracy as merely national sovereignty. Situations like

Brexit, we will go on to suggest, may pose a challenge (or at least give pause) to STS approaches which might take for granted that they are on the side of democracy.

In the first part of this chapter, we consider how political campaign platforms, like the one released by Vote Leave, have been analysed by political sociology, media and communications researchers and STS researchers alike. We argue that existing analyses tend to rely on taken-for-granted notions of various democratic ideals, and we draw on STS discussions of technological controversies and 'anti-politics' to help avoid this trap. We illustrate how democratic ideals are deployed empirically using promotional materials for political campaign platforms. We show how these companies mobilise various notions of democracy in order to sell these software technologies, but do so in highly ambivalent, and arguably, contradictory ways.

The second part of this chapter examines how similarly ambivalent and contradictory democratic ideals emerged in Vote Leave's software release and Cummings' explanation of the campaign's technological strategy, mentioned above. In the blog post accompanying the software release, Cummings makes a series of elaborate claims about technological change and politics but, as we will show, these claims also take on very particular meanings in relation to Brexit as a 'democratic situation' and, specifically, a parliamentary inquiry into misinformation in political campaigning.[4] We suggest that the controversy over the use of technology in Vote Leave's campaign illustrates how moves to democratise technology are not necessarily incompatible with anti-political practices.

In concluding, we discuss the significance of this case for recent STS debates about populism and democracy. Situations like Brexit, we suggest, allow us to see both how political domains are unsettled and reordered by software and data infrastructures, and the consequences of this for democratic political practice. We argue that attending to particular 'gerrymanderings' (Woolgar and Puwluch 1985) of the technical and the political in situations like Brexit can help specify the stakes of contestations over expertise and infrastructures for democratic politics.

CAMPAIGN SOFTWARE AS 'DEMOCRATISING' TECHNOLOGY?

The events introduced above have brought into view just how much technologies orient and organise activities that are typically considered routine features of political processes. For example, in *The Victory Lab*, Sasha Issenberg (2012) catalogues a host of political scientists, data-driven market researchers, advertising consultants and data analytic tools which are now seen as integral to winning elections. While political campaign platforms, like the one released by Vote Leave's director, are often associated with politically mundane or technocratic practices of management and administration, in this section we examine how they also become invested with ideals about democratic politics.[5]

So, what are political campaign platforms? Issenberg (2012) notes that there is a long history of political campaigns using software packages, dating back at least to 1983 with the development of 'Campaign Manager' by John Aristotle Phillips and his brother Dean. These packages have been used to manage volunteers, synch schedules and collate information about supporters or potential voters. It is this latter feature – the ability to house extensive data on people, enabling the practice of 'microtargeting' – which has been at the centre of recent debates. Microtargeting is a process by which potential voters and supporters can be grouped into increasingly narrow subsets (based on psychological profiles, online purchases, cultural interests, behaviours and so on) so that political messages can be tailored to these groups. This requires that data about voters (email addresses, home addresses, demographic information) can be linked up to other types of data (personal data culled from our phones and other devices). Microtargeting dates back to the early 2000s, when the ubiquity of email and email lists offered different possibilities for engaging with supporters, although one might trace back the rationale to theories of mass communication, long critiqued by sociologists (Katz and Lazarsfeld 1955). Today, advocates of microtargeting tend to link these practices to well-worn tropes about 'big data' (Kitchin 2014; Burgess and Puschman 2014) in order to distinguish these campaign technology start-ups from so-called 'traditional' political consultants and political scientists (Ansted 2017).[6,7]

What does perhaps separate the current crop of software packages from their predecessors is the way in which they are often presented as highly networked 'platforms'. While not all of these players refer to their products as platforms, most have adopted key rhetorical and technical features of these Web 2.0 entities (O'Reilley 2005). For example, most of the software specifications we looked at promoted their use of Application Programming Interfaces (APIs), which facilitate the downloading and uploading of data and streaming with other applications, as well as the integration of different software systems (Helmond 2015).[8] It has frequently been highlighted that digital platforms paint themselves as a kind of public utility, like water pipes, which is provided as a service but does not overdetermine how it can be used (Helmond 2015; van Dijck 2013). It has long been argued that this neutral rhetoric conceals both the business models associated with many digital platforms and important asymmetries of access and visibility baked into their technological design (Bucher 2012; Gillespie 2010). As we highlight below, while much software is promoted as applicable to myriad activities, it is also typically coupled with consulting business models and licensing agreements; the technology is offered principally as a service rather than a discrete product.[9]

Much of the scholarship on campaign technologies – which comes mostly from political communications and political sociology – has debated whether forms of interactivity made possible by digital technologies necessarily facilitate the formation of publics or new modes of participation in politics (Bennett and Segerberg 2013). In the context of US political campaigns, Howard (2006) has argued that the development of what he terms 'hypermedia' campaigns led not to broader but rather to more narrow forms of managed interactivity between campaigns and voters. A similar version of Howard's argument can be detected in work by Barocas (2012), which analyses micro-targeting. Where promoters of micro-targeting suggest that such techniques can enhance a campaign's relationship with its audiences (for example, Bartlett, Birdwell and Reynolds 2014), Barocas argues that by allowing campaigns to deliver different messages to different people, they undermine the sense of a common conversation in politics. In this way, micro-targeting is said to contribute to the development of advanced (neo-)liberal forms of democracy in which political participation is reduced to a matter of individual preferences, and in which some individuals (such as swing voters) matter more for campaigns than others.

Kriess (2012, 2016) has chronicled the organisational work involved in integrating data infrastructures within US political parties. Kreiss argues that novel forms of interactivity between campaigns and voters afforded by social media and other Web 2.0 technologies are contingent on the local organisational processes of particular campaigns. In *Prototype Politics*, Kreiss (2016) shows how the two major US parties have developed strikingly different information infrastructures, inheriting many of these specificities from past campaigns, for example, those of Howard Dean and Barack Obama on the Democrat side. Kreiss highlights that the development of interactive networked politics in US elections can be seen as an achievement of the organising practices of campaigns as much as of software development. In other words, these developments are both social and technical.[10]

Both Barocas and Kreiss do an excellent job of politicising these technologies – that is, examining the possible effects of campaign management software on political processes, as well as showing the asymmetries of power that shape their development. However, while they argue that technological change has consequences for democratic politics, they do not show that it fundamentally threatens or reconfigures what counts as democracy, which remains largely assumed. Indeed, we can arguably detect certain normative stances towards democracy in such studies. For instance, Barocas proposes that voters *should* be treated equally, and assumes a common conversation as the aim of democratic politics. For Kreiss this involves positioning interactivity as a positive characteristic of campaigns. Such stances may very well suit the specific political cultures the authors are referencing, but in affirming a particular version of democratic politics they potentially imply that contestations over the capacities of these technologies are not properly political. Empirical sensitivity to the dynamics of technological contestation, we suggest, is therefore crucial to analysing how technologically inflected ideals about interactivity and bottom-up organising can potentially serve what some might see as anti-democratic ends – something we will deal with in the next section.

Democratising science and technology can be understood in various ways: for instance, as holding experts accountable, enhancing the power of publics over technological infrastructures and participation in design and innovation processes – in other words, bringing notions of democracy into science and technology. STS studies have long focused on showing how what counts as the capacities of technologies is always contestable (Bijker and Law 1992; MacKenzie and Wajcman 1999). They highlight how what counts as technical (as opposed to social or political) is contingent and its boundaries often strategically performed by actors in order to remove certain practices and forms of knowledge from scrutiny and contestation. Rather than accepting common sense understandings of what counts as the political, such studies have sought to extend politics to technical expertise and practices. In the analysis that follows, however, we are also interested in how technologies (and related expertise) come to be included in, or are excluded from, the domain of politics, and the extent to which the political practices engaging them are claimed to be democratic or not. In a situation like Brexit, we suggest, such moves are required since technological and political contestations are often difficult to clearly separate from one another; in the case of Vote Leave, technological development is presented by its director Cummings as the primary strategy of the political campaign.

Foucauldian and post-Foucauldian studies have long attended to instruments and techniques which are presented by proponents as facilitating democratic politics. Osborne and Rose's (1999) influential account of the opinion poll, for instance, showed how the proliferation of methods for studying public opinion provided the basis for exchanges and interactions between social science and government in the latter half of the twentieth century. Informed by insights from critical theory, such studies have tended to be cautious about understanding methods like polling as unequivocal agents of democratisation. Osborne and Rose, in particular, highlight why methodological descriptions of polls as procedures for analysing public opinion are, alone, of limited use for analysing the social phenomena polling produces (opinionated societies) and the political practices developed to organise and mobilise them. Their account makes clear why attending empirically to the specific technologies involved in enacting public opinion (for instance, questionnaires, ballots and, in our case, software and machine learning) is critical to a social analysis of contestations like those emerging around the Vote Leave's campaign in the Brexit referendum.

STS studies focused on politics and policy issues have widely attended to technological controversies as occasions when the boundaries between technology and society are unsettled and the political domain is reconfigured (Jasanoff 2020; Nelkin 1979). Much research in this tradition has studied novel participation procedures – often promoted by political scientists as a means by which technical disputes can be democratically resolved. STS studies have shown how, in practice, procedures like juries or consensus conferences can 'frame' the issues at stake and foreclose competing problem definitions and public concerns (see overview in Chilvers and Kearns 2016).[11] Yet critiques of how procedures frame issues and order participation have, arguably, tended to give too much credit to the state agencies and regulatory authorities attempting to govern technological society, and too little to the substantive matters that give rise to public concerns in the first place (Marres 2007). This is a helpful reminder that we can only understand certain consequences of procedures for engaging publics (and other technologies) in relation to particular political events and issues. In some versions of STS research on politics, such questions have been elaborated in discussions about the potential value of technological controversies to enrich democratic politics. Callon, Lascoumes and Barthe (2009) argue that the relationship of technological controversy to democratic politics is poorly understood by political theories that enact demarcations between democracy as a system of governing technological societies, on the one hand, and as a set of ideals about social and technological change, on the other. In other words, questions about whether technological controversies give rise to novel political objects and forms of collectivity are therefore not well served by concepts and analytical tools developed primarily for the study of democratic states (de Vries 2007).

Many STS scholars have therefore turned to approaches that aim to more thoroughly empiricise relations between technology and political ontology (Marres 2013; Woolgar and Lezaun 2013). Marres (2013), for instance, discusses the example of eco-show homes, which are invested with notions of citizenship and environmental participation 'by design'. She argues that it is not enough to note that these objects 'have politics' but that we need to empirically attend to *how* some technologies become politicised and explicitly invested with normative political capacities. Similarly, this approach proposes to attend to how other technologies are rendered as sub-political (Marres and Lezaun 2011) or as mundane aspects of political practice. Woolgar and Neyland, for example, discuss the work that is done when certain technologies of governance – recycling bin bags, security cameras and so on – are rendered as 'mundane' (Woolgar and Neyland 2013). Such sensitivities have analogues in fields such as infrastructure studies. Bowker and Star's (1999) classic *Sorting Things Out,* for example, invites researchers to consider how infrastructures become invisible for some actors while remaining unavoidable for others. Such approaches thus highlight why contestations over democratic politics in technological societies may in practice centre around objects and settings that appear mundane to the institutional forms and procedures associated with the politics of government and state power.

Thus, rather than merely revealing the 'hidden' politics of technology, such approaches also ask *how* certain technologies become politicised by actors in a given situation, while others become taken for granted as background infrastructure. Andrew Barry's (2005) distinction between politics as a commonly understood domain of social life ordered by governmental actors, and 'the political' – which he normatively defines in agonistic terms as a space of disagreement and contestation (see also Mouffe 2005) – is particularly pertinent to the case considered in this paper. Barry's distinction makes clear that activities in the domain of politics can ironically have what he refers to as 'anti-political' effects by circumscribing possibilities for engaging in disputes and debate. This, we argue, provides a helpful guide for our analyses, because even if we need to bracket our own specific political commitments to democracy, Barry reminds us that we are broadly speaking in favour of open contestation, allowing issues to unfold and take their course – even though it is never self-evident how this is to be done. It is also particularly valuable, as we highlight below, for understanding how technological change promoted as having democratising effects can be in principle compatible with anti-political practices.

The marketing materials for some popular campaign software platforms can provide a helpful illustration of how ideals of democracy or participation can be used in ambivalent ways and potentially in the service of anti-political ends.

> Having an organized community gives you an advantage. The concept of community organizing has been around for thousands of years. Moses was a community organizer. The tools of organizing should not be controlled by anyone. The organizing technology that we're building at NationBuilder is helping people come together to support the leaders and the causes they believe in. It's not a weapon to wield; it's infrastructure that's enabling democracy.[12]

In the above statement from NationBuilder, 'community organising' evokes ideas of bottom-up participation: the phrasing 'come together to support' proposes that agency lies with supporters (as opposed to leaders or technocratic campaign managers). In this formulation, NationBuilder is not controlling things; it is 'helping', positioned as merely an infrastructure. NationBuilder is tasked with increasing both the role of supporters in campaigns and also democracy in society, yet at the same time it is depoliticised, distancing the software from connotations of propaganda or control.

Similar uses of 'engagement' are found throughout the publicity materials, again assigning agency to supporters or 'the community', but in ways which also invoke engagement as a marketing term: customers are, for example, encouraged to actively promote products themselves through their networks.

> Share pages tend to make excellent follow-on calls-to-action from other action pages. For instance, after a constituent completes a signup form, you may daisy-chain to a share page which encourages the constituent to encourage their online peers to sign up as well.[13]

Blue State Digital, which (as its name highlights) emerged from the US Democratic party, talks about 'encouraging' constituents. Yet it seems, as suggested by the quote above, that the ways in which supporters can engage are very much set by the platform parameters and the campaign managers (for example, signing up a friend or distributing leaflets). So, while the rhetoric often evokes more active supporters, perhaps even to the extent of making it appear that the campaign is accountable to them, the architecture of the platforms also appears equally compatible with campaigning styles long critiqued as 'machine politics': organising public opinion and manufacturing the consent of the governed (Lippmann 1922).

While participation and interactivity are often invoked, specific political stances and potential disagreements seem to be actively supressed. The Groundwork, a (now defunct) software company linked to Google's Eric Schmidt, represents a particularly conspicuous example. Although associated with Hillary Clinton's presidential campaign, the company made no mention of political parties or politics in general in its publicity, instead presenting its software as a tool for social movements, community organisers and non-profit campaigns alike.[14] This flexibility is possible because of the way these platforms are typically presented as a neutral (apolitical) infrastructure (as in the quote from the NationBuilder website above), to be used in any particular political context. This assumes that technology can remain politically neutral regardless of the place, process or regime in which it is instrumentalised. As we will go on to illustrate, the limiting of politics to a mere context for technology is empirically problematic in a situation like Brexit where both constitutional matters and what counts as legitimate political practice are at stake in the controversy.

To make this even more apparent, many of these companies offer versions of their platforms which are geared toward (non-political) marketing as well. Where political advertising is today often seen as the application of marketing principles to the practices of political campaigning, several software companies also trade on specific notions of politics, prompting advertisers to run their campaign 'like a candidate' or promote products 'at the speed of politics'.[15] This invokes a version of politics as mobilising followers (in contrast to audiences or consumers). So, these particular presentations of the software as a democratising infrastructure could also, arguably, be seen as anti-political in Barry's sense by flattening out radically different ways of doing political engagement and disagreement.

Marketing materials for these platforms also frequently claim to level the playing field of the political landscape in general; that is, they assert the technologies to be inherently democratising. In doing so, they often evoke notions of equal access to software common in the Free Libre and Open Source Software (FLOSS) community. For instance, by offering their software at a supposedly low price, many platforms claim not to discriminate between wealthy political campaigns (such as those backed by major US political parties) and other types of NGOs and issue-based initiatives. This is to call forth a notion of democracy as fundamentally 'fair', in which particular parties or candidates are not given an advantage over others. Yet alongside such egalitarian gestures, other technological divisions may be created: several firms might price their service based on the total number of subscriber email addresses being stored, but at the same time these more established organisations are more likely to receive bespoke support and ultimately shape the development of further software features.

The above brief examples highlight some of the ways in which democracy is performed as a marketing device for technology firms aiming to sell software and computational expertise to political actors. These companies trade on fuzzy ideals of democracy, in which interactivity, grassroots organising and civic participation are moral constructs unmoored from any particular instantiation or struggle. Notice how in some cases the platforms themselves are invested with the capacity to increase democracy (or install democracy) while at other times they are made to fade into the background as a neutral infrastructure for politics. It's not hard to see how such deployments of democracy could be made compatible with anti-political practices, delimiting politics as simply a market segment and context for technology deployment.

In the next section, we discuss in detail the campaign software used by Vote Leave (called VICS) during the UK's EU referendum, critically attending to how similar-sounding claims about the democratising influence of technology take on a distinctively anti-political significance in relation to debates about the legitimacy of the referendum process and Brexit.

VOTE LEAVE'S (ANTI-)POLITICAL SOFTWARE RELEASE

The UK's EU referendum arguably unsettled many taken for granted ideas about the role political campaigns play in processes like referendums. With its high voter turnout, the referendum is widely considered to have been an occasion in which new sorts of actors and groups participated, outside traditional partisan lines (Davies 2016). Although the referendum may have increased participation, debate still rages about its effects on, and consequences for, democratic politics in the UK. We thus propose to approach Brexit as a 'democratic situation' in the sense proposed by the editors of this volume (Birkbak and Papazu 2022).

The primary material we use to analyse this democratic situation is the blog post by Dominic Cummings[16] (Director of the Vote Leave campaign) which accompanied the open-source release of Vote Leave's campaigning software, as well as correspondence with campaign personnel and details of the software itself, which we also attempted to set up ourselves (see p. 246, below). The software release coincided with the aforementioned investigations into Vote Leave's campaigning practices by regulators, specifically the Digital, Culture, Media and Sport Committee (2019) inquiry on disinformation during the referendum. This latter inquiry (which concluded several years later) explicitly highlighted the lack of transparency around Vote Leave's campaigning practices and judged the campaign, in addition to its violating laws relating to campaign spending, to have been complicit in the data protection violations of the consultants it employed. The inquiry's final report notes that Cummings refused to give oral evidence to the inquiry and ignored a formal order requiring him to appear before the committee. Against this backdrop, Cummings' software release could be seen as an attempt to stage a counter-demonstration of transparency, purporting to lift the hood on the inner workings of Vote Leave's campaign and contradict criticisms, later formalised by the parliamentary inquiry, that the campaign deliberately misinformed the electorate.

What we are interested in here is the way notions of the democratising influence of technology, and arguments about the social construction of expertise, can (potentially at least) be made compatible with what others claim are anti-political practices. Cummings' account draws on many of the same tropes about the democratising influence of technology as the software firms discussed above but, as we show here, these have very particular *consequences* in a situation like Brexit.

In the blogpost, which was released shortly after the referendum result, Cummings announced the open-source release of a piece of software, called the Voter Intention Collection System (VICS), that he claimed enabled an interactive approach to campaigning and was able to mobilise the 'silent majority' of eurosceptic voters. Crucially, Cummings argued, the software allowed the Vote Leave campaign to develop data analytics and test predictive models that would inform, in real-time, the campaign's social media messaging approach.

In a text laced with popular anti-establishment rhetoric, Cummings presented Vote Leave's use of data science expertise as an attack on an out of touch political class and the 'traditional' expertise of its political machinery:

> This included a) integrating data from social media, online advertising, websites, apps, canvassing, direct mail, polls, online fundraising, activist feedback, and some new things we tried such as a new way to do polling ... and b) having experts in physics and machine learning do proper data science in the way only they can – i.e. far beyond the normal skills applied in political campaigns (Cummings 2016).

In a broadside against metropolitan pollsters, economic forecasters and marketing specialists, Cummings proposed that campaigns no longer need to rely on traditional techniques of political strategy and should instead 'hire physicists' to mine data. Extolling the novelty of VICS, he stated that:

> Amazingly there was essentially no web-based canvassing software system for the UK that allowed live use and live monitoring. There have been many attempts by political parties and others to build such systems. All failed, expensively and often disastrously (Cummings 2016).

Cumming's claims about the ascendance of data science and the decline of what is positioned as 'traditional' polling or campaign tactics mirrors much of the positioning we find in the campaign software publicity, discussed in the previous section. Yet, when we approached the data scientists working with Cummings for an interview, they declined, saying their firm did not 'talk about the polling it does'. This may be taken to suggest that the analysts themselves do not see such a clear separation between polling and data analytics. Similarly, a blog by an ex-Labour staffer who set up the software suggests many commonalities with the technologies used by conventional political party bureaucracies. He notes: 'For all talk about how radical and new this software is, this is worse than other parties' alternatives'.[17]

Cummings' claims to inject science into politics, demarcating a new data science from the old polling, have broader connotations in relation to the referendum process. While such invocations of science-led politics are in many senses simply technocratic, they are clearly intended by Cummings to be continuous with Vote Leave's broader attack on the EU. In one of the most publicised moments of the campaign, the leader of Vote Leave, MP Michael Gove, announced on prime-time television that 'the British people have had enough of experts'. Conflations between policy experts and political elites have subsequently played a central role in populist stagings of Brexit as a victory for the people against an out-of-touch political class. In this sense, the drive to replace political scientists with data scientists is not only an issue related to knowledge about voter behaviour but also invokes images of the political elite that were the target of the Leave campaign's anti-EU rhetoric. While we are accustomed in STS to showing the politics of different ways of constructing knowledge claims, we can see here how some actors might leverage similar arguments to reduce such contestation to simplistic oppositions – a hallmark of populist thought.

Not unlike the marketing materials surveyed above, Cummings adopts many tropes relating to grassroots mobilisation, emphasising the role of Vote Leave in mobilising 'people who usually ignore politics' against 'the Government machine supported by almost every organisation with power and money'. Such populist political rhetoric also appears to inform the ways that other, more technically literate, actors involved in the campaign understood the VICS software. One of its developers, for instance, described VICS in the following way:

> People on the ground would ... gather data to enrich the model in an iterative process, so the model improved organically over time as more data came in from the ground team. VICS facilitated the whole thing – highlighting [sic] key geographical areas to volunteers and telling them which streets to go to (based on the evolving model) (Personal communication 16 December 2016).

In this account, the software is presented as enhancing interactivity between campaign managers and volunteers via improved feedback. However, reading through the software code, we found a pdf guide designed for activists on the ground canvassing for the campaign. The data gathering process appears distinctly inflexible and closed to a range of bottom-up forms of political interaction. Much as with the other software, individual views were sought only on predefined issues prioritised by the directors of the campaign;[18] what counts as interactions appeared delimited by the management.

It is also worthwhile interrogating similar claims about how VICS promoted interactivity between Vote Leave and its supporters. Cummings deploys many tropes of grassroots political activism, but it is also clear that part of Vote Leave's strategy was to *discover* potential supporters. Indeed, in the blog post Cummings outlines one strategy the campaign developed for discovering potential Leave voters which involved a seemingly unrelated competition in which players were asked to predict sporting results. This allowed Vote Leave to gather data about a specific type of participant (sports fans) who they believed traditionally ignored politics and used this data to train their models. Despite the implication that data analytics allows campaigns to expand what counts as politically active people, financially incentivising groups to participate passively, or unknowingly, in campaigns implies a distinctly technocratic and paternalistic view of political mobilisation. Vote Leave's analytics models might be responsive but gathering data about people surreptitiously hardly seems interactive. While we can only speculate on the inner workings of the campaign, our point is that these claims about the politics of science and expertise take on distinctively populist meanings in relation to Vote Leave's claims to be wrestling back democracy from a technocratic elite.

Much like the marketing materials of other platforms, Cummings' account of VICS paints the software as 'levelling the playing field' for diverse political movements. In announcing the release of Vote Leave's software, Cummings referred to some basic tenets of the open-source movement, stating that its release was '…strictly on the basis that nobody can claim any intellectual property rights over it'. However, as with the other platforms, open-source software can be made available in different sorts of ways; the openness of software is in practice shaped by its ongoing maintenance as much as its legal status (Kelty 2008).

We attempted to set up VICS ourselves.[19] However, in its open-source form, the software is missing a key module and in its released form doesn't perform its basic functionality. According to one of the developers we spoke to: 'VICS depends on a [sic] upstream application which we called the "Voter API". This API sits in front of a database which contains information about the voters, and some aggregated measures (scores) to enrich the data and is essential for allowing the platform to communicate with the database. Without it the software is effectively an empty shell. By announcing its open-source release as a contribution to democratising the field of campaigning technology, Cummings seems to draw on a similar understanding of democratising as 'fair' used by firms like NationBuilder. However, there is no obvious community of coders contributing to or forking the code, and the ReadMe begins with the disclaimer 'This project is no longer maintained'. The incomplete VICS code and lack of engagement with its release suggests that Cummings' claims to be open-sourcing Vote Leave's technology fall considerably short of open-source conventions.

What is interesting about Cummings' blog post accompanying the software release is that it could be said to perform moves similar to those that many STS scholars have been seen to make in the past. Cummings is claiming that Vote Leave's approach was democratising; releasing VICS software, he claims, demonstrates not only that Vote Leave had the technology to understand the electorate better than its rivals, but that the software enabled Vote Leave to upend the traditional hierarchical way of involving experts in campaigns and make the campaigning process interactive and responsive. By releasing its software open-source, Cummings suggested, Vote Leave's campaign developed a technology that could expand participation, to open the door to novel interactions between a new breed of experts and the voters marginalised from existing political processes. While we do not think that STS researchers would ever fall into such blatant technological-determinism, STS notions associated with democratising science and technology, such as 'public engagement' or 'counter-expertise', are clearly not immune to populist variants of political thought.

As our analysis suggests, there are many reasons to be sceptical regarding Cummings' claims about the software, and against the backdrop of various inquiries into Vote Leave, we have suggested that the blog could also be read as a superficial attempt to demonstrate transparency and to justify campaigning practices that critics claimed deliberately misinformed the electorate. Indeed, based on the materials we have, Vote Leave's approach appears to have been more concerned with fitting voters into pre-defined framings of issues than with articulating their specific concerns. However, even though we are sceptical about the substantive claims Cummings makes, his text should still be sobering for an STS audience because it (rhetorically) claims to be enacting a democratising move on campaigning technology – in both senses of making technology available to more people and making it political. While we might disagree with Cummings' politics or position on the EU, we still might concede that his account draws attention to the importance of technology in the political arena and the ways in which it is often bracketed as a mundane aspect of political processes.

DISCUSSION AND CONCLUSIONS

Brexit is a situation that has brought into centre stage the kinds of relations between technology and politics which STS scholars have long raised, but it has also provoked questions about what makes specific political forms, like campaigns, democratic. Much of the debate about the referendum has focused on misinformation on social media, and in STS this has been discussed in the context of concepts like 'post-truth' and a populist rejection of expertise (Jasanoff and Simmet 2017; Sismondo 2017). Some (e.g., Fuller 2016, cited in Sismondo 2017) have raised questions about constructivist approaches to knowledge in STS, given that all sorts of actors in politics now seem to be using constructivist arguments for partisan political gain (see also Latour 2004). Such debates highlight that STS analysis of politics cannot be entirely agnostic when it comes to matters of epistemology in deciding what counts as a knowledge claim and what is simply myth, rumour, slander or lying. However, the focus on prominent scandals around firms like Cambridge Analytica has tended to bring only certain technologies into the foreground of these debates, while rendering other technologies as merely the background infrastructure of political practice.

Our analysis of Vote Leave's software release has shown that online misinformation is not only (and not even primarily) a matter of epistemology (how we know facts from falsehoods) but an issue that emerges alongside attempts to technologically innovate traditional formats of political practice. Vote Leave may well have used social media adverts to peddle myths about the EU, although in many respects this could be seen as simply a longstanding political campaigning technique deployed in a novel medium. What is more interesting for STS, we suggest, is the way in which an actor like Cummings deploys a gesture of open sourcing the campaign's software as a means of justifying such political practices as democratic. Claims made by Cummings about how technological innovation made the campaign interactive and responsive to voter concerns appear hard to substantiate from the software release. Yet the open-sourcing move by Cummings makes clear that technology lies at the heart of Vote Leave's politics: the campaign's relationship to voters, the referendum process, government and the EU are all, in Cummings' account, refracted through ideas about relations between science, technology and democracy, albeit that these may sometimes be considered contradictory. This case, we suggest, demonstrates why the political aims of democratising science and technology cannot be taken for granted, and why attending to the situations in which science and technology become invested with political capacities is crucial.

We have argued that, in analysing the role played by campaigning technologies in the referendum process, it is important to look at how actors draw boundaries between the technical and the political. It is not just important to question the tendencies of actors to fetishise technology and reduce democracy to a mere ideal, but also to attend closely to the political practices that such notions are deployed to justify. For example, Vote Leave's open-source software release claims to demonstrate transparency, yet this gesture towards technological openness (which we don't find particularly convincing) coincides with Cummings' refusal to give evidence before a parliamentary inquiry into misinformation during the referendum. One way to distinguish what Cummings is doing from our STS-informed position is through the concept of 'ontological gerrymandering' (Woolgar and Pawluch 1985), to bring a political term, appropriated by STS, back into the political arena. In STS, this term was used to describe how, in literature on social problems, an arbitrary division was created between 'social' factors and other, 'natural' or 'technical' factors. Similarly, in the case we have presented here, certain technologies are rendered as political, but not others, and this division affects claims about what counts as legitimate (or illegitimate) political practice. What this means for the present analysis is that STS scholars should not find themselves confronted with a choice between advocating for the democratising of technology or not; they should instead take a position on particular gerrymanderings of technology and politics. While in other situations, we might be able to get behind a critique of experts, or advocate for the open-source release of proprietary software, we have shown that Cummings' use of both of these moves – the staging of technology as a site of politics – is here compatible with a form of anti-political action.

We reserve a few final words for the substantive matter of Brexit. While the European Union has been widely understood as a primarily technocratic endeavour that suffers from democratic deficits, it has arguably also occasioned novel forms of politics (see Ehrenstein, this volume). As Barry's (2001) study of the EU highlighted, an analysis of the politics of European integration requires attending to technological controversies, from bathing water to air quality standards, and the contestations that emerge around practices like demonstration or testing that take place beyond the traditional sites of government and administration. The EU may be built on political talk about technological innovation and networks, but in practice the political contestations that shape it, Barry argues, are far more situated around sites where measurements are made or infrastructure is being developed. Such a view of EU politics was largely bracketed by the main protagonists in the Brexit referendum. As far as we can see, few attempts were made by any campaign to connect the sociotechnical issues underpinning EU politics to referendum debates about democracy. There was a missed opportunity, in other words, to connect public concerns about EU politics to issues (like air pollution) that shape the technological infrastructures and environments of everyday social life and have material consequences for democracy in the UK. Instead, somewhat ironically given the campaign's populist rhetoric of 'taking back control', the case of Vote Leave illustrates precisely why attempts to technologically innovate traditional forms of politics, like campaigns, are likely to simply reinstate expert-centric forms of political practice that may have little to do with addressing the democratic deficits between governing authorities and the publics they claim to represent.

ENDNOTES

1 See, for example: https://www.theguardian.com/technology/2017/may/07/the-great-british-brexit-robbery-hijacked-democracy (accessed 30 Jun 2018).
2 For example, the investigative journalist Carole Cadwalladr. See: https://www.ted.com/talks/carole_cadwalladr_facebook_s_role_in_brexit_and_the_threat_to_democracy#t-903238 (accessed 08 May 2020).
3 The software was released on the open-source platform GitHub and can be accessed here: https://github.com/celestial-winter/vics/ (accessed 02 May 2018)
4 We use the term 'misinformation' in a broader sense than is defined in the parliamentary inquiry (Digital, Culture, Media and Sport's Select Committee, 2019), which distinguishes between 'disinformation' and 'misinformation' as, respectively, the intentional or unintentional propagation of 'false information'. For our purposes the notion of 'false information' is unhelpful because it suggests that misinformation can be easily separated from contestations over expertise and the knowledge infrastructures of political campaigns.
5 It is notable that to date we have come across less than a handful of political commentaries written about Vote Leave's software. A blog by the BBC's Laura Kuenssberg, for instance, largely repeats the claims made on Cummings' blog, albeit with a few qualifying 'maybes'. See: https://www.bbc.co.uk/news/uk-politics-37841605 (accessed 30 Jun 2018).
6 The 2016 US election saw a series of particularly strong attacks on traditional polling methods and the use of aggregate pollsters like Nate Silver to predict election results (Loukissas and Pollock 2017). There is also a range of longstanding problems recognised by the polling industry, including low response rates, tensions between representative phone and unrepresentative internet polling, and public distrust of pollsters.

7 Such distinctions between 'new' data science expertise and 'traditional' political science techniques like polling, presented as a fait accompli, are harder to substantiate in terms of their applications to campaign management. Many of the tools we looked at centre on the not-so-ground-breaking technique of A/B testing, a longstanding practice within market research, used to test and trial messages and advertisements but also assign 'responsiveness scores' to contacts in the database.

8 Making them a 'type 1' API (Helmond 2015).

9 In its basic premise, 'software as a service' is not unlike the dominant business models of the software industry, which are widely organised around licensing agreements rather than individual ownership.

10 In the UK context, Anstead (2017) has similarly interviewed politicians and campaign managers on the effects of data driven campaigns in the 2015 general election.

11 Such studies, importantly, make clear why participation should not be conflated with democratisation.

12 Available at: https://nationbuilder.com/myths (accessed 30 April 2020)

13 Available at: https://tools.bluestatedigital.com/kb/article/what-is-a-share-page (accessed 20 April 2020)

14 Available at: https://www.thegroundwork.com/ (accessed September 2017, site no longer accessible)

15 Available at: https://nationbuilder.com/allsaints (accessed 30 April 2020)

16 Since we started working on this topic in 2016, Cummings has gone from being a little-known campaign director to the UK Prime Minister's Chief Adviser, a position that he left during the Covid pandemic. He is now a polemical media figure who is both credited as a mastermind strategist behind Brexit and caricatured as a Silicon Valley-inflected Rasputin in equal measure.

17 Available at: https://twitter.com/jshmrtncrrngtn/status/793845659946266624 (accessed 10 May 2021).

18 This point is also raised by the ex-Labour staffer introduced above, who wrote up his blog in an article for the *New Statesman* (Carrington 2016)

19 We set up the software on a virtual machine, using the Ubuntu 16.04 operating system with some help from our colleague Marcus Burkhardt.

ACKNOWLEDGEMENTS

We are grateful for the comments and feedback provided by participants at the authors' workshop convened by the editors in November 2017, as well as those of the editors themselves and the anonymous reviewers.

REFERENCES

Anstead, N., 'Data-driven Campaigning in the 2015 United Kingdom General Election', *The International Journal of Press/Politics*, 22 (2017), 294–313.

Barocas, S., 'The Price of Precision: Voter Microtargeting and its Potential Harms to the Democratic Process', *Proceedings of the First Edition Workshop on Politics, Elections and Data*, (2012), pp. 31–36.

Barry, A., *Political Machines: Governing a Technological Society*, (London: The Athlone Press, 2001).

Bartlett, J., J. Birdwell, and L. Reynolds, *Like, Vote, Share*, (Demos, 2014), <https://www.demos.co.uk/files/Like_Share_Vote_-_web.pdf?1415749150> [accessed 3 July 2018].

Bennett, W. L., and A. Segerberg, *The Logic of Connective Action: Digital Media and the Personalization of Contentious Politics* (New York: Cambridge University Press, 2013).

Birkbak, A., and I. Papazu, 'Introducing Democratic Situations' in A. Birkbak, and I. Papazu, eds, *Democratic Situations*, (Manchester: Mattering Press, 2022) [this volume]

Bijker, W. E., and J. Law, *Shaping Technology/Building Society: Studies in Sociotechnical Change*, (Cambridge, MA: The MIT Press, 1992).

Bowker, G., and S. L. Star, *Sorting Things Out*, (Cambridge, MA: The MIT Press, 1999).

Bucher, T., 'Want to Be on the Top? Algorithmic Power and the Threat of Invisibility on Facebook'. *New Media and Society*, 14 (2012), 1164–1180.

Callon, M., P. Lascoumes, and Y. Barthe, *Acting in An Uncertain World: An Essay on Technical Democracy* (Cambridge, MA: The MIT Press, 2009).

Chilvers, J., and M. Kearnes, *Remaking Participation: Science, Environment and Emergent Publics* (London: Routledge, 2016).

Carrington, J., 'The Vote Leave Campaign Wasn't as Clever as It Thinks It Was', *The New Statesman*, 10 July 2016, <https://www.newstatesman.com/politics/staggers/2016/11/vote-leave-campaign-wasn-t-clever-it-thinks-it-was> [accessed 3 July 2018].

Cummings, D., 'On the Referendum #20: The Campaign, Physics and Data Science – Vote Leave's 'Voter Intention Collection System' (VICS) Now Available For All. In: *Dominic Cummings's Blog*, 20 October 2016, <https://dominiccummings.com/2016/10/29/on-the-referendum-20-the-campaign-physics-and-data-science-vote-leaves-voter-intention-collection-system-vics-now-available-for-all/> [accessed 30 June 2018].

Davies, W., 'Thoughts on the Sociology of Brexit', in Verso Books, eds, *The Brexit*

Crisis: A Verso Report. (London: Verso, 2016), <https://www.versobooks.com/books/2352-the-brexit-crisis> [accessed 30 June 2018].

De Vries, G., 'What is Political in Sub-Politics? How Aristotle Might Help STS', *Social Studies of Science* 37, (2007), 781–809.

Digital, Culture, Media and Sport Committee., *Disinformation and 'Fake News': Final Report.* (House of Commons, 2019), <https://publications.parliament.uk/pa/cm201719/cmselect/cmcumeds/1791/1791.pdf> [accessed 1 November 2019].

Ehrenstein, V., 'Technocratic Activism: Environmental Organisations, Carbon Markets and European Bureaucracy' in A. Birkbak, and I. Papazu, eds, *Democratic Situations,* (Manchester: Mattering Press, 2022) [this volume]

Gillespie, T., 'The Politics of "Platforms"', *New Media & Society*, 12 (2010), 347–364.

Helmond, A., *The Web as Platform: Data Flows in Social Media* (PhD Thesis, University of Amsterdam, 2015).

Howard, P. N., *New Media Campaigns and the Managed Citizen* (Cambridge: Cambridge University Press, 2006).

Howard, P. N., and B. Kollanyi, 'Bots,# Strongerin, and# Brexit: Computational Propaganda During the UK-EU Referendum', (2016), <https://ssrn.com/abstract=2798311> [accessed 30 June 2018]

Information Commissioners Office, 'Investigation into the Use of Data Analytics in Political Campaigns: A Report to Parliament', (2018) <https://ico.org.uk/media/action-weve-taken/2260271/investigation-into-the-use-of-data-analytics-in-political-campaigns-final-20181105.pdf> [accessed 1 November 2019]

Issenberg, S., *The Victory Lab: The Secret Science of Winning Campaigns* (New York: Broadway Books, 2012).

Jasanoff, S., 'Science and Democracy', in U. Felt, R. Fouché, C. A. Miller, and L. Smith-Doerr, eds, *The Handbook of Science and Technology Studies,* (Cambridge, MA: The MIT Press, 2020), 259–288.

Jasanoff, S., and H. R. Simmet, 'No Funeral Bells: Public Reason in a "Post-Truth" Age', *Social Studies of Science*, 47 (2017), 751–770.

Katz, E., and P. Lazarsfeld, *Personal Influence: The Part Played by People in the Flow of Mass Communications,* (Columbia University: Bureau of Applied Social, 1955; repr. Taylor & Francis Group, 2005).

Kelty, C. M., *Two Bits: The Cultural Significance of Free Software* (Durham, NC: Duke University Press, 2008).

Kitchin, R., *The Data Revolution: Big Data, Open Data, Data Infrastructures and Their Consequences.* (London: Sage, 2014).

Kreiss, D., *Taking Our Country Back: The Crafting of Networked Politics from Howard Dean to Barack Obama* (Oxford: Oxford University Press, 2012).

———, *Prototype Politics: Technology-intensive Campaigning and the Data of Democracy* (Oxford: Oxford University Press, 2016).

Latour, B., 'Why Has Critique Run out of Steam: From Matters of Fact to Matters of Concern', *Critical Inquiry*, 30 (2004), 225–248.

Lippmann, W., *Public Opinion* (New York: Harcourt, Brace and Company, 1922; repr. Jefferson Publication, 2015).

Loukissas, Y., and A. Pollock, 'After Big Data Failed: The Enduring Allure of Numbers in the Wake of the 2016 US Election', *Engaging Science, Technology, and Society*, 3 (2017), 16–20.

MacKenzie, D., and J. Wajcman, *The Social Shaping of Technology: How the Refrigerator Got Its Hum* (Milton Keynes: Open University Press, 1985).

Marres, N., 'The Issues Deserve More Credit: Pragmatist Contributions to the Study of Public Involvement in Controversy', *Social Studies of Science*, 37 (2007), 759–780.

———, 'Why Political Ontology Must be Experimentalized: On Eco-Show Homes as Devices of Participation', *Social Studies of Science*, 43 (2013), 417–443.

Marres, N., and J. Lezaun, 'Materials and Devices of the Public: An Introduction', *Economy and Society*, 40 (2011), 489–509.

Mouffe, C., *On the Political* (London: Routledge, 2005).

Nelkin, D. E., *Controversy: Politics of Technical Decisions* (London: Sage Publications, 1979).

O'Reilley, T., 'What is Web 2.0: Design Patterns and Business Models for the Next Generation of Software', (2005) <http://oreilly.com/ web2/archive/what-is-web-20.html> (Accessed 11 May 2020).

Osborne, T., and N. Rose, 'Do the Social Sciences Create Phenomena? The Example of Public Opinion Research', *The British Journal of Sociology*, 50 (1999), 367–396.

Puschman, C., and J. Burgess, 'Metaphors of Big Data', *International Journal of Communication*, 8 (2014), 1690–1709.

Sismondo, S., 'Post-Truth?', *Social Studies of Science*, 47 (2017), 3–6.

The Electoral Commission., *Investigation: Vote Leave Ltd, Mr Darren Grimes, BeLeave and Veterans for Britain*, (2018a) <https://www.electoralcommission.org. uk/who-we-are-and-what-we-do/our-enforcement-work/investigations/ investigation-vote-leave-ltd-mr-darren-grimes-beleave-and-veterans-britain> [accessed 1 November 2019]

———, *Investigation: Leave.EU Group Limited*, (2018b) <https://www. electoralcommission.org.uk/who-we-are-and-what-we-do/our-enforcement-work/investigations/investigation-leaveeu-group-limited> [accessed 1 November 2019]

van Dijck, J., *The Culture of Connectivity: A Critical History of Social Media*, (Oxford: Oxford University Press, 2013).

Woolgar, S., and J. Lezaun, 'The Wrong Bin Bag: A Turn to Ontology in Science and Technology Studies?', *Social Studies of Science*, 43 (2013), 321–340.

Woolgar, S., and D. Neyland, *Mundane Governance: Ontology and Accountability*, (Oxford: Open University Press, 2013).

Woolgar, S., and D. Pawluch, 'Ontological Gerrymandering: The Anatomy of Social Problems Explanations', *Social Problems*, 32 (1985), 214–227.

THE CONCEIVED CHILD: MATERIAL POLITICS IN THE POLISH 'WAR ON GENDER'

Andrzej W. Nowak

INTRODUCTION: FROM HEGEMONIC TO ONTOLOGICAL POLITICS

IN THIS CHAPTER, I FOCUS ON THE INSTALLATION OF A SPECIFIC OBJECT IN the ongoing, so-called 'war on gender' in Poland (Duda 2016, Kováts et al. 2015). The object is material-discursive. It is based on the narrative of a 'conceived child' (or 'nasciturus'), which is the Catholic-conservative framing of the foetus as a child already at the moment of conception. This narrative gains material form in the shapes of a plastic figurine and a Tamagotchi-like app. My suggestion is that in order to understand the Polish 'war on gender', it is necessary to pay attention to how political campaigns are grounded in material objects and how these objects take part in shaping democratic situations.

As Gramsci theorised, 'winning common sense' is a key aspect of gaining hegemony (Gencarella 2010). In my understanding of hegemony, I follow Laclau and Mouffe's reinterpretation of Gramsci's (2014) classic approach. I also draw on Laclau and Mouffe's concept of 'radical democracy'. In their perspective, democracy is an always fragile and unstable result of pro-democratic hegemonic actions under constant threat from counter-hegemonic activities. Here, hegemony is understood as a discursive formation that manages to unify a social and political space through the establishment of 'nodal points' and 'chains of equivalence' defining this space (Laclau and Mouffe 2014: 136).

This understanding of the production of networks of power is not without similarities to the foundational actor-network theory (ANT) concept of 'translation' (see, for example, Latour 1988). Laclau and Mouffe, however, remain attached to the analysis of discourse and language, thus losing the material and institutional moment central to understanding how the democratic situation studied in this chapter unfolds in practice, as the 'war on gender' is to a large extent a war fought by material means. In Laclau and Mouffe's (2014: 151–152) language of radical democracy, the process of gaining nodal points is based on appropriating and redefining central linguistic terms and concepts present in public discourse. Against this understanding of radical democracy, I argue that struggles to 'win common sense' with regard to gender in Poland in recent years are not primarily discursive, but happen through ontological politics (See also Mol 1999).

In Annemarie Mol's (1999: 74) words, ANT underlines 'that the reality we live with is one performed in a variety of practices', with the radical consequence that reality has become multiple. What follows is that 'there are *options* between the various versions of an object: which one to perform'? To supplement Mol, I propose my own concept of 'ontological imagination' (Nowak 2013), which underlines the need for an activist positioning requiring 'a radical, adventurous imagination, complemented by a purposive will to act' (Nowak 2016: 377). If we understand ontological politics as performative and able to influence future states of the world by means of crafted objects and practices, this means we must go beyond the purely analytical level, as the political moment of ontological imagination is equally important (Nold 2018). With this imagination we must (re-)construct ontological assemblies in a politically desired direction. In the face of conflicts such as the 'war on gender', it is my position that STS researchers ought to dare to design and install socio-material objects around which democratic onto-hegemonic networks can develop and transform our communities.

In this, I follow Papadopoulos' idea of 'alterontologies': alternative 'ways of life' which can be crafted and performed (Papadopoulos, 2018: 19). Ontologies are an important aspect of 'more-than-social movements' (ibid.). As Papadopoulos puts it: 'The political organisation of a social movement does not preexist the making of alternative forms of life; rather, political organising is the crafting of alterontologies' (ibid: 22). However, contrary to Papadopoulos' emphasis on emancipatory movements, I claim that alterontologies may also be created by anti-democratic movements. Here, the terms 'craft' and 'caring', which are important for Papadopoulos, cease to have a self-evident, positive connotation (ibid: 23; see also Papazu, this volume). With inspiration from Laclau and Mouffe, I suggest that the production of the 'worlds we live in' is done by various forces, often in agonism (2014). In the clash of alterontologies, their agonistic incompatibility requires that ontological politics are not only crafted and taken care of, but also made part of a struggle.

To put it in Gramsci's terms, a discussion about democracy requires hegemony to be addressed, as democracy is always fragile and contested. This is not too far from the perspective of Andrew Barry, who argues that 'politics is not something that should be grounded. On the contrary, a radical democratic politics is one which has to live with the fact that the grounds of politics are not given' (Barry 2007: 288). The 'disenchanted' analysis of democratic processes that I am putting forward in this chapter draws on the idea that democracy emerges as a result of hegemonic struggles (Laclau and Mouffe 2014) and that these struggles have a strong material and ontological dimension (Asdal 2008; Huvila 2011). In this approach, I am indebted to Clegg's proposition that Laclau and Mouffe's theory of hegemony can be complemented by an STS/ANT-inspired material analysis (Clegg 1989).

I approach democracy as something that constantly needs to be constructed, installed, enacted and stabilised (see also Barry 2007). Accordingly, in this chapter, I do not treat the notion of 'gender ideology' simply as a '(mis)interpretation or (mis)representation of (de)constructivist feminist and queer theories, which is used as a background story to delegitimise all kinds of progressive policies in the fields of gender and sexuality' (Mayer and Sauer 2017: 24). My argument is that the emphasis should be shifted from the epistemological level (that is, talking about misinterpretation) – on which Laclau and Mouffe also find themselves – to the ontological level. In the case of the Polish 'war on gender' I suggest it is less important who is epistemologically right than what makes ontological might. That is, it is crucial to appreciate how the world is transformed through processes of embodiment and the incorporation of policies into material and ontological infrastructures, and who benefits from these transformations (Latour 2000: 216–235; Oreskes and Conway 2010).

By asking the two sides of the 'war', I show how and why the counter-movement to the Catholic-conservative 'anti-gender' hegemony does not manage to successfully mobilise beyond discursive-symbolic politics. With its protests, it enacts something akin to the radical democratic politics suggested by Laclau and Mouffe, which lacks a powerful material-ontological element. Contrarily, and perhaps surprisingly, the conservatives seem to have recognised the value and potential of an ontological politics grounded in material artefacts that become endowed with great significance and are capable of a wide public reach and influence.

THE 'WAR ON GENDER'

Before I turn to the case of the 'conceived child', a few remarks about the 'war on gender' in Poland are called for. This 'war' can be traced back to the Polish government's rejection of the Istanbul Convention on violence against women in April 2012, initiating a three-year period of heated debate (Szczygielska 2019). The most intense phase of the 'war on gender' began on 29 December 2013, when an 'anti-gender' message was read out during the sermons in all Poland's parishes. The controversy reached a climax in 2016 with the so-called Black Protest organised by women and feminist activists, the largest mass protest in Poland since the communist collapse (Suchanow 2020). This protest, and subsequent women's strikes, caused the government to retreat and freeze a restrictive anti-abortion law that was in the works.

During the 'war on gender', the notion of an 'ideology of gender' became dominant in the Polish public sphere (Duda 2016: 137–408). The notion was circulated through the infrastructure of the Catholic church: in parishes, on the radio station 'Radio Maryja' and in public lectures. The number and intensity of these lectures was much greater than the activity of academic gender studies (Duda 2016: 402–403; Graff and Korolczuk 2017: 182–186). 'Anti-gender' books were published and circulated in large quantities, printed on good quality paper and in hardcover. Anti-gender activists clearly understood the performativity of books as political objects. For instance, the book 'Dyktatura gender' ('Gender dictatorship') was published in an encyclopaedia style with a preface by Pope Benedict XVI, on expensive chalk paper and with high quality illustrations and photos.

As observed by Mayer and Sauer (2017), the conservative construction of 'gender ideology' 'is a crucial notion in the establishment of a "chain of equivalences" that links concerns over anti-abortion and women's rights to anti-LGBTIQ and anti-feminist agendas, as well as to Catholic-conservative, right-wing and neoliberal stances on social policies in general' (ibid: 24). As such, while the case I discuss in this chapter has to do with abortion, it should be understood in the context of a wider controversy and struggle over gender and sexuality in Poland in recent decades. This is a key site of democratic politics, insofar as the conflict between 'progressive' and 'conservative' forces is shaping and transforming Polish society in a struggle for hegemony.

THE CASE OF THE 'CONCEIVED CHILD'

The concept of a 'conceived child' has been present in Poland since the beginning of the 1980s through social campaigns, posters, lectures, articles, radio and television. As a notable example, the movie *The Silent Scream* – screened during religious lessons and in churches – shows how, during an abortion, the unborn child dies in pain, after which the surgeon throws the dismembered body into a cold metal vessel. As Petchesky (1987: 264) puts it:

> The Silent Scream marked a dramatic shift in the contest over abortion imagery. With formidable cunning, it translated the still and by-then stale images of foetus-as-'baby' into real-time video, thus (1) giving those images an immediate interface with the electronic media; (2) transforming antiabortion rhetoric from a mainly religious/mystical to a medical/technological mode; and (3) bringing the foetal image 'to life'.

In Poland, this message was circulated first in catechetical rooms, then in schools. In the movie, the narrator claims that the foetus tries to 'escape' from the surgical instrument. The images in the film are slowed down, and then – when the surgeon's tools are introduced – accelerated to create the impression of anxiety and dramatic escape. The mass reception of this film and its ability to intertwine the anti-abortion narrative with Polish common sense and folklore is evidenced by the creation of the song *Ballada o nienarodzinym dziecku* [Ballad of the Unborn Child], which paraphrases scenes from the movie (Gencarella 2010). The song is still popular among Catholic youth, scout associations and right-wing anti-abortion movements in Poland.

The 'conceived child' narrative redefined the concepts of foetus, conception and child, and became an important reference point in Polish debates on LGBT questions, women's rights, abortion and the position of the Catholic Church in public life. The installation of the 'conceived child' in political imaginaries and common sense in Poland is arguably part of the reason why it was possible for the government to ignore a petition with 1.3 million signatures and pass a 1992 law that was extremely restrictive in comparison to other European standards. Abortion was forbidden and criminalised except when pregnancy is a threat to the mother's life or a result of rape (see also Mayer and Sauer 2017; Hodžić and Štulhofer 2017). In practice, legal abortion is almost banned in Poland.

The corporeality and apparent objectivity of the 'conceived child' is sustained by a variety of strategies. Particularly interesting are the plastic figurines distributed among school children by the Catholic organisation Bractwo Małych Stópek (Little Feet's Brotherhood). An idealised plastic model of a foetus called 'Jaś' ('Johnny') is presented on their website as follows:

> Meet Johnny! Although only 5 cm in size, he is a great defender of life. Thanks to him, many unborn children have been saved from abortion – this educational model makes us aware of the 10-week-old unborn child. Most people who see or hold a faithful model of a child in their own hands in the 10th week of their foetal life change their minds about abortion, among other things. Johnny can also reach your hands and save another unborn life together with you.

Gadżety

Model edukacyjny „Jaś"

Poznaj Jasia! Jaś, choć mierzy zaledwie 5 cm, jest wielkim Obrońcą Życia. Dzięki niemu wiele nienarodzonych dzieci zostało ocalonych od aborcji – ten edukacyjny model uświadamia, jak wygląda 10-tygodniowe nienarodzone dziecko. Większość osób, które na własne oczy zobaczy, bądź potrzyma w ręku wierny model dziecka w 10 tygodniu życia płodowego, zmienia swoje zdanie na temat m.in. aborcji. Jaś może trafić również do Twoich rąk i razem z Tobą ocalić kolejne nienarodzone życie.

Chcesz zorganizować wydarzenie pro-life? Skorzystaj z materiałów ed Powiadomienia zostały zablokowane Małych Stópek

FIG. 12.1 'Little Johnny' figurine as an anti-abortion gadget and 'Fighter for Life' in an online shop: https://fundacjamalychstopek.pl/product/pakiet-akcji-kup-pieluchy-podaj-jasia-2-jasie/

The materiality of the plastic figurine reinforces the effect that the use of ultrasound scans have had on the anti-abortion movement globally (Burri and Dumit 2008: 307). Now, thanks in part to 3D-printing technology, anti-abortionists can move beyond pictures and change the relationship between children and early pregnancy, turning foetuses into children from the moment of conception.

The flagship product of the Little Feet's Brotherhood is a Tamagotchi-like mobile phone application called 'Adoptuj życie' (Adopt a Life), which allows users to 'adopt' and 'grow' a nasciturus on their phone. For the purpose of this chapter, I adopted three virtual 'conceived children'. Two of them are now 'born', while the last one is in its fourth week of pregnancy. The app feeds the user daily quasi-biological stories about how your virtually adopted 'conceived child' is growing and changing. Furthermore, your 'conceived child' will receive your 'daily prayer', which you are reminded about through a pop-up message in the app. You can also observe a 'scan' of your 'conceived child', and even interact with it in various ways (see screenshots below).

As these screenshots illustrate, the application mimics scientific visualisations. A person adopting a 'conceived child' has the impression of participating in a quasi-experiment of growing virtual life. The full name of this unexpectedly

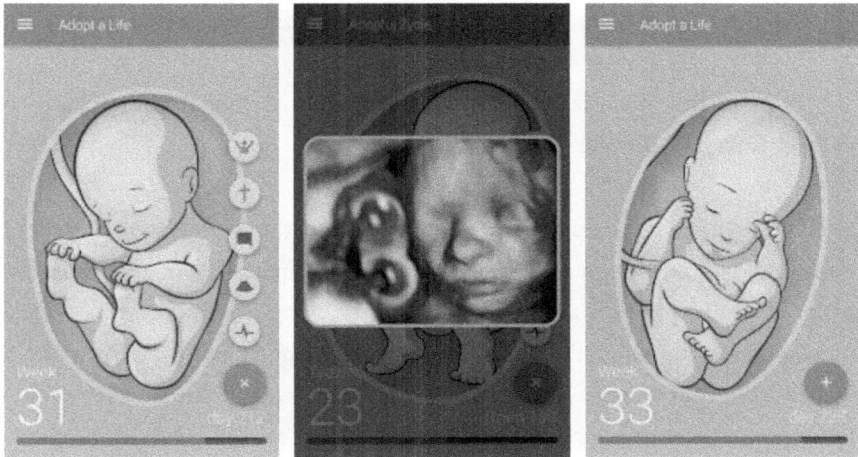

FIG. 12.2   The app offers a 'scan' of your virtually adopted 'conceived child'. Different options are available at different stages of development. At 6 weeks, for example, you can listen to the heartbeat by pressing an icon with an ECG/EKG symbol. Screenshots from the app Adopt a Life, with permission from the maker Bartosz Scheuer.

intriguing post-human character is 'a mobile assistant for the spiritual adoption of the conceived child'. By virtue of this object, seemingly traditional, even conservative, political forces are able to use the affordances of modern communications infrastructures for their purposes. In a similar way, anti-gender forces used the popularity of the Pokemon game to produce their own application in which Pikachu is saved from abortion (Neil Datta 2018: 23).

The materiality of the smartphone application also created unexpected effects. The power of the application was paradoxically revealed in a situation where the digital quality of the intervention could have become its greatest weakness. An unsuccessful software update triggered a series of strong reactions from users who felt like a virtual abortion was taking place (quotes from the app store; author's translation):

ANKA xD: 12 June 2017: The application was great in itself, but I was in the 11th week and lost everything, and I felt some kind of bond with this child. I've lost precious time which will not come back, and I hope that somebody will advise you on these unfortunate updates.

Smerfetka Smerf 12 June 2017: The application is great, but after an upgrade, the child has reset itself.

Laura L.: Everything is great, but after an update it has reset itself and this is very unpleasant.

By using the application myself, I became aware of similarities to processes of identity-creation through self-tracking (Bode and Kristensen 2016). By measuring the user's physical activity, digital self-tracking devices create a virtual *doppelgänger* with which the user lives, negotiates and enacts their lives with a new awareness of their physicality. In the case of this application, a virtual *doppelgänger-foetus*, the ideologised political object of a 'conceived child', becomes part of the life of the user in a similar way: it lives with the user and negotiates and enacts his or her own life in a certain register. The temporary breakdown of the application revealed how strongly intertwined some users had become with their virtual 'child'. The unpleasant experience of the unplanned technical failure of the update that caused the 'conceived children' to 'reset themselves' may have instilled an even greater animosity against abortion in the users who had now, so to speak, lived through 'something similar'.

In sum, the Catholic Church used the app and the figurine to establish robust political-hegemonic networks, combining new and previously installed political objects, such as the *Silent Scream* movie from the 1980s. The 'conceived child' gained the constancy of a fact – an object strong enough to offer new stability to the anti-abortion agenda.

MATERIAL TACTICS OF THE PRO-ABORTION MOVEMENT

The 'conceived child' offers an example of how politics can be ontologised through the creation of durable objects which can resist discursive struggles and to which political ideas and projects can be delegated. The sturdiness of the figure is apparent not least in the way the failed app update did not turn the users off the app (or the cause), but instead served to strengthen the users' anti-abortion sentiments and attachment to the 'conceived child' of the app. I suggest that STS scholars, as well as (other) progressive actors, may have something to learn from this seemingly conscious use of ontological politics: namely, how to produce more effective democratic situations by grounding these materially, rather than relying on more traditional symbolic-linguistic politics of resistance.

In this last part of the chapter, I turn to clashes between the pro- and anti-abortion movements, where pro-abortion and feminist activists in Poland attempt to also use material interventions, partly in response to the interventions made by the anti-abortion movement. During a pseudo-scientific lecture with the title 'Gender as a destruction of a human being and the family', delivered on 5 December 2013 by a priest and lecturer from the Theology Department at Adam Mickiewicz University, a young man in a golden dress jumped onto a table and started to parody the lecture. At the same time, a group of young women started chanting pro-equality slogans. The 'boy in a dress' figure was a reference to previous attempts by the anti-abortion movement to undermine the legitimacy of a programme for more 'gender-sensitive' kindergartens in Poland. Undercover police officers quickly suppressed the protesters with tasers, and a riot police squad was called. The events triggered intense media discussions. Three months after the event, the lecturer-priest published a mass-distributed booklet presenting his version of the events with the emblematic 'boy in a dress' activist on the cover with the title: *Gender exposed – A story of a lecture* (Bortkiewicz 2014). Due to asymmetries in access to resources between the pro-abortion activists and the well-established anti-abortion movement, this type of mass-distribution tactics is not available to the protesters. As such, this unequal battle reveals the material power of artefacts as carriers of politics. The anti-abortionist booklet is likely to have had a larger impact than the protest that inspired it.

Another intriguing situation is the series of 'Black protest' demonstrations held across the country against the tightening of the anti-abortion law (Bielinska-Kowalewska 2017; Korolczuk 2017; Petö, Grzebalska, and Post 2016; Szczygielska 2019). As mentioned, the protest was fuelled when the Polish Parliament received a draft abortion law which tightened the already restrictive law from 1992. On 3 April 2016, demonstrations against the law were held in big cities all over Poland. In Warsaw, several thousand protesters gathered in front of the parliament. A Facebook group, *Dziewuchy dziewuchom* ('Girls for Girls'), launched on 1 April, gained 100,000 fans in ten days (Bielinska-Kowalewska 2017). In the beginning, protestors used various symbols, with the clothes hanger being used as an unpleasant sign of illegal home abortions. However, an unplanned material contribution shaped the 'Black Protest' marches on 3 October 2016. On this day, which is now referred to as 'Czarny Poniedziałek' ('Black Monday'), thousands of Polish women went on strike to oppose the proposed legislation for a total ban on abortion (Korolczuk 2016). It happened to be raining, and most protesters carried umbrellas. The media coverage of the gatherings showed a massive number of unfolded black umbrellas, which came to play their own performative role as they became a new symbol of the movement (Sieracka 2018: 25).

The crowd of women with umbrellas, often black due to the colour code of the black protest, took on a performative quality in Polish public life. Photos distributed on social media depicting squares filled with umbrellas were suggestive of the strength of the protest and influenced its later representations. The protests followed the well-recognised dynamics of the materiality of public demonstrations in urban squares (Kowalewski 2018). At the same time, the mass presence of umbrellas redefined this type of expression. The combination of political mobilisation (based partially on the party 'Razem') and the mass use of social media (such as the Facebook group 'Girls for Girls') created a temporary network that could 'collide' with and challenge the hegemonic infrastructure created by the anti-abortion movement and the Catholic Church (Szczygielska 2019). Although initially only by accident, the black umbrella became a symbol of resistance and created an ideological generator so strong that it lent its strength to other feminist initiatives. The umbrella decisively replaced the clothes hanger ('wieszak'), the symbol disseminated during earlier protests. The clothes hanger, with its direct connection to the procedure of illegal abortion, is a dramatic symbol that can mobilise strong emotions, but it can be problematic for women with more moderate political stances. The use of umbrellas as the primary symbolic object turned out to be much more useful as a less loaded signifier. Women (and the men supporting them), regardless of the spectrum of views on abortion, could literally fit under the umbrella of the protest.

An example of a more direct counter-strategy to the 'conceived child' as an ontological generator is the campaign 'Far From the Hospital', which focused on combating anti-abortion posters depicting foetuses. Instead of attacking human political opponents, the activists focused on the destabilisation of the political object itself, that is, the 'conceived child'. A similar but more radical (and humorous) campaign is the 'Make jam at home, do not buy it in a store', organised by a radical feminist group.

The group creates banners similar to those made by anti-abortion organisations, which depict foetuses after an abortion. On the feminist banners, these visuals are mimicked and replaced by portions of red fruit jam. The action is accompanied by slogans encouraging home-made jam products. This action suggests that activists have recognised pictures co-producing and sustaining the metaphysics of the conceived child in relation to (gory) abortions to be a node stabilising the hegemonic anti-abortion network.

In sum, the emergence of a heterogeneous ontological counter-network began with the power of the umbrellas in the Black Protest, which then lent their power to an initiative fighting photos of foetuses in the public space. The latter initiative combines the strength of a political party, a social movement and media attention to destabilise the political object of 'the conceived child', as well as to enrol new allies. However, these examples of counter-reactions are all fairly unplanned, as well as reactive, and as such they do not set the agenda, nor do they constitute a coherent and institutionalised strategy. There remain significant asymmetries in the material politics surrounding abortion in Poland.

CONCLUSION

My purpose in this chapter has been to explore the material objects of a recent wave of political-ideological struggle taking place in Poland around the issue of abortion. In order for STS scholarship to relate to these unruly and problematic democratic situations, I propose a radicalised version of ontological politics, where the emphasis is placed both on ontological reconfigurations of power and on transforming these in order to strengthen the sort of democratic policies desired by the analyst. This approach can draw on the project of political design outlined by Christian Nold (2018: 60):

> I suggest a practice-based notion of ontology from STS offers strong potential for politically transformative design. This approach sees socio-material design as enacting multiple realities. Instead of metaphysical commitments, this presents a pragmatic focus on everyday practices that allow political choices to be made between multiple realities.

Such 'political choices' are not readily available in the material-semiotic entanglements of ontological politics (Mol 1999). As the last part of the analysis has shown, ontological politics is dependent both on the availability of resources and on the strength and reach of the networks employed. However, as I have indicated in this chapter, Catholic-conservative forces in Poland are currently deploying significant and widespread material-political interventions, including 3D-printed plastic figurines of foetuses accompanied by smartphone apps. The counter-struggles by the women's movement are loosely assembled, and although they deploy artefacts such as umbrellas and banners, these continue to work more on the conventional symbolic level of social movement politics, as described by Laclau and Mouffe, allowing the Catholic-conservative forces a somewhat surprising role as the more 'technologically enhanced' actor. To act in relation to this kind of onto-hegemonic politics, STS scholars, as well as emancipatory movements, must sensitise themselves to ontological political situations and explore the political subjectivities associated with them in order to contribute more effectively to shaping material realities that make their goals and values achievable.

REFERENCES

Asdal, K., 'On Politics and the Little Tools of Democracy: A Down-to-Earth Approach', *Distinktion: Scandinavian Journal of Social Theory*, 9 (2008), 11–26.

Barry, A., 'Political Invention', in K. Asdal, B. Brenna, and I. Moser, eds, *Technoscience: The politics of interventions* (Oslo: Unipub, 2007).

Bielinska-Kowalewska, K., '# czarnyprotest: The Black Protest for Abortion Rights in Poland', *New Politics*, 16 (2017), 53.

Beynon-Jones, S. M., 'Re-visioning Ultrasound through Women's Accounts of Pre-abortion Care in England', *Gender & Society: Official Publication of Sociologists for Women in Society*, 29 (2015), 694–715.

Bode, M., and D. B. Kristensen, 'The Digital Doppelgänger within: A Study on Self-Tracking and the Quantified Self Movement', in R. Canniford and D. Bajde, eds, *Assembling Consumption: Researching Actors, Networks and Markets*, (London: Routledge, 2016), pp. 119–134.

Bogost, I., *Alien Phenomenology, or, What It is Like to Be a Thing* (Minneapolis, MN: University of Minnesota Press, 2012).

Bortkiewicz, P., *Historia jednego wykładu czyli gender zdemaskowany* (Warsaw: Prohibita, 2014).

Burri, R. V., and J. Dumit, 'Social Studies of Scientific Imaging and Visualization', in U. Felt et al., eds, *The Handbook of Science and Technology Studies* (Cambridge MA: The MIT Press, 2008), pp. 297–317.

Clegg, S. R., *Frameworks of Power* (London: Sage, 1989).

Duda, M., *Dogmat płci: Polska wojna z gender* (Gdansk: Wydawnictwo Naukowe Katedra, 2016).

Gencarella, S. O., 'Gramsci, Good Sense, and Critical Folklore Studies', *Journal of Folklore Research*, 47 (2010), 221.

Graff, A., and E. Korolczuk, '"Worse than communism and Nazism put together": War on Gender in Poland', in R. Kuhar, and D. Paternotte, eds, *Anti-Gender Campaigns in Europe: Mobilizing against Equality.* (London, New York: Rowman & Littlefield International, 2017), pp. 176–194.

Hodžić, A., and A. Štulhofer, 'Embryo, Teddy Bear-Centaur and the Constitution: Mobilizations against "Gender Ideology" and Sexual Permissiveness in Croatia', in R. Kuhar, and D. Paternotte, eds, *Anti-Gender Campaigns in Europe: Mobilizing against Eequality.* (London, New York: Rowman & Littlefield International, 2017), pp. 59–79

Huvila, I., 'The Politics of Boundary Objects: Hegemonic Interventions and the Making of a Document', *Journal of the American Society for Information Science and Technology*, 62 (2011), 2528–2539.

Joerges, B., 'Do Politics Have Artefacts?', *Social Studies of Science*, 29 (1999), 411–431.

Korolczuk, E., 'Explaining Mass Protests against Abortion Ban in Poland: The Power of Connective Action', *Zoon Politikon*, 7 (2016), 91–113.

——, 'Explaining "Black Protests" against Abortion Ban in Poland: The Power of Connective Action', https://www.researchgate.net/publication/314232114_

Explaining_black_protests_against_abortion_ban_in_Poland_the_power_ of_connective_action, (2017), [accessed 18 August 2021].

Kováts, E., and M. Põim, 'Gender as Symbolic Glue: The Position and Role of Conservative and Far Right Parties in the Anti-Gender Mobilizations in Europe; France; Germany; Hungary; Poland; Slovakia', http://library.fes.de/pdf-files/ bueros/budapest/11382.pdf, (2015), [accessed 18 August 2021].

Kowalewski, M., 'Emergent Political Spaces in the Post-Socialist City: Solidarity Square', *Space and Polity*, 22 (2018), 328–341.

Laclau, E., and C. Mouffe, *Hegemony and Socialist Strategy: Towards a Radical Democratic Politics*, 2nd ed., (London: Verso, 2014).

Latour, B., *The Pasteurisation of France* (Cambridge, MA: Harvard University Press, 1988).

——, *Pandora's Hope: Essays on the Reality of Science Studies* (Cambridge, MA: Harvard University Press, 2000).

Lynch, M., 'Ontography: Investigating the Production of Things, Deflating Ontology', *Social Studies of Science*, 43 (2013), 444–462.

Mayer, S., and B. Sauer, '"Gender ideology" in Austria: Coalitions around an Empty Signifier', in R. Kuhar, and D. Paternotte, eds, *Anti-Gender Campaigns in Europe: Mobilizing against Equality* (London, New York: Rowman & Littlefield International, 2017), pp. 23–41.

Mol, A., 'Ontological Politics. A Word and Some Questions', *The Sociological Review*, 47 (1999), 74–89.

Neil, D., '"Restoring the Natural Order": The Religious Extremists' Vision to Mobilize European Societies against Human Rights on Sexuality and Reproduction, https://www.epfweb.org/node/175, (2018), [accessed 18 August 2021].

Nold, C., 'Practice-Based Ontological Design for Multiplying Realities', *Strategic Design Research Journal*, 11 (2018), 58–64.

Oreskes, N., and E. M. Conway, *Merchants of Doubt: How a Handful of Scientists Obscured the Truth on Issues from Tobacco Smoke to Global Warmin.* (New York: Bloomsbury Press, 2010).

Papadopoulos, D., *Experimental Practice: Technoscience, Alterontologies, and More-Than-Social Movements. Experimental Futures, Technological Lives, Scientific Arts, Anthropological Voices* (Durham, NC: Duke University Press, 2018).

Petchesky, R. P., 'Fetal Images: The Power of Visual Culture in the Politics of Reproduction', *Feminist Studies*, 13 (1987), 263.

Petö, A., W. Grzebalska, and H. Post, 'How Hungary and Poland Have Silenced Women and Stifled Human Rights', *Transitions Online* (2016), 28–31.

Planned Parenthood Federation of America. *The Facts Speak Louder: Planned Parenthood's Critique of "The Silent Scream"*, (New York: Planned Parenthood

Federation of America, 1985). Retrieved from http://stummeschrei.info/ wp-content/uploads/sites/2/2015/11/Silent_Scream_facts.pdf [accessed 18 August 2021].

Sieracka, J., 'Strong, Independent Women Who Know Their Worth and Shrug at the Very Idea of Discrimination. The Black Protest in the Context of Changing Ideals of Femininity in Poland', *Władza Sądzenia*, 14 (2018), 14–29.

Suchanow, K., *To jest wojna: Kobiety, fundamentaliści i nowe średniowiecze* (Warszawa: Agora SA, 2020)

Szczygielska, M., '"Good change" and Better Activism: Feminist Responses to Backsliding. Gender Policies in Poland', in A. Krizsán, and C. Roggeband, eds, *Gendering Democratic Backsliding in Central and Eastern Europe: A Comparative Agenda* (Budapest: Central European University Press, 2019), pp. 120–160.

MATTERING PRESS TITLES

Concealing for Freedom: The Making of Encryption, Secure Messaging and Digital Liberties
KSENIA ERMOSHINA AND FRANCESCA MUSIANI

Engineering the Climate: Science, Politics and Visions of Control
JULIA SCHUBERT

With Microbes
EDITED BY CHARLOTTE BRIVES, MATTHÄUS REST AND SALLA SARIOLA

Environmental Alterities
EDITED BY CRISTÓBAL BONELLI AND ANTONIA WALFORD

Sensing In/Security
EDITED BY NINA KLIMBURG-WITJES, NIKOLAUS POECHHACKER & GEOFFREY C. BOWKER

Energy Worlds in Experiment
EDITED BY JAMES MAGUIRE, LAURA WATTS AND BRITT ROSS WINTHEREIK

Boxes: A Field Guide
EDITED BY SUSANNE BAUER, MARTINA SCHLÜNDER AND MARIA RENTETZI

An Anthropology of Common Ground: Awkward Encounters in Heritage Work
NATHALIA SOFIE BRICHET

Ghost-Managed Medicine: Big Pharma's Invisible Hands
SERGIO SISMONDO

Inventing the Social
EDITED BY NOORTJE MARRES, MICHAEL GUGGENHEIM, ALEX WILKIE

Energy Babble
ANDY BOUCHER, BILL GAVER, TOBIE KERRIDGE, MIKE MICHAEL, LILIANA OVALLE, MATTHEW PLUMMER-FERNANDEZ AND ALEX WILKIE

The Ethnographic Case
EDITED BY EMILY YATES-DOERR AND CHRISTINE LABUSKI

On Curiosity: The Art of Market Seduction
FRANCK COCHOY

Practising Comparison: Logics, Relations, Collaborations
EDITED BY JOE DEVILLE, MICHAEL GUGGENHEIM AND ZUZANA HRDLIČKOVÁ

Modes of Knowing: Resources from the Baroque
EDITED BY JOHN LAW AND EVELYN RUPPERT

Imagining Classrooms: Stories of Children, Teaching and Ethnography
VICKI MACKNIGHT

www.ingramcontent.com/pod-product-compliance
Lightning Source LLC
Chambersburg PA
CBHW031426270326
41930CB00007B/593